SEX AND SUFFRAGE
IN BRITAIN,
1860-1914

Susan Kingsley Kent

SEX AND SUFFRAGE
IN BRITAIN,
1860-1914

PRINCETON

UNIVERSITY PRESS

Copyright © 1987 by Princeton University Press
Published by Princeton University Press, 41 William Street,
Princeton, New Jersey 08540
In the United Kingdom: Princeton University Press, Oxford

All Rights Reserved
Library of Congress Cataloging in Publication Data will be
found on the last printed page of this book

ISBN 0-691-05497-5
ISBN 0-691-00852-3, pbk.

First Princeton Paperback listing, 1990

Publication of this book has been aided by a grant
from the Paul Mellon Fund of Princeton University Press

This book has been composed in Linotron Bulmer
Clothbound editions of Princeton University Press books
are printed on acid-free paper, and binding materials are
chosen for strength and durability

Printed in the United States of America by Princeton University Press,
Princeton, New Jersey

Designed by Laury A. Egan

10 9 8 7 6 5 4 3 2

For
Anne Kent and Michael Mendelsohn
in memory of their daughter
Elisa

CONTENTS

ACKNOWLEDGMENTS ix

INTRODUCTION 3

CHAPTER I "THE SEX" 24

CHAPTER II PROSTITUTION 60

CHAPTER III MARRIAGE 80

CHAPTER IV THE DOCTORS 114

CHAPTER V THE LAW 140

CHAPTER VI SEX WAR 157

CHAPTER VII SUFFRAGE 184

EPILOGUE 220

NOTES 233

BIBLIOGRAPHY 269

INDEX 287

ACKNOWLEDGMENTS

AFTER SIX YEARS, I take great pleasure in thanking the many individuals whose assistance and generosity made this book possible. I am especially grateful to Eugene Black for his much-needed guidance and direction during the earliest phases of this project and for his support and encouragement throughout. A Brandeis University Summer Grant and a Sachar International Fellowship enabled me to carry out the necessary research in London. The library staff at the British Museum, the London School of Economics, and the Fawcett Library, especially, could not have been more helpful. David Doughan, in particular, served as a constant source of expertise and good cheer. His deep commitment to "the Cause," the quite evident joy with which he collects and preserves the materials of the Fawcett, and his desire to see archival research made as painless as possible transformed what could have been a tedious task into a positive experience.

The comments and suggestions offered by a number of people strengthened the manuscript significantly. With keen historical and personal sensitivity John Demos asked questions about interpretation that compelled me to clarify much of my thinking and to elucidate greater meaning from the words or actions of the feminists and their opponents. I deeply appreciate his help. For their close readings of drafts of the book, and for the generous spirit in which they offered their criticisms, I thank Martha Vicinus, Suzanne Lebsock, Ellen Carol DuBois, Ben Barker-Benfield, Bill Angel, Molly Shanley, and Bonnie Smith. Many of their suggestions have been incorporated into the text, enhancing it considerably. I also wish to thank Joanna Hitchcock, who shepherded the manuscript through its various stages with unerring good sense and professionalism, and my editor, Cathie Brettschneider, whose care and expertise have proved

invaluable. I, of course, am solely responsible for any errors or
faults that remain in my work.

My family and friends gave much moral, emotional, and material support. Although I cannot possibly cite them all, I do
wish to thank Jack Kent, Barbara Kent, Margaret Ley Kent, Eileen D. Taggart, Winifred Altree, Margaret Kent Kinton, Ina
Malaguti, Deborah Heller, Judy Brown, and Laura Rood.

To Joan Scott—teacher, critic, mentor, colleague, friend—I
owe an enormous debt of gratitude. I first encountered Joan at
the 1981 Berkshire Conference of Women's Historians, where,
in her keynote address, she called for a reaffirmation of feminist
ideals in academia. If ever we needed to be supportive of one
another, she reminded us in this era of budget cuts and threats
to affirmative action programs, it was now. Two years later,
when I sought her help as a reader of my dissertation, she
agreed without hesitation, despite considerable obligations and
commitments to her own students and to her own work. Since
then, she has never failed to give generously of her time, her
energy, and her profound learning. Joan taught me to approach
my subjects in such a way as to make it possible—indeed necessary—to rewrite conventional history. Most important, Joan
proved by her own example that the affirmation and application
of feminist ideals in the academy can ultimately transform it.
This book has benefited immeasurably from her contributions,
as have I.

Finally, I wish to express my deepest appreciation to Anne
Davidson, whose support and confidence never wavered, and
whose sense of humor and perspective enabled me to complete
this book. For her wisdom and her constancy—for all that she
has been and done for me—I offer my profound thanks.

SUSAN KINGSLEY KENT
Natick, Massachusetts
June 1986

SEX AND SUFFRAGE
IN BRITAIN,
1860-1914

INTRODUCTION

> For—let there be no mistake about it—this move-
> ment was not primarily political; it was social,
> moral, psychological and profoundly religious.
>
> HELENA SWANWICK, 1935

Until very recently, historians have tended to characterize the women's suffrage campaign in England as an exclusively politi-cal movement, as merely an attempt on the part of women to share in the general enfranchisement that occurred throughout the nineteenth century. Feminists did, indeed, demand recog-nition from and participation in the political process, but to stop here is to describe, not to understand, the feminist movement. In fighting for enfranchisement, suffragists sought no less than the total transformation of the lives of women. They set out to redefine and recreate, by political means, the sexual culture of Britain. Though suffragists repeatedly made this clear to the British public—and their opponents did not fail to take them at their word—the image of the suffrage campaign as a conserva-tive, limited, purely political movement has remained intact. In one of the most recent claims, Patricia Stubbs, echoing the con-ventional wisdom, asserted in 1981 that the feminist movement "was entirely civic in its aims and organization."[1]

Within the last few years, historians such as Olive Banks, Les Garner, and Brian Harrison have acknowledged that the suffrage campaign went beyond the strictly political, but they have not adequately analyzed the primary connections between sexual is-sues and the demand for the vote.[2] Richard Evans, for instance, defining feminism as the doctrine of equal rights for women, has stated that moral reform movements such as that seeking to end the state regulation of prostitution "further contributed to the extension of the feminist movement in a radical direction."[3] He has not pursued the ramifications of this insight by defining the nature of that radicalism and has thus missed an opportunity to see how the suffrage campaign furthered other feminist aims.

Evans has conceded that "people do not . . . commit themselves to political action and suffer the scorn, contempt, ridicule and hatred which the feminists were forced to endure, merely out of intellectual conviction."[4] He discerned the motives for feminism in the social and economic developments of the nineteenth century that gave rise to the middle class. The professionalization of medicine, education, and business, he has stated, forced women to adjust by seeking higher educational standards in order to qualify for admission to the new professions. The increasing importance of property and wealth as the foundation of status in society led women to seek the legal right to an independent share of that wealth. Finally, as it became increasingly offensive for the aristocracy to maintain and pursue a life of leisure, it became impossible for self-respecting middle-class women to share that idle existence.[5]

Evans's analysis, though accurate, is limited. It fails to account for the agency of women and ascribes motivation to amorphous economic and social development. Moreover, it does not explain satisfactorily why feminists provoked and, by Evans's admission, endured "scorn, contempt, ridicule, hatred," and violence. Above all, Evans has not listened to the arguments the women themselves advanced as they explained their justification and goals. An important key to understanding the persistence of feminist agitation lies in analyzing not only the social and economic developments of the nineteenth century but the ideological developments as well. The domestic ideology proclaimed in this period associated women not only with the household but also with biological characteristics that objectified them as "the Sex." The feminist movement, especially the campaign for the suffrage, aimed to alter that perception so that women would no longer be objectified or defined essentially in terms of their biology and would no longer be victims of what they deemed to be male sexual tyranny.

The difficulty for historians in hearing the explanations advanced by feminists lies in their conception of the relation of sexuality to politics. In keeping with the notions elaborated so effectively in the nineteenth century, sexuality and politics are each assigned a separate sphere, one private, one public. According to this ideology, if women are seeking change in the political, public sphere, they cannot be motivated by private issues such as sexual identity. Nineteenth-century feminists argued, however, that the public and the private were not distinct spheres but were inseparable from one another; the public was private, the personal was political. Suffragists perceived their campaign as the best way to end a "sex war" brought about by separate sphere ideology—an ideology that finally reduced women's identity to a sexual one, encouraged the view of women as sexual objects, and perpetuated women's powerlessness in both spheres. Historians have not been able to see beyond their categorizations, which firmly separate politics and sexuality into different realms of thought and activity. They have dismissed the "sex war" as an aberration or a titillating sidelight. But for contemporaries—men as well as women, parliamentary leaders as well as suffragists—the "sex war" formed the crux of the suffrage campaign and provides one of the keys to comprehending the true nature of the women's movement.

Most historians have described as anomalous or bewildering certain features of the suffrage campaign that were, in fact, integral to its aims and meaning. The most conspicuous example is the treatment of Christabel Pankhurst's "Great Scourge" articles in the *Suffragette* in 1913, in which she asserted that from 75 percent to 80 percent of all men in England suffered from some form of venereal disease, and she pointed out the consequent dangers of marriage for women. The solution, she insisted, was "Votes for Women, Chastity for Men." Roger Fulford baldly stated that Pankhurst's "arguments and facts fortunately need not detain the reader."[6] Andrew Rosen, while devoting a chapter to "The Great Scourge," expressed incredulity at the failure of members of the Women's Social and Political Union (WSPU) to repudiate Pankhurst's leadership after publication of the articles. "It is not easy to explain," he announced, "why the officials and the ordinary members of the WSPU neither took exception to Christabel's allegations nor questioned seriously her fitness to continue to set WSPU policy."[7] Completely disregarding the possibility that her followers might have agreed with her, he hinted that some insidious lesbianism attached to the militant movement might explain the "idiosyncratic" aspects of "The Great Scourge."[8] Finally, he concluded that

> it is possible that ready acceptance of Christabel's ideas stemmed in part from many unmarried WSPU members' desires to legitimize the socially and economically precarious role of the unmarried woman. WSPU members had often alluded to heterosexual activity as a vehicle for the satisfaction of selfish male pleasure, and frequently associated active heterosexuality with either immorality or the male domination involved in marriage. If marriage was as intensely dangerous as Christabel claimed, then fortunate the woman who had not married![9]

Rosen intimated that feminist charges of immorality and sexual oppression within the marriage bond were disingenuously marshaled in order to justify what appeared to him to be the rather bizarre desire of women to remain single. His exclamation point belies the seriousness with which he treated a matter that held profound importance for nineteenth- and early twentieth-century feminists and, indeed, for society in general.

Rosen stated—correctly—that Pankhurst's "factual assertions regarding the prevalence and consequences of venereal disease were grossly exaggerated."[10] O. R. McGregor spoke of the "fantastic idiocy of Miss Pankhurst's belief that three-quarters of the male population suffered from venereal disease."[11] Neither writer informed the reader that Pankhurst's misleading figures and descriptions of the consequences of such disease for women were those widely propagated by the medical profession.[12] The establishment of a Royal Commission on Venereal Disease in 1913 demonstrates the degree to which medical and governmental authorities were alarmed by the incidence of venereal disease. Worse, in reading Pankhurst's words literally and dismissing her argument because it lacks statistical veracity, Rosen and McGregor have subjected a historical problem to a test of statistical truth instead of analyzing Pankhurst's language to get at the meaning of her statements.[13] Pankhurst is made to appear ridiculous—a fanatic—and is therefore to be dismissed, along with issues that, in actuality, pervaded and informed the entire suffrage movement. Although one must acknowledge the air of the dramatic, even of the absurd, about Pankhurst, it is a mistake to deprecate the views she communicated to the public in "The Great Scourge." For she only presented in a highly visible and provocative manner concerns that many suffragists had explicitly stated were at the heart of their agitation: the double standard of morality, prostitution, and the sexual objectification and abuse of women. But when traditional historians approach the issues of sex and sexuality raised by suffragists, they treat the women either as deranged, à la Rosen and McGregor, or as perverse. David Mitchell's biography of Pankhurst, for instance, has presented suffragists as sex-starved and masochistic.[14] George Dangerfield labeled the militant suffrage campaign a movement of "pre-war lesbianism."[15]

While Evans and others such as William O'Neill have pointed to the moral ties between sexual issues and feminism,[16] Judith Walkowitz, in her ground-breaking study of Victorian prostitution, has forged direct links between the Contagious Diseases (CD) Acts repeal campaign of the 1870s and 1880s and the suffrage movement.[17] Passed by Parliament to regulate prostitution and reduce the incidence of venereal disease in garrison towns, the CD Acts gave police the authority to arrest any woman suspected of being a prostitute and compelled the women to submit to an examination by speculum. Feminist advocates of repeal, inspired and led by the eminently respectable Josephine Butler, labored tirelessly for sixteen years to eradicate the laws and attitudes that conspired to make women "safe" for male vice and to subject women to the "instrumental rape" of the compulsory examination. Walkowitz has noted that Edwardian suffragists used many of the tactics first practiced by the repealers—militant acts, by-election campaigning, and extraparliamentary activity—and referred to Butler as the "great founding mother of modern feminism."[18] More important, Walkowitz has pointed out, "the repeal campaign firmly committed later feminists to an attack on the double standard and 'male vice.' The sixteen-year campaign against state regulation ingrained the theme of the sexual wrongs perpetrated against women by men on later feminist consciousness." She has argued that many of the actions of the militants—arson and window-breaking, for example—were "part of a real sex war, whose explicit political precedent may be traced to the campaign against the C. D. Acts."[19]

Walkowitz's study constitutes the first comprehensive treatment of English feminists as active agents in a political campaign to transform sexual mores rather than as passive victims of ideological prescriptions. "The repeal campaign," she has argued,

> has occupied an important niche in the history of nineteenth-century feminism, although its contributions to the emerging feminist movement have never been satisfactorily explored. As conventionally depicted in the historiography of feminism, the Ladies' National Association's attack on male vice and the double standard is made to seem out of place next to the more decorous struggles for the franchise, property rights, and access to higher education.[20]

In fact, the women's battle against state-regulated prostitution and the double standard was an integral aspect of a movement that included the other "decorous struggles," specifically the suffrage campaign. It struck at the heart of women's difficulties: their sense of sexual objectification and victimization. The franchise movement—as well as the campaigns for property rights and access to medicine and higher education—were all of a piece; they aimed at a redefinition of the roles of and relationships between women and men in English society.

The campaign for repeal of the Contagious Diseases Acts explicitly identified for thousands of women the socio-sexual structure set up by patriarchal society. It crystallized for women their status as sexual objects and catapulted many complacent, mild-mannered women into the public sphere to discuss a heretofore unmentionable issue. The leadership of the Ladies' National Association (LNA) was committed to feminism before its involvement with the repeal campaign, but that was not the case for thousands of women who were propelled into the movement as a result of Butler's activities on behalf of prostitutes and other victims of the double standard. Madame Emilie Venturi, an LNA member, confided in 1872 to Henry Wilson, a steadfast proponent of repeal, that "until roused up by the CDA infamy, I confess that I never took any part in political life in England."[21] Her epiphany was typical. Walkowitz has asserted that the "LNA attracted hundreds of middle-class women to the political arena for the first time."[22] Many women told Millicent Garrett Fawcett, president of the National Union of Women's Suffrage Societies (NUWSS), that they came to the suffrage movement after working with, knowing, or hearing of Josephine Butler.[23]

The momentum created by the CD Acts repeal campaign and the issues it raised for women spread to and influenced many other reform movements. "The vitality of our Crusade," wrote Butler, "appeared . . . to cause it to break through the boundaries of its own particular channel and to create and fructify many movements and reforms of a collateral character. We felt it necessary, while combatting the State Regulation of vice . . . also to work against all those disabilities and injustices which affect the interests of women."[24] In many instances, however, feminists were compelled by the ferocity of the opposition to the repeal effort to understate their auxiliary demands. For the attacks on the repealers were vituperative in the extreme. One Member of Parliament declared that Butler—a member of the Grey family that produced a Prime Minister—was "worse than the prostitutes."[25] A journalist described her as "an indecent maenad, a shrieking sister, frenzied, unsexed, and utterly without shame."[26] Butler lamented that "motives of the worst kind were sometimes imputed, among the most frequent being that of a lurking sympathy, not with the sinners alone, but with their most hateful sin."[27] This kind of abuse and language constituted more than simple insult or defamation. The language of sexuality employed by extentionists joined that of the feminists—suggesting that the opposition recognized feminist intentions and purposes. Many historians, however, have dismissed this language as insult; they have not regarded it as serious political discourse and so have missed the connection between sex and politics.

The furor raised by the repeal campaign was so great that until 1877 feminists felt it necessary—for strategic reasons—to divorce Butler's crusade from other feminist reform movements. Neither Fawcett nor Emily Davies, leader of the struggle for higher education, wanted a breath of scandal attached to her cause.[28] They did not, however, repudiate the work of Butler and the LNA. On the contrary, they regarded it as of the utmost importance. Butler confided to Maria Grey in 1871, "Some of my best friends have frankly told me that they must get rid of my name in their schemes or committees for good objects, although *they* heartily follow me in my special work."[29] Ray Strachey, a suffragist and intimate of Fawcett, stated that the repeal campaign was a movement that Fawcett supported with "her whole heart," despite the fact that her sister, Elizabeth Garrett Anderson, one of the first female physicians in England, supported the acts on the grounds that they would protect innocent women and children from venereal disease.[30] Fawcett herself, in tribute to Butler, asserted that "the long years of [CD Acts] propaganda had been invaluable . . . in shedding light on the wider aspect of women's place as responsible citizens in the body politic."[31]

For, despite strategic differences, the suffrage campaign itself espoused the same ideas and sought the same ends as the campaign for repeal of the CD Acts. "It cannot be," wrote Frances Swiney, President of the Cheltenham branch of the NUWSS, in 1908,

> that, in England, for the simple possession of the political vote, the woman question should absorb the thoughts and attentions of so many able minds; there must be in the logical nature of things an ulterior motive, an underlying force, that is the foundation for one of the most noticeable features of the end of the nineteenth century. This unrest, this straining forward, this earnestness and unity of purpose in woman, must be for a certain goal towards which the franchise is but a means to an end.[32]

Ethel Colquhoun, an avowed anti-suffragist, recognized in 1913 that "such surface manifestations as the franchise agitation" were "only superficial expressions of something deeper." She found that underlying motive in what Olive Schreiner had spoken of in 1911 as "dis-co-ordination, struggle and consequent suffering which undoubtedly exist when we regard the world of sexual relations and ideals."[33]

Many feminists testified that their movement was at bottom a struggle for sexual autonomy. Helena Swanwick, a member of the NUWSS and editor of *Common Cause*, the NUWSS's official newspaper, remembered that during her childhood she spent many hours reading novels depicting the plight of women. "I must have been still a child," she wrote, "when I rebelled against the common morality of the day in regard to respectability in sex relations."[34] Her resentment continued in her teens, when she discovered that "I could not be allowed out after dark, even in frequented thoroughfares. When it was explained to me that a young girl by herself was liable to be insulted by men, I become incoherent with rage at a society which, as a consequence, shut up the girls instead of the men."[35] Cicely Hamilton, a militant suffragist, attributed her feminist beliefs to the fate of women in a society that operated under a double standard of morality. "I believe my youthful thoughts and views on the relations of the sexes were a good deal influenced by the story of Lucrece [a Roman woman who committed suicide after being raped]," she stated,

> and that, all unconsciously, I became a feminist on the day I perceived that—according to the story—her "honour" was not a moral but a physical quality. Once that was clear to me my youthful soul rebelled; it was insulting to talk of "honour" and "virtue" in a woman as if they were matters of chance—things which she only possessed because no unkind fate had thrown her in the way of a man sufficiently brutal to deprive her of them by force.[36]

Teresa Billington-Greig, an early member of the WSPU and later of the Women's Freedom League (WFL), listed "my mother's position and resentment" as the foremost factor in "the genesis of my personal rebellion."[37] Billington-Greig's mother, Helen Wilson, had been educated in a Catholic convent school and hoped to become a nun. When the sisters refused her, she was expected to marry William Billington. Helen shrank from the intimacies of married life. "[A]ll [her] life she remained a rebel in sex matters[,] submitting only so far as her own interpretation of her Church's teaching committed her, and no farther," her daughter recalled.

> With the church and the law and the convention behind him [William] was yet never able to win more than indignant acquiescence from his wife; and their years together therefore were a succession of battles. . . . The experience

of [the marriage's] day by day working was a crucial part
of my home environment[,] one of the strange and distress-
ing elements that subdued and invaded the centre of my
world, a mystery, a menace which always hung like a potential disruption of family peace. Naturally as a child I did
not know the cause or meaning of this enduring conflict.
There was no clear knowledge of some mysterious wrong—
a sort of imprisonment or servitude which was somehow
imposed by William upon Helen but there was the indelible impression that such wrong existed.[38]

These feminists intended to create a society that would eliminate sexual wrongs through the elevation of women to human
status. Beatrice Forbes-Robinson Hale, involved in both the
English and the American suffrage movements, insisted that
"the first axiom of Feminism" is "that the majority of human
attributes are not sexual."[39] Ethel Snowdon explained that the
feminist "asks for freedom for women in the exercise of those
gifts and in the use of those qualities of soul and mind which
are apart from the consequences of the sex-act. She objects to
the forcing of woman's interests into one groove."[40] Snowdon
saw that the definition of woman as only a reproductive/sexual
being held all sorts of opportunities for the degradation, even
the brutalization, of women. "For the woman as a human being,
and not as an animal, the feminist demands opportunity and
freedom," she asserted.[41]

The vote became both the symbol of the free, sexually autonomous woman and the means by which the goals of a feminist
sexual culture were to be attained. The ultimate source and
embodiment of patriarchal power was seen to lie in political
expression, or law, and the vote was perceived as a strategic tool
for changing law. Thus, the demand for women's enfranchisement was a direct strike at the very seat and symbolic locus of
patriarchal power. Josephine Butler had originally believed that
all the reforms feminists were fighting for in the legal and po-

litical realm could have no real impact on the lives of women if the more fundamental issue of the relations between men and women was not first addressed and resolved.[42] She soon realized that sexual autonomy and political rights could not remain separated from one another.[43] "We shall never have faith and courage enough in Parliament," she maintained, "to attack this monster evil [of prostitution] in its sources until the convictions of women as well as of men are represented there."[44]

For Fawcett the suffrage campaign and the franchise were "a still further strengthening of the foundations on which [Butler] had been building."[45] She described suffragists as those who were "trying to preach and live the gospel of a nobler and truer relationship between the sexes."[46] Strachey noted that Fawcett saw the suffrage as a means to eliminate prostitution, ease divorce constraints upon women, and raise public morals generally. She insisted that women's disenfranchisement was directly connected to the existence of prostitution, a double standard of divorce, and low public morals that victimized women, so she concentrated her energies in the battle for the vote.[47]

Partisans of women's suffrage who were less reticent than Fawcett described more explicitly the motives and aims of the suffrage movement.[48] Elizabeth Wolstenholme Elmy, active in all aspects of the feminist movement—suffrage, higher education and medicine for women, property rights, and divorce reform—from its inception in the 1860s to the granting of limited suffrage to women in 1918, summed up the entire issue of women's suffrage in a letter to Harriet McIlquham in 1897. "It is the fear of men that women will cease to be any longer their sexual slaves either in or out of marriage that is at the root of the whole opposition to our just claim," she asserted. "No doubt their fear is justified, for that is precisely what we do mean."[49]

How do we explain all this talk of sex and sexuality by women involved in a political struggle? The hypotheses advanced by Michel Foucault in *The History of Sexuality* suggest an approach to understanding the sexual issues that so permeated the suffrage campaign. Foucault noted that during the nineteenth century the discussion of sex and sexuality flourished, that the era witnessed "the great process of transforming sex into discourse." The discourses on sexuality, the primary articulators of which were scientists and doctors, expressed "a cluster of power relations." The "explosion of distinct discursivities," *the multiplication of discourses concerning sex*," served as a means of "exercising power itself," Foucault maintained. Power, he suggested, was not a thing located in any particular place but was the possession of knowledge.[50]

Physicians played a major role in the creation and multiplication of the sexual discourse. In the course of the nineteenth century, Foucault argued, doctors took it upon themselves, employing "science," to discover and guard "the truth of sex," to act as arbiters in formulating sexual norms and the sexual identity of individuals. In the hands of physicians, sexuality became transformed from one element of individual identity to a major determinant of personal identity; sexuality was used "as a mode of specification of individuals."[51]

Doctors defined sexuality as being "by nature . . . a domain susceptible to pathological processes, and hence one calling for therapeutic or normalizing intervention." Foucault found that this assumption operated especially frequently in the case of women, the hysterization of whose bodies served as one of the "great strategic unities which . . . formed specific mechanisms of knowledge and power centering on sex." In the hands of the medical profession, "the feminine body was analyzed—qualified and disqualified—as being thoroughly saturated with sexuality; whereby it was integrated into the sphere of medical practices, by reason of a pathology intrinsic to it."[52]

The deployment of sexuality was used "in the formation of a political ordering of life," Foucault contended.[53] Although referring specifically to a political ordering involving the bourgeoisie and the working classes, Foucault's analysis is perhaps even more appropriate for the dynamics of power ordering men and women. As sexuality constituted personal—including political—identity, and as female sexuality was said to contain an intrinsic pathology, women's continuing disqualification from the political process now rested upon their sexuality and sexual organization. In order, therefore, to be recognized as individuals qualified to participate in political life, suffragists had, necessarily, to challenge and overturn cultural constructions of femininity and female sexuality. They did so utilizing what Foucault called "reverse discourses," or discourses of resistance that often incorporated the vocabulary and categories of the dominant discourse. In this context, given, as Foucault argued, that sexuality is one of those power relations "endowed with the greatest instrumentality: useful for the greatest number of maneuvers and capable of serving as a point of support, as a linchpin, for the most varied strategies," the suffragist preoccupation with sexual issues takes on immense significance. Feminists recognized that sexuality serves, as Foucault declared, "as an especially dense transfer point for relations of power," and they focused their demands for power in the political sphere around demands for power in the private, sexual sphere, where they perceived power and powerlessness to have their roots.[54]

THIS STUDY represents another approach to the suffrage movement—indeed, to the entire women's movement of the second half of the nineteenth century. I have listened to the arguments of the women as they presented their ideas and explained and justified their efforts, and I have analyzed the language they employed in the course of their movement. The individuals presented here belong overwhelmingly to the middle classes. Despite the contributions made to suffrage by working-class women, middle-class women constituted the vast majority of suffragists. As Jill Liddington and Jill Norris have demonstrated, working-class feminists often advanced an agenda quite different from that of the feminists discussed here; their demands centered on work-related issues such as equal pay.[55] Moreover, this is not a social history of feminism but an intellectual/cultural history. Because I am interested in "discourses" and ideology, this work focuses upon the articulate leaders of the feminist movement, those who led organizations or wrote about their cause. When I refer to "feminists," I necessarily mean these articulate women, not the rank and file. (Though the term "feminism" did not come into general use until 1890 or so, I employ "feminist" to describe individuals who were active in the women's movement before that date.) Though few, they were the ones who defined the issues; though unrepresentative of even those women who followed them, they were the ones whose debates and arguments composed the feminist discourse.

Some of the leaders and theorists of the women's movement were active for the fifty-odd years required to win the vote. Most of them, though certainly not all, belonged psychologically as well as generationally to one of three cohorts of suffragists: those who pioneered in the struggle for women's rights, born before 1850; those born between 1850 and 1870, thus coming of age before 1890; and those born after 1870, who cut their first political teeth after 1890. Differences of attitude and behavior between and among the individuals of these three groups certainly did exist. But all the women grappled with the same issues pertaining to sexuality, and though they might disagree fundamentally with one another over certain points, all involved themselves in an attack upon the ideology of separate spheres.

The views and beliefs held by feminists reflected, for the most part, those of society at large. As general social values altered, so—often—did the mores of a new cohort of feminists. This situation might have produced problems within the movement, but it also stimulated growth and development.

The pioneers of the feminist movement included Elizabeth Blackwell (1821-1910), Elizabeth Garrett Anderson (1836-1917), and Sophia Jex-Blake (1840-1912), the three women most instrumental in breaking down the barriers to women in the profession of medicine in the 1860s and 1870s. Though preoccupied with the medical movement, they gave much time, energy, and support to other feminist campaigns. Garrett Anderson, for instance, joined the WSPU, marched on Parliament, and was spared a prison term only through the intervention of her sister, Millicent. Frances Power Cobbe (1822-1904), Josephine Butler (1828-1906), Elizabeth Wolstenholme Elmy (1834-1919?), Millicent Garrett Fawcett (1847-1929), and Frances Swiney (1847-1922) were active from the beginning in demanding and organizing for educational and employment reforms for women, the Married Women's Property Acts, the suffrage, and various social purity causes—such as the repeal of the Contagious Diseases Acts or the passage of the Criminal Law Amendment Act of 1885. Almost all of them came from respectable, middle-class, Dissenting or Evangelical families. For women of their time, they were unusually well educated, though not necessarily formally so, and they tended to espouse a Liberal or Radical philosophy. Members of their family were very often politically active and were even political and social "insiders."

Three of these pioneers—Blackwell, Cobbe, and Jex-Blake—never married, which no doubt facilitated their ability to devote so much time to the Cause. Garrett Anderson married only after she completed the arduous preparation for her degree. Fawcett, although she participated in various campaigns in the 1870s and 1880s, did not take on the full-time responsibilities of the presidency of the NUWSS until after her husband, Henry Fawcett, had died. Butler had been active in the North of England Council, which sought to increase educational opportunities for women, in the 1860s, but she did not immerse herself in the CD Acts repeal campaign until after (and as a result of) her young daughter's death. Her sons lived at school by that time, and her husband, George Butler, subordinated his personal and professional needs to those of his wife's great crusade. Swiney's six children had become adults by the time she presided over the Cheltenham Affiliated Society of the NUWSS. Where there were demanding husbands or small children, these women could not direct all their attention to feminist demands. As a result of Elmy's attempt to do justice to both the Cause and her young son, the latter, according to Sylvia Pankhurst, did not fare as well as he might have.[56]

Writing in 1916, Wilma Meikle identified this group of women as the "old" suffragists. Referring specifically to issues of sex and sexuality, she explained that "the old were women who had concealed their sufferings in youth and had nervously whispered their complaints in middle age, until at last they impetuously gave tongue. They were women who might be vulgar for a cause and in the exalted spirit of martyrdom (and quite frequently were), yet remained essentially ladies or 'ladylike.' " In contrast to younger feminists, these older suffragists, by virtue of the "gentility of their minds[,] shrank from much that for a later generation was part of the essential tissue of feminism."[57]

Despite "the gentility of their minds," and the intolerance of society, many of these women did participate in public discussion of sexual issues. In its earliest days, however, the organized feminist movement consisted of a number of discrete campaigns. Property rights, higher education, admission to the medical profession, the vote, and custody rights to children made up much of the feminist agenda; but matters such as the age of consent, the double standard of morality, and prostitution also commanded a great deal of the pioneers' time and energy. Because they feared that demands pertaining to sexuality might negatively influence the success of their campaigns for more conventional rights, feminists at first kept the two sets of demands separate, even though the personnel involved in each campaign were often the same. Gradually, as the legal and institutional obstacles to women's equality with men fell, sexual issues and the vote came increasingly to occupy center stage.

By the 1880s, in large part because of the impact of the campaign to repeal the Contagious Diseases Acts, public discussion of sexual problems and issues had become more acceptable. The second cohort of feminists—those born between 1850 and

1870—both benefited from and contributed to this looser atmosphere. These were the "New Women," less reticent than many of the earlier feminists to complain of sexual wrongs or to make demands pertaining to women's sexual needs. With the passage of the Criminal Law Amendment Act in 1885, which raised the age of consent for girls and made procuring a criminal offense, and the repeal of the CD Acts in 1886, social purity concerns that had so dominated the feminists' discourses of resistance gave way to attacks on marriage and the double standard of morality. The participating women included Sarah Grand (1854-1943), Olive Schreiner (1855-1920), Mona Caird (1858-1932), Helena Swanwick (1864-1939), Nina Boyle (1866-1943), and Emmeline Pethick Lawrence (1867-1954).

Grand, who left her husband in 1890, wrote prolifically and served as the mayor of Bath six times.[58] Schreiner, a radical feminist and a writer, was the confidante and intimate friend of such diverse personalities as Havelock Ellis, Eleanor Marx, and Cecil Rhodes. Her most famous work, *The Story of an African Farm*, was published in 1883. Caird, who married in 1877, was a journalist who scandalized the British public with her assault on marriage in the 1880s. Swanwick was one of the first to obtain a college degree from Girton at Cambridge. She served as editor of *Common Cause* from 1909 until 1912 when she left, "too advanced" for the rest of the Executive Board of the NUWSS.[59] Boyle, carrying her demand for the inclusion of women in the power of the state to a degree beyond most other suffragists, helped to found the first women's police force in England during the First World War.[60] Pethick Lawrence, with her husband Frederick, virtually financed the WSPU until their ouster by the dictatorial Pankhursts.

The youngest generation of suffragists was born roughly between 1870 and 1880; these women were in their twenties when militancy burst upon the Edwardian scene, bringing excitement and urgency to the Cause. Among them were Cicely Hamilton (1872-1952), A. Maude Royden (1876-1956), Teresa Billington-

Greig (1877-1964), Christabel Pankhurst (1880-1958), and F. W. Stella Browne (1882-1955). They were, for the most part, college-educated, affiliated in some fashion with the Labour Party, and—out of either necessity or political commitment—worked to support or to help support themselves.

Hamilton, an actress, playwright, and novelist, never married. Nor did Christabel Pankhurst, who held a law degree from Owens College, a precursor to the University of Manchester. Teresa Billington, who received her education through Manchester University extension classes, taught in the Manchester elementary-school system until recruited by Emmeline Pankhurst to establish a branch of the WSPU in London. She later married Frederick Greig. Maude Royden received her B.A. from Lady Margaret Hall, Oxford, and became an Anglican preacher. She served on the Executive Committee of the NUWSS. For some forty years she lived in the home of the man she loved, Hudson Shaw, and his wife Effie in what can only be described as a platonic *menage à trois*. When Effie died in 1944, Royden and Shaw, an ordained Anglican minister, married; he died two months later.[61] Browne had joined the Divorce Law Reform Union by 1912, the Malthusian League by 1914, and helped to found the Abortion Law Reform Association in 1936. Clearly far more radical than the feminists of the mainstream suffrage campaign, she represents rather the branch of the women's movement associated with *The Freewoman*, a provocative newspaper that appeared in November of 1911.

This newest generation of suffragists distinguished themselves from their foremothers by their great willingness to discuss and tackle—in public—problems relating to sex and sexuality. Meikle related that these women, as university students, had "pored over" the works of George Bernard Shaw and H. G. Wells "and at last came out into the world earnestly convinced that there was something certainly wonderful and possibly glorious about this mystery called sex and that it was their business to discover it." Armed with these ideas, and observing around them a great

deal of dissatisfaction with sexual relations as they currently existed, these suffragists "saw that sexual problems were the core
of feminism."[62] Because the suffrage campaign had become a
mass movement by 1910, feminist concerns about sex and sexuality permeated social discourse and sometimes dominated
public debate. Those problems articulated by older feminists—
prostitution, venereal disease, marriage, and the legal and moral
double standard—were now joined by discussions of menstruation, child-bearing, sexual assault, incest, homosexuality, sexual
pleasure for women, and birth control, and were aired in a
manner and to a degree not possible earlier.

The period covered in this study then, 1860-1914, spans three
generations of feminists. Despite the differences among and between the women of each group, however, the feminist critique
of separate sphere ideology embodied a certain consistency.
Chapter I identifies the ideological context within which physicians and scientists branded women "the Sex." Chapters II
through V show how feminists sought to eliminate such a characterization by attacking the institutions of power (knowledge)
that embodied and perpetuated it. According to the feminist
analysis, these institutions—prostitution, marriage, medicine,
and law—enslaved women and provided a protective cover under which men were able to indulge their sexual proclivities in
violation of the very terms of their profession, be it husband,
doctor, lawyer, or Member of Parliament. In launching their
critique, feminists focused on the inherent hypocrisy and con-
tradictions of separate sphere ideology in both theory and practice, arguing that it permitted and encouraged attitudes and behavior diametrically opposed to those it purported to assert.

Chapter VI explores the feminists' depiction of a society
preyed upon by a self-interested male sexuality justified by a set
of binary definitions—cultural constructions of masculinity that
were established by contrast to but interdependently with ideas
about female sexuality. In the end, the feminists argued, these
definitions of sexuality had to be changed if the relations be-

tween men and women were to be characterized by peace and complementarity rather than by "sex war." Chapter VII looks anew at the suffrage campaign in light of the insights gained by examining the voices, language, and ideas of the feminists, concluding that it was a part of, in fact a culmination of, the sexual discourses articulated in the nineteenth and early twentieth centuries. Finally, the epilogue examines feminism after 1914 and addresses the question of why the suffrage movement failed to alter the gender system and the sexual culture of Britain.

CHAPTER I

"THE SEX"

Man possesses sexual organs; her sexual organs
possess woman.
                    OTTO WEININGER, M.D., 1906

Though the term was not introduced until 1890 or so, the movement that came to be called "feminism" became large and outspoken during the second half of the nineteenth century. Feminists sought to reverse what they deemed to be the declining role of the middle-class woman. They reserved their most furious objections for representations that equated the female with the sexual. Feminists cast their arguments in the context of a larger discussion about the value and function of the family and its individual members' roles in industrial capitalist society.

The dominant theme of middle-class ideology stressed women's roles as wife and mother to the exclusion of all other functions and invested in women the responsibility of upholding morality and purity. While denying middle-class women sexuality, nineteenth-century bourgeois society paradoxically heightened an awareness of women as primarily reproductive and sexual beings. Increasingly during the nineteenth century, women became symbols of their husbands' wealth and success—objects of conspicuous consumption—and this inexorably made them and their sexuality a kind of objectified commodity.[1] Although these views seemed to predominate in public discussion, significant dissent arose to challenge them. The "revolt of women" produced a critique and an alternative to these ideas. Formulated within what Foucault termed the "dominant discourse," the women's movement articulated a number of pointed "discourses of resistance."

The discussion of gender roles took place within a framework of centuries of political and economic change. Some of the changes were defined in terms of analogies to marital or sexual relations. Mary Lyndon Shanley has demonstrated, for example, that seventeenth-century antagonists in the debate over Parliament's relation to royal authority used an analogy to the relationship between husband and wife in order to buttress their respective positions. Royalists pointed to the hierarchical and irrevocable nature of the marriage contract to justify absolutism. Such arguments compelled advocates of parliamentary rule to discredit the royalist conception of both marriage and monarchy. They applied their individualistic premises about government to the sphere of domestic organization as well.[2] Randolph Trumbach and Lawrence Stone have pointed to more literal links between politics and gender. Speaking of the domestic relations of the eighteenth-century aristocracy, Trumbach has argued that as the patriarchal household as a system of economy and authority lost predominance, relationships within the household became more egalitarian. The patriarchal household had rested on the presumption that the male head of the household owned his wife, his children, his tenants, his animals and tools, and his land. By the eighteenth century, patriarchal authority and control had given way to the assertion that "all men were created equal." Ownership of individuals had been discredited, and "the equality of men and women was declared."[3] The notion of equality between all men and between men and women was still very far from complete in the eighteenth century, but it had entered the lexicon of socio-political thought, and it continued to dominate political, economic, and social discussions in the nineteenth century.

The substitution of egalitarian relations for patriarchal patterns of authority in formal politics had profound ramifications for the household, as Stone has demonstrated. The necessary political, social, and economic changes took a century to implement. Property ceased to be the *raison d'être* of marriage and was replaced by notions of romantic love and companionship. Marriage became emotionally rather than economically based, and the family was transformed from an economic to a sentimental unit.[4] Divorce became possible because marriage was no longer a question of property, and—ideally—women were no longer the property of their husbands.

In reality, however, as Trumbach has shown, men were severely constrained in the degree to which they could consider women their equals, and the idea of women as property remained strong throughout the nineteenth century. In 1789, an observer of the position of women commented, "Though the idea of being property, or parts of our goods and chattels, be exploded from our philosophy and from some of our laws, it still remains in our pre-possessions or customs, counteracted by a little senseless and romantic gallantry."[5] Property in women was institutionalized in the parliamentary divorce law and enshrined in the double standard of morality.[6] Until 1857, the divorce law granted the right of a husband to petition Parliament to divorce his wife if he could prove her adultery, yet wives had no such rights over their husbands. Not simply in 1789 but until very recently in this century, the double standard remained inviolate.

The debate over absolute authority in the seventeenth and eighteenth centuries carried over from political organization to marriage law, and the acceptance of the social contract in the political realm had its limited counterpart in the marriage contract in the domestic realm. The debate was advanced significantly in the late eighteenth and nineteenth centuries as industrial capitalism altered the political, economic, and social structures of England. By the 1780s, men of new wealth were challenging the legitimacy of government by limited monarchy and landed aristocracy. The victory they realized in 1832 with the Reform Act signaled the emergent ascendancy of industrial and manufacturing wealth over the heretofore dominant landed and commercial elites. Throughout the nineteenth century, England experienced the dismantling of aristocratic, patriarchal institutions and concentrated on building a society based on liberal, individualistic, egalitarian philosophies. Middle- and working-class groups of men agitated and asserted their rights to participation in the new industrial order, basing their claims on the ideology of liberalism. With traditional forms of power and authority facing challenge from insubordinate groups, women, too, joined the fray, seeking out changes in law and custom that would more clearly reflect their changing role in the family. For if marriage and the family were now firmly based on ideals of romantic love, companionship, and some notion of equality between men and women, the legal, economic, and social position of women had yet to affirm that fact.

Under the law of coverture, married women had no rights or existence apart from their husbands. "By marriage," opined Sir William Blackstone, "the very being or legal existence of a woman is suspended, or at least it is incorporated or consolidated into that of the husband, under whose wing, protection and cover she performs everything, and she is therefore called in our law a *feme covert*."[7] The popular aphorism "my wife and I are one, and I am he" described a situation in which a married woman had no legal rights to her property, her earnings, her freedom of movement, her conscience, her body, or her children; all resided in her husband. Throughout the nineteenth century women and their male allies challenged these holdovers of aristocratic patriarchal society, largely successfully.

The first such challenge to property in women and children occurred in the 1830s, when Caroline Norton sued for control over her children after her husband absconded with them. The Custody Act of 1839 gave women custody of their children under the age of seven in cases of divorce or separation. Thereafter, the husband resumed control, though visitation rights were secured for his wife. The act modified but did not overturn paternal control, for any father had complete authority over his children, determining their domicile, the extent and location of their schooling, their religion, and their guardianship. The Guardianship of Infants Act of 1886 gave mothers the guardianship of their children upon the death of the father; and in 1925 women obtained full custody rights to their children.[8]

Barbara Leigh Smith Bodichon's *A Brief Summary in Plain Language of the Most Important Laws Concerning Women*, published in 1854, laid out in a systematic fashion the legal situation that condemned women to a position of chattel of men. An advocate of women's economic independence, Bodichon helped to set in motion the campaign for women's property rights. With the passage of the Married Women's Property Acts of 1870 and 1882, married women secured the right to retain and own any property or earnings they might bring to their marriage; husbands no longer enjoyed full and free access to their wives' assets.

The economic position of women independent of men was enhanced by the movement for women's education. In 1848, Queen's College was founded and began to grant degrees to women. In the 1850s, Mary Frances Buss and Dorothea Beale opened the North of London Collegiate School for Ladies and Cheltenham, respectively, so that single middle-class women might qualify for employment that would provide an income to support them. Girton College at Cambridge in 1871, the University of London in 1878, and Newnham College at Oxford in 1879 admitted women to examination.

Patriarchal laws and the idea of property in women changed slowly during the course of the century. In 1884, Parliament rescinded the law that allowed men to have their wives jailed if they refused sexual intercourse.[9] In 1891, with the decision of *Queen v. Jackson*, a man could no longer imprison his wife in his home in order to enforce restitution of conjugal rights. The *Times* lamented, in response, that "one fine morning last month marriage in England was suddenly abolished."[10]

Women obtained some amelioration even from the law that most symbolized their status as property of men—that of divorce. Until 1857, divorce could be obtained only by Act of Parliament and was available only to the wealthy elite. The Matrimonial Causes Act of 1857 created a court for divorce and established the grounds for the procedure. Men could divorce their wives, as before, on the basis of adultery alone; women, however, had to prove their husbands' adultery in addition to cruelty, desertion, incest, rape, sodomy, or bestiality. The Royal Commission on Divorce, reporting in 1850, had recommended that adultery was much more serious on the part of the wife than on the part of the husband.[11] The underlying tenet of the double standard in law and custom, as Keith Thomas has suggested, incorporated the "view that men have property in women and that the value of this property is immeasurably diminished if the woman at any time has sexual relations with anyone other than her husband."[12] The Matrimonial Causes Act, however inequitable, did allow divorce for women, and women continued to challenge the double standard until the Matrimonial Causes Act of 1923 established a single standard for divorce for both sexes.[13]

The most radical challenge of the women's movement to patriarchal control consisted of demands for enfranchisement on the same lines as men. The Reform Acts of 1832, 1867, and 1884 had afforded to increasing numbers of men the opportunity for political participation, until virtual universal manhood suffrage prevailed. When women began to agitate for inclusion in the public arena in the 1860s, their claim was denied, and continued to be denied, on the basis of their sex. Though the liberal state embraced the notion of equality and individuality, Trumbach's observation of eighteenth-century aristocrats holds true for nineteenth-century men as well, that "in the end, the traditional means by which the adult male's identity was formed placed serious restrictions on the extent to which a man could treat a woman as his equal."[14] The patriarch, having been deprived of his identity as the master and owner of men, reclaimed at least part of his identity by maintaining possession of women.

The ruling elites of England had neutralized somewhat the threat they perceived from the inclusion of the lower orders in the political process by means of education acts that required at least some schooling in middle-class values. The threat posed by women's challenges to patriarchal order was seen to be even greater than that of the working classes. The potential contradiction between, on the one hand, a liberal ideology that had legitimated the dismantling of aristocratic power and authority and the enfranchisement of most men and, on the other, the denial of the claims of women to full citizenship was resolved by appeals to biological and characterological differences between the sexes. Definitions of femininity evolved whose qualities were antithetical to those that had warranted widespread male participation in the public sphere. Men possessed the capacity for reason, action, aggression, independence, and self-interest. Women inhabited a separate, private sphere, one suitable for the so-called inherent qualities of femininity: emotion, passivity, submission, dependence, and selflessness, all derived, it was claimed insistently, from women's sexual and reproductive organization. Upon the female as a biological entity, a sexed body, nineteenth-century theorists imposed a socially or culturally constructed "femininity," a gender identity derived from ideas about what roles were appropriate for women. This collapsing of sex and gender—the physiological facts with the normative social creation—made it possible for women to be construed as at once pure and purely sexual; although paradoxical, these definitions excluded women from participation in the public sphere and rendered them subordinate to men in the private sphere as well.[15]

The language and images used to define gender reasserted the bases for patriarchal control, but now they did so in bourgeois terms. Theories of middle-class professionals—scientists, doctors, lawmakers, and sociologists—spoke directly to the

question, incorporating older notions of a hierarchical relationship between the sexes in their discussion of the direction and
meaning of social change. As the debate advanced, women succeeded in eliminating laws that made them the property of men,
and in 1918 they were granted the vote. But at the same time,
the ideology of "woman's sphere" and "woman's nature," legitimated by science and medicine, circumscribed their actions
and limited the possibility of women sharing real power with
men. Consequently, the vote, perceived by feminists to be the
means of bringing about a total transformation in the lives of
women, turned out to be nothing of the sort.

These notions of femininity that prescribed "woman's sphere"
and "woman's nature" were used metaphorically as various
groups vied for control in this period of great social change.
The metaphors were not necessarily consistent, but they played
on "natural dichotomies" expressed in the opposition of male
and female. L. J. Jordanova had noted that "our entire philo-
sophical set describes natural and social phenomena in terms of
oppositional characteristics," or dichotomies, "where the two
opposed terms mutually define each other."[16] Many nineteenth-
century theorists appropriated an idea of the feminine to justify
the middle classes' acquisition of power in the private and public spheres. In the struggle to eliminate or neutralize traditional,
aristocratic forms of power and authority, for instance, bourgeois
protagonists often described the aristocracy as "feminine," lacking in those masculine qualities of strength, resolve, and discipline that were indispensable to the creation and maintenance
of the industrial order. Aristocrats were by contrast weak, dis-
solute, and depraved, that is, "feminine," and their fitness to
govern was brought into question.

These notions were used to justify opposition to the demands
of the women's movement, but other arguments were added as
well. Though sharing the same objective, these arguments were
superficially inconsistent, for they at once idealized women and
expressed profound fear of them. On the one hand, women were

aligned with morality and religion, whereas men represented corruption and materialism. Women were construed as occupying the ethical center of industrial society, invested with the guardianship of social values, whereas men functioned in a world of shady dealings, greed, and vice, values generally subversive of a civilized order. On the other hand, women were also identified with nature—wild, unruly, yet to be explored and mastered; whereas men belonged to culture—controlled, systematic, symbolic of achievement and order. Correspondingly, women were assigned an exclusively reproductive function, in contrast to men, who allegedly held a monopoly on productivity. In each case, notions of femininity, or female nature, ultimately rested on the perceived sexual organization of women, who were construed to be either sexually comatose or helplessly nymphomaniacal. Whether belonging to one category or the other, women were so exclusively identified by their sexual functions that nineteenth-century society came to regard them as "the Sex." This in turn set up yet another dichotomy, which offered only two possible images for women: that of revered wife and mother, or that of despised prostitute. Both roles effectively disqualified women from public, political activity. At the same time, as feminists argued, the characterization of women as "the Sex" created the potential for the sexual abuse of women.

These notions of femininity first appeared in romantic prescriptive literature. The medical profession, in the course of its creation of a "science of sexuality," took the stereotypes and metaphors offered by prescriptive literature and grounded them in so-called objective scientific observation, thus creating practical prescriptions for women's behavior. Politicians seized upon these biologically determined aspects of femininity and implemented in legal "fact" what had been idealized ways of talking about men and women, male and female nature, and middle-class identity. The contradiction between the ideal mother on the one hand and the degraded prostitute on the other, however, was simply too extreme to reflect the real experiences of women.

Nineteenth-century women were, indeed, participants in and agents of culture; they did operate in the material and productive world of industrial society; and their contribution to the economic sphere was not limited to the reproduction of babies or the servicing of men's sexual needs. Many middle-class women protested that the gender construction assigned to them by the exigencies of nineteenth-century political economy rendered them powerless and sexually vulnerable, and they set out to construct a society and culture that reflected the realities of their lives. Feminists embarked on a campaign to gain recognition for their full and complete humanity and thereby eliminate the reductively sexualized definition of femininity that threatened their integrity and dignity.

NINETEENTH-CENTURY ideology eliminated the economic function of middle-class women and created the notion of the perfect wife and mother, or "the angel in the house," as she was described by Coventry Patmore. In the competitive, unsettling, and sometimes brutal world of nineteenth-century industrial society, it fell to women to provide a haven of peace and security, a repository of moral values. The home became a place of refuge from what Sarah Stickney Ellis called "those eager pecuniary speculations" and "that fierce conflict of worldly interests, by which men are so deeply occupied as to be in a manner compelled to stifle their best feelings."[17] John Ruskin referred to the home as "a walled garden"; inside, the wife and mother ruled as queen. Outside,

> the man . . . must encounter all peril and trial; to him, therefore, must be the failure, the offence, the inevitable error; often he must be wounded or subdued; often misled, and *always* hardened. But he guards the woman from all this; within his house, as ruled by her, unless she herself has sought it, need enter no danger, no temptation, no cause of error or offense. This is the true nature of the

home—it is the place of Peace; the shelter, not only from all injury, but from all terror, doubt, and division.[18]

Nineteenth-century romantics and moralists assigned to woman the task of creating a sanctuary from the harsh realities of the industrial world. Her feminine virtues of gentleness, sympathy, purity, and piety provided her husband and children with the emotional security necessary to face the hardships of modern life. One writer, Mrs. J. Stanford, believed that domestic comfort was "the greatest benefit [woman] confers upon society." "The sphere of Domestic Life is the sphere in which female excellence is best displayed," asserted another, the anonymous author of *Woman as She is, and as She should be*.[19]

"Female excellence," for authors of Victorian prescriptive literature, consisted largely of women's submissiveness to men. "Her part is to make sacrifices, in order that his enjoyment may be enhanced," advised Stickney Ellis of the duties of women, explaining that "the humblest occupation, undertaken from a sense of duty, becomes ennobled in the motive by which it is prompted, and that the severest self-denial may be blessed and honoured by the Father of mercies, if endured in preference to an infringement upon those laws which he [sic] has laid down for the government of the human family." Those laws reduced women to the role of helpmeet of men and succinctly stated that "the man naturally governs: the woman as naturally obeys."[20]

The romantic stereotypes of Victorian men and women and the underlying assumptions about human nature logically delineated and justified for each sex their ordained sphere in life: to men, the public realm; to women, the private one. These stereotypes and separate sphere ideology received scientific validation in the nineteenth century as sociologists such as Herbert Spencer and biologists such as Patrick Geddes and J. Arthur Thomson sought to explain and justify social organization through the application of biological principles.

Spencer attributed the differences between the sexes to a

"somewhat earlier-arrest of individual evolution in women than in men; necessitated by the reservation of vital power to meet the cost of reproduction." Because the energy spent by women in reproduction was not available for intellectual activity, they were said to be less developed, less evolved than men, whose limited role in reproduction—fertilization—permitted the expenditure of energy in more physical and cerebral areas. The capacity for the development of abstract reasoning and abstract justice by men, and the complete inability of women to contribute to this line of development, had been evolutionarily determined, Spencer maintained.[21]

Geddes and Thomson, in *The Evolution of Sex*, carried Spencer's ideas to a more primitive level, again rooted in the male and female roles in reproduction. Not simply in human and animal societies but among the simplest forms of life, male organisms exhibited a tendency toward dissipation of energy, whereas females inclined toward its conservation. Men were thus aggressive, women passive, creatures whose roles had been assigned in the earliest stages of life. Change in this regard, whether political or technological, was neither possible nor desirable, Geddes and Thomson argued. "What was decided among the prehistoric *Protozoa*," they asserted, "can not [sic] be annulled by act of Parliament."[22] As Jill Conway has observed, scientific explanations for the contemporary organization of society expiated any "guilt to be felt over the inferior position of women. It was a function of natural laws which operated well beyond the boundaries of human society."[23]

The ideology of the Victorian lady, or the "angel in the house," contained the notion of the inherently "passionless" woman. Though utilized by Nancy Cott to describe the American case, passionlessness was a transatlantic phenomenon, reflecting the view that "women lacked sexual aggressiveness, that their sexual appetites contributed a very minor part (if any at all) to their motivations, that lustfulness was simply uncharacteristic." Until the eighteenth century, it was believed that women's lust, as personified by Eve, was insatiable, but that women could become spiritual through God's grace, and hence less carnal. During the eighteenth and nineteenth centuries, the dominant definition of women as especially sexual was reversed and transformed into the view that women were less carnal and lustful than men.[24]

The prescriptive literature of the early eighteenth century recognized that women's sexual appetites were comparable to, if not greater than, men's. Such a view, as Cott has noted, created the "vast potential for sexual exploitation in a society in which women's sexual nature was considered primary and their social autonomy was slight." When, therefore, the notion of women's passionlessness was promulgated throughout the late eighteenth and nineteenth centuries, women had a stake in its acceptance and perpetuation.[25]

Cott has attributed the development of the ideology of passionlessness in America to three separate phases of British opinion, whose impact at home was no less significant. In the late eighteenth century, spokesmen for the new professional and commercial classes sought to discredit the aristocracy by decrying its pretensions, vanity, and libertinism. They "portrayed sexual promiscuity as one of those aristocratic excesses that threatened middle-class virtue and domestic security. . . . By elevating sexual control highest among human virtues the middle-class moralists made female chastity the archetype for human morality." Another contribution to passionlessness came from the etiquette manuals of the upper classes, which encouraged the development of an artificial modesty and demureness in women so that they would be more attractive to men, for whose pleasure and service they were created. These prescriptions, with their "underlying theme that women had to appeal to men," Cott has argued, "turned modesty into a sexual ploy, emphasizing women's sex objectification."[26]

The Evangelicals of the late eighteenth and early nineteenth centuries then transformed the notion of an affected modesty and purity of women into one of a natural or inherent modesty. In asserting that "Christianity had raised women from slaves in status to moral and intellectual beings," Evangelical Protestants insisted upon the suppression of female sexuality as a "tacit condition" of women's improved status. "The clergy . . . renewed and generalized the idea that women under God's grace were more pure than men," Cott has stated, "and they expected not merely the souls but the bodies of women to corroborate that claim." The clergy emphasized the moral rather than the sexual features of woman's nature for two reasons. First, as men's religious commitment diminished, women's agency in the cause of Protestantism became increasingly necessary. Second, the eclipsing of woman's sexual nature by moral and spiritual qualities undermined her primitive, original power over men—that of her sexuality.[27]

IN ITS original manifestations, the ideology of passionlessness seemed to offer positive rewards for women. The substitution of moral for sexual motives and qualities undermined the identification of women with sexual treachery and helped to engender power and self-respect for women. It also, Cott noted, "served women's larger interests by downplaying altogether their sexual characterization, which was the cause of their exclusion from significant 'human' (i.e., male) pursuits."[28] As physicians took up the notion of passionlessness in the mid-nineteenth century, however, they reduced it from its moral and spiritual connotations to a world view involving scientific, biological principles. Their rendering of the passionlessness of women once again imposed an exclusively sexual characterization; it placed women in a position of sexual vulnerability and at the same time justified anew their exclusion from "human" pursuits.

In developing a "science of sex," physicians involved themselves in a discourse on sexuality pertaining to women that contained paradoxical inconsistencies. One line of the argument insisted upon women's utter lack of sexual feeling; the other, as

Foucault and others have observed, asserted that their bodies were saturated with sex.

William Acton, in *Functions and Disorders of the Reproductive Organs*, published in 1857, declared that

> the majority of women (happily for society) are not very much troubled with sexual feeling of any kind. What men are habitually, women are only exceptionally. . . . There can be no doubt that sexual feeling in the female is in the majority of cases in abeyance, and that it requires positive and considerable excitement to be roused at all; and even if aroused (which in many instances it can never be) it is very moderate compared with that of the male.

Acton believed that women's "indifference to sex was naturally ordained to prevent the male's vital energies from being overly expended at any one time."[29] His concern for the overexpenditure of male sexual energies supports Foucault's contention that the deployment of sexuality is a technique for "maximizing life," creating a political order of life "through an affirmation of self." The fundamental concern of the scientists of sex was "the body, vigor, longevity, progeniture, and descent of the classes that 'ruled,' " Foucault wrote. Equipped with a "technology of sex," rulers isolate themselves from others so as to retain their differential value, and hence their position of power in the political ordering of life.[30]

As Jean L'Esperance has demonstrated, not all British physicians accepted Acton's dictum concerning female sexuality. Dr. George Drysdale, for one, believed that sexual pleasure was natural and beneficial to both sexes; in *The Elements of Social Science* (1859), he advocated more frequent sexual intercourse for married couples as a means to prevent disease. Of the "inherent" purity of the female, Drysdale wrote, "If we examine the origins and meaning of these singular ideas with regard to women, we shall find that they are based upon no natural distinction between sexes, but upon the erroneous views of man, and especially upon the mistaken ideas as to the virtue of female *chastity*."[31]

But Drysdale was, in many respects, a man ahead of his time. Other physicians shared his ideas about the naturalness of female sexuality, but, as L'Esperance has contended, "there seems little doubt that Acton's views were widely accepted and well received by the profession at large."[32] In the late nineteenth century, when the passionlessness of women began to be seriously challenged by such theorists as Havelock Ellis and even Geddes and Thomson, scientists and physicians minimized the extent to which a woman might experience sexual feeling. The latter two, as Jeffrey Weeks has pointed out, acknowledged that female sexuality rested upon a "physiological base," but they argued that morality and the perceived consequences of sexual activity exerted far greater control over women's behavior than was true for men. The sexuality of women "is so constituted," they proclaimed, "that from wooing to consummation it takes longer for the brain to become eroticised."[33]

The doctors' insistence on the purity of women reflected attempts on the part of Victorians to give order to a society that had undergone and continued to display great change, socially, economically, and politically. Anthropologists regard symbols of purity as means of controlling dirt or pollution. Dirt, Mary Douglas has noted, is "essentially disorder. Dirt offends against order. Eliminating it is . . . [an] effort to organise the environment."[34] Carroll Smith-Rosenberg has suggested that the purity literature of nineteenth-century America was designed to root out the threat posed to society by adolescent boys and single men, "individuals who remained outside recognized [social] structures."[35] Drawing upon the works of Douglas and Victor Turner, Smith-Rosenberg has argued that

the body . . . serves as a symbol of society, its members representing different groups or institutions within that society. If the body is symbol, then a determination to control bodily functions, to legislate, and to punish indicates a desire to control or protect specific institutions and groups within that society. If the body is seen as endangered by uncontrollable forces, then presumably this is a society or social group which fears change—change which it perceives simultaneously as powerful and beyond its control.[36]

When women began to participate in the demands for change that characterized the end of the aristocratic order in Britain, they were perceived as a powerful and potentially uncontrollable threat to society. Defining women as pure mitigated against the danger of dirt, of pollution, of the untidiness they represented in a male-directed and male-defined world. "[I]deas about separating, purifying, demarcating and punishing transgressions," Douglas has asserted, "have as their main function to impose system on an inherently untidy experience. It is only by exaggerating the difference between within and without, above and below, male and female, with and against, that a semblance of order is created."[37] With traditional, aristocratic, and patriarchal patterns of control and authority falling away, and women challenging those patterns that continued to exist, new means of control were necessary. The notion of the "great unwashed," applied to the formerly deferential lower classes, found its counterpart in the traditional emphasis on "the polluting, dirty, dangerous and thus anti-social character of women's sexuality."[38] No longer the property of men, women held an ambiguous and threatening position. By defining women as pure, men could render them relatively harmless. "[O]ur pollution behaviour," Douglas has written, "is the reaction which condemns any object or idea likely to confuse or contradict cherished classifications."[39]

Traditional society had regarded women as sexually treacherous. Modern, industrial society defined them as pure. The correlations are not meaningless. The symbol of Mary, and "the idea of the high value of virginity," Douglas has argued, "would be well-chosen for the project of changing the role of the sexes in marriage and in society at large. The idea of woman as the Old Eve, together with fears of sex pollution, belongs with a certain specific type of social organization. If this social order has to be changed, the Second Eve [Mary], a virgin source of redemption crushing evil underfoot, is a potent new symbol to present." For "purity is the enemy of change, of ambiguity and compromise."[40] "Pure woman" was used as a metaphor for dealing with the general disorder of the nineteenth century and for creating new forms of definition and control in the "real" or culturally prescribed relations between men and women. In their development of the "science of sex," in the process of creating a discourse of sexuality, physicians converted the metaphorical pure woman to one of flesh and blood, imposing upon women an identity composed solely of sexuality.

In asserting the nonsexuality of women, doctors helped to encourage the establishment of prudery in social interactions and the idea that ignorance of sexual matters was tantamount to sexual innocence. But, as Cott has pointed out, "when prudery became confused with passionlessness, it undermined women physically and psychologically by restricting their knowledge of their own sexual functioning."[41] As Foucault suggested, knowledge is power. Denial of knowledge is denial of access to power. Moreover, the definition of women as pure and asexual, while men remained passionate and lustful, set up a "hostility between the sexes which was to have overwhelming psychological and social ramifications . . . : man as aggressor, woman as victim."[42]

The doctors' characterization of women as nonsexual involved another element: fear of women's sexual power. At the same time that they announced that women had no sexual feeling at all, physicians also insisted that women were governed by their sexual and reproductive organs. So exclusively were women represented as "the Sex" in the nineteenth century that any behavior on their part that deviated from the functions of the woman as wife and mother was denounced as "unsexed."

– 41 –

One English gynecologist, Dr. Bliss, articulated in 1870 the general view of women as "the Sex" when he referred to the "gigantic power and influence of the ovaries over the whole animal economy of woman."[43] Dr. Horatio Storer, an American physician writing a year later, concurred. "Woman was what she is [sic]," he insisted, "in health, in character, in her charms, alike of body, mind and soul because of her womb alone."[44] Storer had frequent contact and close ties to British doctors. A member of the Medico-Chirurgical and Obstetric Societies of Edinburgh, he co-edited with an Edinburgh physician *The Obstetric Memoirs and Contributions of James Y. Simpson, M.D., F.R.S.E.* This type of collaboration between British and American medical men occurred regularly. A kind of transatlantic medical culture ensured that doctors in America and Britain shared an almost identical view of women as "the Sex."[45]

With menopause, Dr. W. Tyler Smith had warned in the *London Medical Journal* in 1848, "the death of the reproductive faculty is accompanied . . . by struggles which implicate every organ and every function of body [sic]." He alerted his colleagues to the "attacks of ovario-uterine excitement approaching to nymphomania" that occurred among menopausal women.[46] The American doctor A. K. Gardner considered women past the age of childbearing to be "degraded to the level of a being who has no further duty to perform in this world."[47]

Gynecologists identified women with reproduction and sex to the point that they likened women's sexual organs to the features that one ordinarily associates with the face and head. Dr. T. Clifford Allbut, in a lecture before the Royal College of Physicians, described the female patient at the mercy of her gynecologist, "who finds her uterus, like her nose, a little on one side, or again like that organ is running a little."[48] Dr. J. Marion Sims's *Clinical Notes on Uterine Surgery*, published in America in 1866, represented the vagina as having a "mouth," the womb a "neck" and "throat," and described the cervix as comparable to "the tonsils."[49]

Women were not simply defined by their reproductive systems; they were, in the language of nineteenth-century physicians, controlled by them as well. Henry Maudsley, M.D., an eminent British psychiatrist, wrote in an 1874 issue of the *Fortnightly Review* that "the male organization is one, and the female organization another . . . it will not be possible to transform a woman into a man . . . she will retain her special sphere of development and activity determined by the performance of those [reproductive] functions."[50] Drawing heavily upon the influential work by the American physician Edward Clarke, *Sex in Education*, Maudsley sought to justify attempts to exclude women from education and the professions and to limit their role to a reproductive rather than a productive one. He asserted that women, by virtue of their reproductive functions, could not stand up to the rigors of higher education or sustained cerebral activity. According to Maudsley, nature had endowed women with a finite amount of energy, and its proper use belonged to reproduction. Reproductive processes demanded all the energy a woman could muster; to spend it in another direction would inexorably undermine the very functions that gave woman her only *raison d'être*. If women foolishly attempted to undertake study, he concluded, they risked ruining forever their childbearing capacities, thus endangering the future of the race.

Real educational strain began to take place, insisted Maudsley, just at the time of puberty, "when, by the development of the sexual system, a great revolution takes place in the body and mind, and an extraordinary expenditure of vital energy is made." Education continued after puberty, "when by the establishment of periodical functions, a regularly recurring demand is made upon the resources of a constitution." Any interference with the development of the processes of reproduction, especially in the critical years during and immediately following puberty, threatened to destroy women's health completely, that is, destroy their ability to bear children. The *healthy* performance of women's reproductive functions, maintained Maudsley, determined that they could not succeed in following men's paths or striving for men's goals. "They cannot choose but to be women; cannot rebel successfully against the tyranny of their organization." He concluded that a woman should not be permitted to undertake any form of education that would "unsex her," for "sex is fundamental, lies deeper than culture, cannot be ignored or defied with impunity . . . if the attempt to do so be seriously and persistently made, the result may be a monstrosity—something which having ceased to be woman is not yet man."[51] Conceived as sexual beings and determined by reproductive functions, women who deviated the slightest from their assigned roles as wife and mother were stripped of any trace of personhood.

The development of the reproductive system in women was so delicate a process that even the tiniest complication rendered them quite susceptible to mental and physical disease. Maudsley advised that "their nerve-centres being in a state of greater instability, by reason of the development of their reproductive functions, they will be more easily and the more seriously deranged."[52] Almost every female disease, claimed the doctors, derived from some disorder of the reproductive system.[53] Usually the "disorder" consisted of a refusal on the part of a woman to perform her duties as wife or mother, or, conversely, a tendency of the woman to exhibit an unwomanly interest in sex. Dr. T. S. Clouston's *Clinical Lectures on Mental Diseases* (5th ed., London, 1898), for instance, diagnosed as "Ovarian Insanity" or "Old Maid's Mania" the passion of an unmarried woman "for some casual acquaintance of the opposite sex, whom the victim believes to be deeply in love with her."[54]

After the turn of the century, scientific advances slowly replaced the model of physiological causation upon which earlier physicians had based their theories—what Weeks has called a model of "closed energy systems"—with one founded upon the significance of hormonal activity. Nevertheless, these advances in knowledge failed to rupture the tie between sexual physiology and social characteristics; in fact, they strengthened it. For instance, by 1908, ovarian hormones were acknowledged to be vital to the reproductive process. In 1916, W. Blair Bell used this information to formulate an "essential fact" about women: that "femininity itself is dependent on all the internal secretions." The "female mind," he continued, "is specifically adapted to her more protracted part in the perpetuation of the species."[55]

The theories of Spencer and the doctors moved the argument about woman's nature from metaphor to practical application. The association of women with nature—Maudsley's statement that sex lies deeper than culture—as opposed to the association of men with culture proved to be a powerful agent in arguing for the subordination of women. Anthropologist Sherry Ortner has asserted that the symbol of woman as nature meant her identification with "something that every culture devalues, something that every culture defines as being a lower order of existence than itself." Men, on the other hand, are associated with culture, or "the notion of human consciousness, or with the products of human consciousness (i.e., systems of thought and technology), by means of which humanity attempts to assert control over nature." Since it is culture's task to overcome and transcend nature, and since women are associated with nature, "then culture would find it 'natural' to subordinate, not to say oppress, them," Ortner has reasoned.[56]

The connection of women with nature originates, Ortner has maintained, with "the body and the natural procreative functions specific to women alone . . . woman's *body and its functions*, more involved more of the time with 'species life,' seem to place her closer to nature, in contrast to man's physiology, which frees him more completely to take up the projects of culture." The association of woman with nature and man with culture not only places woman on a lower level than man, it also gives way to the tendency of culture "to circumscribe and restrict her functions, since culture must maintain control over its (pragmatic and symbolic) mechanisms for the conversion of nature into culture."[57]

The dichotomy of woman as nature and man as culture enabled men to develop a greater sense of identity in a period of vast social change. Jordanova has noted that "debates about sex and sex roles, especially during the nineteenth century, hinged precisely on the ways in which sexual boundaries might become blurred. . . . At certain times (perhaps times of perceived rapid change), physicians were deeply concerned about . . . the masculinization of women, which they believed could result from excessive physical or mental work." Maudsley's dire predictions about the consequences of educating women reflected the desire, in Jordanova's words, for "clarity in areas of life which appear constantly subject to change." The woman/man, nature/culture dichotomy was, for Maudsley, expressed concretely in terms of the distinctions between men's work and women's work. "Men were . . . potential members of the broadest social and cultural groups," Jordanova has pointed out, "while women's sphere, it was constantly insisted, was the private arena of home and family." Confining women to the home, as wives and mothers, might disarm them of some of their power and danger, for "women as *sexual beings* carry danger; it is really only as *mothers* that they are safe."[58]

Women who refused the duties of motherhood or who exhibited "unwomanly" sexuality, manifested in female illness, were indeed perceived by doctors to be unsafe. It was a short distance from defining all female illness as a disorder of the reproductive system to using gynecological surgery to cure those ills. Some doctors recognized the connection feminists made between the women's movement and sexual revolution: "any demand for social or political rights on the part of a being construed as entirely body was a sexual rebellion," Barker-Benfield has argued persuasively about the reaction of American physicians to feminism.[59]

The doctors' solution to the threatened overthrow of patriar-

chal society was the castration and sexual mutilation of women
who displayed any tendency to step out of their ordained sphere
of innocence, purity, and submissiveness to men. Isaac Baker
Brown, a London gynecologist, reported in 1866 a number of
successes in curing various illnesses through clitoridectomy. In
the case of a young woman of twenty, who had for two years
"suffered from almost constant menorrhagia, during which time
she had suffered great irregularites of temper, been disobedient
to her mother's wishes, and had sleepless nights," Baker Brown
discovered that "all these symptoms arose from peripheral excitement [masturbation]." He prescribed his "usual plan of
treatment"—clitoridectomy—which resulted in "the most rapid
and marked success" in ridding the woman of her ills. Another
woman came to him suffering from menorrhagia, which manifested itself in a "great distaste for her husband." This, too,
Baker Brown found, resulted from "peripheral excitement." "I
pursued the usual surgical treatment," he reported, "which was
followed by uninterrupted success, and after two months treatment, she returned to her husband, resumed cohabitation, and
stated that all her distaste had disappeared; soon became pregnant, and resumed her place at the head of the table, and became a happy and healthy wife and mother."[60]

Clitoridectomy was performed to cure dysuria, amenorrhea,
sterility, epilepsy, masturbation, "hysterical mania," and various
manifestations of insanity.[61] The source of these diseases was
thought to be sexual arousal; the termination of sexual arousal
through clitoridectomy cured the disease. One historian has estimated that some 600 such operations were performed between
1860 and 1866, at which time they were discontinued in England.[62] Ovariotomies may have been performed even more often,
and for the cure of diseases that were nonovarian in nature.[63]

Given the view that women were defined and controlled by
their reproductive and sexual organs, gynecological surgery for
any number and variety of problems was a logical procedure.
But it served another purpose as well. "The gynecologists' un-

derlying aims," Barker-Benfield has contended, "cannot be separated from the society in which they moved: these aims were retaliation against and control of women, and the assumption of as much of their reproductive power as possible, all part and parcel of the projective meaning of the subordination of 'the sex.' " The American Dr. Arnold Praeger, in 1895, asserted that the "principles of [gynecological] surgery . . . resemble justice." His colleague, Dr. David Gilliam, in 1896, compared the advantages of castrating animals to those of castrating women. "Why do we alter our colts and calves?" he asked. "Not that we expect to abate strength or endurance, nor yet to render them less intelligent; but that we may make them tractable and trustworthy, that we may convert them into faithful, well disposed servants."[64] The Englishman Allbut, mentioned earlier, described his archetypal patient as "entangled in the net of the gynecologist." She found relief from her doctor's ministrations only when he was engaged in his ancillary occupation, "during the long vacation when the gynaecologist is grouse shooting or salmon catching."[65] The metaphors of breaker and animal, of hunter and prey, permeate the gynecological literature.

Again drawing upon the symbolic interpretations made available by anthropologists, we may better understand the doctors' fear of, and attempts to neutralize or eliminate, any manifestation of female sexuality. The female, Simone de Beauvoir suggested, by virtue of her reproductive functions, "is more enslaved to the species than the male, her animality is more manifest."[66] A woman, then, is less than human and exists on the periphery of what is human, or culture.[67] For illustrative purposes, Ortner has described culture "as a small clearing within the forest of the larger natural system. From this point of view, that which is intermediate between culture and nature is located on the continuous periphery of culture's clearing; . . . it is simply outside and around it."[68] In other words, women exist on the margins of culture and society, and as Douglas and Smith-Rosenberg have argued, margins are dangerous and powerful. Using Douglas's insights, Smith-Rosenberg has explained that "marginal . . . figures by their very nature lie outside and thus are alien to order and control. In cultures which perceive their traditional order as endangered, marginal figures appear particularly dangerous."[69]

The attitudes of the doctors support Jordanova's contention that "science and medicine as activities were associated with sexual metaphors which were clearly expressed in designating nature as a woman to be unveiled, unclothed and penetrated by masculine science." Woman was nature, and "nature was taken to be that realm on which mankind acts, not just to intervene in or manipulate directly, but also to understand and render it intelligible."[70] The depiction of the female reproductive organs as similar to facial features can be seen as an attempt to give familiarity, or humanness, to what is otherwise perceived as sexual, animal, natural. Gynecological surgery is a more radical approach to the elimination of the sexual danger posed by women to the order of society. Praeger's statement that gynecological surgery resembles justice constitutes a desire to bring the dangerous woman into the realm and control of the man, justice being, as Spencer maintained, a male construct.

MIDDLE-CLASS ATTITUDES toward sexuality—marriage, birth control, prostitution, and sexual relations—changed over the fifty-odd years under study. Throughout the entire period, for example, the deliberate refusal of a woman to marry, as Jane Lewis has noted, "signified a revolt against the prescribed feminine role." But those women who did seek marriage and "got left on the shelf," as the saying went, realized some improvement in their situation. In the nineteenth century, they would have been regarded, and would have regarded themselves, as failures. By the early twentieth century, with the increase in respectable occupations available to women, judgment would not have been quite so harsh, and perhaps not so readily internalized.[71]

The institution of marriage itself underwent some modification. Though challenged by feminists in the 1890s, the traditional, patriarchal marriage, characterized by inequality between spouses and the notion of the "natural" subordination of the wife, remained the accepted norm throughout the Victorian and Edwardian eras. Ignorance about sex, unreliable methods of contraception, and the ever-present dangers of childbirth often meant that the intimate aspects of marriage for women could be quite unpleasant. "During the late nineteenth century," Lewis has asserted, "many husbands and wives must have met in the marriage bed as two separate races." But at least partly as a result of such reforms as the Married Women's Property Act and the Matrimonial Causes Act of 1857, the spread of contraceptive information among the middle classes after 1876, and the feminist attack on marriage as a trade, matrimony slowly took on a new meaning, one that emphasized companionship and partnership. This trend continued with the establishment of the Royal Commission on Divorce, whose recommendations for equalization of grounds in 1912 became law in 1923. "By the inter-war years married women were no longer regarded primarily as ornamental and sexually innocent creatures; the ideal companionate marriage also involved an expectation of sexual harmony. The sexes no longer led the uncommunicative, separate lives, which is perhaps the most striking characteristic of middle class Victorian autobiographies and popular literature."[72]

In the realm of sexuality, some fairly clear demarcations are visible. Although at no time in the nineteenth century do we find any notion of women's sexuality that is independent of men's, attitudes toward sex and related issues varied. Social purity campaigns, the idea of the passionless woman, and repression dominated the culture until the 1880s or so, although as Weeks has observed, "social purity never succeeded in totally silencing its opponents." In fact, the repressive ways of the Victorians probably stimulated, by the 1880s, a "new mood." Victorian society witnessed "a significant expansion of writings on sexuality in the late nineteenth and early twentieth centuries."

Edward Carpenter, Havelock Ellis, and the "New Women" authors arose to challenge the advocates of sexual ignorance and innocence, of passionless women, commencing a contest for the hearts and minds of society between social purity and greater liberalization that lasted until the First World War.[73]

By the twentieth century, sex theorists such as Ellis and even the conservative Geddes and Thomson had begun to recognize an autonomous female sexuality, though they continued to insist that it was harder to arouse than that of the male. Moreover, it remained dependent upon male initiative. "The female responds to the stimulation of the male at the right moment just as the tree responds to the stimulation of the warmest days in spring," wrote Ellis, maintaining that while the boy spontaneously develops into a man, the girl "must be kissed into a woman."[74]

The notion of passionless women and the interdependence of constructions of male and female sexuality rendered Victorians utterly incapable of conceiving of female sexual activity that did not involve a male partner. While male homosexuality was acknowledged and condemned in the nineteenth century, lesbianism was not only ignored, it was actively denied, despite the fact that romantic friendships of great intensity flourished between women. "These romantic friendships were love relationships in every sense except perhaps the genital," Lillian Faderman has argued,

> since women in centuries other than ours often internalized the view of females as having little sexual passion. Thus they might kiss, fondle each other, sleep together, utter expressions of overwhelming love and promises of eternal faithfulness, and yet see their passions as nothing more than effusions of the spirit. If they were sexually aroused, bearing no burden of visible truth as men do, they might deny it even to themselves if they wished.[75]

Victorians tolerated and even encouraged these passionate friendships between women, confident that they could only be innocent, pure relationships that were wholly compatible with heterosexual marriage. They never entertained the possibility that these might involve a sexual component, for the dominant discourse defined women as without passion. Thus, Faderman has pointed out, "a sexual act without a male initiator, one which required autonomous drive, would be unthinkable."[76]

The early reforms achieved by feminists, especially those that expanded employment and education opportunities, spurred a slight alteration in the perception of passionate friends. The fact that women could now claim an existence independent of men seems to have inspired a new apprehension. As early as 1880, Eliza Lynn Linton, a notorious anti-feminist, hinted in her novel, *The Rebel of the Family*, that the "Lady President of the West Hill Society for Women's Rights," Mrs. Bell Blount, engaged in deviant behavior with her followers. Blount, separated from her husband, lived with Miss Connie Taylor, whom she called her "little wife." Taylor, in turn, referred to Blount as her "husband." When Bell brought Perdita, the heroine, into the movement, she did so by "suddenly taking her in her arms and kissing her with strange warmth." Later, having left town, she wrote to Perdita every day letters of great "warmth of her expressions of affection," which "made Perdita's cheeks burn, she scarcely knew why; but certainly with more pain than pleasure. . . . Half-attracted and half-repelled—fascinated by the woman's mental power and revolted by something too vague to name yet too real to ignore."[77] The inference is clear, for as Vineta Colby has pointed out, Lynn Linton's feminists, whom she called "wild women," always seemed to know too much about sex.[78]

Lynn Linton's dark intimations of sexual deviance were not representative of late nineteenth-century observers, but they foreshadowed society's response in the twentieth century. As Faderman has noted:

Perhaps love between women was permitted to flourish unchecked in the nineteenth century because the fact of the

New Woman and her revolutionary potential for forming a permanent bond with another woman had not yet been widely impressed upon the popular imagination, as after World War I when New Women emerged in great numbers. It was then that love between women came to be generally feared in America and England. The emotional and sensual exchanges between women, which correspondence and fiction tell us were a common form of affectional expression for centuries, suddenly took on the character of perversion.[79]

Physicians played a significant role in the establishment of a lesbian identity and its characterization as pathological. Nineteenth-century doctors such as Carl von Westphal and Richard von Krafft-Ebing believed that lesbianism resulted from "cerebral anomalies"; it was the mark of "an inherited diseased condition of the central nervous system" and a "functional sign of degeneration." Havelock Ellis, whose wife, Edith Lees, was a lesbian, accepted this disease model; through his influential writings on sexuality he transmitted the model to twentieth-century society. The new scientific "knowledge" defining lesbianism as a medical problem, combined with society's anxieties over women's increased independence, ensured that romantic friendships, previously tolerated and encouraged, would now be regarded as deviant, anti-social, and dangerous. Ellis himself clearly discerned a connection between feminism and "sexual inversion," as he called it, maintaining that the women's movement "involved an increase in feminine criminality and in feminine insanity. . . . In connection with these we can scarcely be surprised to find an increase in homosexuality, which has always been regarded as belonging to an allied, if not the same, group of phenomena."[80]

POLITICIANS drew upon all the feminine stereotypes in their refusal to admit women to the franchise. The exclusion of women rested on their disqualification by sex. The franchise was based on property qualifications; anyone meeting those criteria could exercise the prerogative to vote except criminals, lunatics, idiots, children, or women. Governed by their reproductive systems, women were thought to be too emotional, too unstable, too lacking in intellectual capacity to participate in the running of government. F. E. Smith, announcing his opposition to women's suffrage in the House of Commons, quoted H. G. Wells on women's disabilities. "The trend of evolutionary forces through long centuries of human development," he read,

> has been on the whole towards differentiation. An adult white woman differs far more from a white man than a negress or pigmy woman from her equivalent male. The education, the mental disposition of a white or Asiatic woman reeks of sex; her modesty, her decorum, is not to ignore sex but to refine and put a point to it; her costume is clamorous with the distinctive elements of her form.[81]

Austen Chamberlain, in the debate on the second reading of the Conciliation Bill in 1910, argued that nature had distinguished between men and women, stating "it is on that ground that I am an opponent of woman suffrage. In my opinion the sex of a woman is a disqualification in fact, and we had better continue to so regard it in law."[82]

Smith and Chamberlain identified women with the concept of nature as that, to quote Jordanova, "which has not yet been penetrated (either literally or metaphorically), the wilderness and deserts, unmediated and dangerous nature." In this sense of woman as nature,

> it was woman's emotions and uncontrolled passions which gave her special qualities. Women, being endowed with less reason than men, indeed with less need for reason since their social lives required of them feeling and not thought, were more easily dominated by extreme emotions. Women

were therefore conceptualized as dangerous because less amenable to the guiding light of reason. . . . Their potential for disorder can be minimised by drawing and maintaining strong social boundaries around them.[83]

Opponents of women's suffrage marshaled all sorts of sentiments in support of their refusal to grant women the vote. Women had no need for the vote, they insisted; men—husbands, fathers, or brothers—had always protected their interests and would continue to do so. Smith argued that "after centuries of man-made law . . . woman today occupies a position so preferential that no parallel can be discovered in any civilised country in the world." Voting was unfeminine and unnatural; participation in the sordid affairs of government would sully the purity of women's character. "The fear I have," Gladstone stated, "is, lest we should invite her unwittingly to trespass upon the delicacy, the purity, the refinement, the elevation of her own nature, which are the present sources of its power."[84]

As Gladstone hinted here, the sources of female power, as granted by men, lay in women's submissiveness to men in all spheres of life. Agitation for enfranchisement threatened male dominance, not simply in the political and public realm but in the domestic and private realm as well. In 1867, in a speech before the House of Commons, John Stuart Mill charged that objections to enfranchisement for women went far deeper than the mere participation of women in politics. "I know," he stated, "there is an obscure feeling—a feeling which is ashamed to express itself openly—as if women had no right to care about anything except how they may be the most useful and devoted servants of some man."[85] Votes for women would raise them from "the stultifying servitude of sex," as *Common Cause* put it; would bring about their descent from the pedestal of "the angel in the house"; in short, would confer upon them a humanity, a reality as human beings.[86] The anti-suffragists feared that votes for women would constitute a revolutionary transformation of the relations between the sexes, a transformation that would permeate every aspect of society, including that of sexual relations.

Frederic Harrison acknowledged the radical nature of the suffrage campaign when, writing in 1909, he observed, "great as is the revolution in the constitution demanded to-day by some Women, it is but an incident in a social problem far vaster and more deep. . . . It cuts down to the roots of our family life." Greater manhood suffrage, he argued, did not pose the peril to the state that votes for women entailed; it concerned only politics. Harrison cautioned that female suffrage would "disintegrate families" and "plant anarchy in the Home." "No thoughtful man or woman," he warned,

> denies that the cry of "Votes for Women" cannot be separated from the entire consensus of the domestic, social, and spiritual existence of Woman as a sex distinct from Man. Education, manners, social philosophy, religion, are all essentially involved in the change. It is no mere affair of Constituencies and House of Commons. It affects life on a thousand sides.[87]

Describing militant suffragettes as "viragoes," Harrison revealed his fear that votes for women would upset the dominant/submissive character of male/female roles in the family and usurp the power over their wives that men enjoyed.

Men feared the use to which women would put the vote if it were granted them, particularly in sexual matters. F. W. Pethick Lawrence, a primary contributor to the WSPU, recalled that antis believed that "if women came to share the political, intellectual, and occupational life of men they would lose their special charm and attraction."[88] That special charm and attraction were expressed in terms of complementarity, but ultimately they came to mean complete submission to men, involving especially submission to men's sexual demands. Votes for women, argued the antis, would overturn the sexual order that gave men complete control over women's bodies. The opposition often pointed

out—though not always openly, Pethick Lawrence reported—
that "on sex matters women were narrower and harder than
men; and that if they were given power they would impose im-
possibly strict standards of morality, and endeavour to enforce
them by penalties for non-observance."[89] William Acton, as early
as 1875, had warned his readers that the campaigners for wom-
en's rights posed a grave threat to male domination in sexual
matters. He revealed the case of a "lady who maintains women's
rights to such an extent that she denied the husband any voice
in the matter, whether or not cohabitation should take place."[90]

Finally, antis insisted that women's suffrage would bring
about a "sex war." "We have seen how easily in the more excit-
able natures the agitation for female suffrage stiffens into a kind
of sex-war," Harrison wrote.

> This sex-war calls out all the latent discontent which too
> many women unconsciously nurse, and is often a mere
> mask to the wish for separation in families on more or less
> equal grounds. Equal electoral rights could not fail to in-
> flame a standing war between the sexes, by giving equal
> power to man and woman where the practical responsibil-
> ities and capacities are not equal.

Women were made to bear children; men were made to rule
them. Harrison and others intimated that any deviation from the
model of the sexually submissive woman and the dominant man
would occur only at great risk to women. "The universal and
inevitable result of female franchise would be a subtle weakening
of men's respect for women's opinion—and, indeed, soon a
weakening of men's respect for women," Harrison threatened.[91]

Feminists countered that relations between men and women
already resembled a "sex war" because of the separation of the
sexes in distinct spheres. The ideology of women's private
sphere rested on definitions of female sexuality; indeed, it was
always depicted in those terms. It is not surprising, then, that
women who challenged the ideology of separate spheres ad-

dressed the central premise of the ideology—the question of women's, and men's, sexual identity. As Olive Banks has observed, "the feminists who claimed for women the right to break out of both their confinement to domesticity and their legal and political subordination to man . . . had to re-examine for themselves both the cult of domesticity and its corollary, the doctrine of true womanhood, because these were not only the justification for woman's separate sphere but the basis on which the antifeminists attacked the feminists' cause."[92]

As the following chapters will illustrate, feminists charged that in presenting women as "the Sex," the ideology did not protect them and enshrine their virtue but permitted the abuse of women by men. As "the Sex," women had not been elevated to a pedestal as the moral guardians of hearth and home but had been dragged through the mire either as prostitutes or as "respectable" receptacles for male sexuality. Feminists sought to eliminate the stereotypes of women—both the idealized and the feared—that rendered them inhuman and, through the weapon of the vote, to create a society that was consistent with their needs, interests, and self-defined reality. In the process, however, they did not entirely reject cultural stereotypes. Instead they formulated their arguments in terms of and in relation to prevailing ideas as expressed in prescriptive, scientific, and political discussion. As Lewis has pointed out, "feminists who made women's right to enter the public sphere a priority never really addressed the issue of women's role as wives and mothers, which late nineteenth-century doctors and scientists held to be the chief and necessary constraint on women's achievements. They acknowledged the importance of motherhood. . . . To all intents and purposes, however, they *ignored* the implications of their demand to enter the public sphere for the role of women in the private sphere of home and family, and chose not to confront the emphasis doctors and scientists placed on the latter."[93]

Feminists spoke the language of their time, even as they

sought to alter the meaning of some of its terms. They did not mean by the elimination of separate spheres that women should no longer marry and bear children or abandon the home, nor did they suggest that men should participate equally in child-rearing and other domestic chores. "Women are . . . in a special degree the guardian of the home and family," wrote Millicent Fawcett to Asquith in 1913, "a fact recognised by suffragists and anti-suffragists alike."[94] But feminists did intend to eliminate separate spheres through "the attempted invasion of the mas-culine world not simply by women but, potentially even more revolutionary in its impact, by womanly values," as Banks has argued.[95] In their vocabulary—as in the society at large—sex and politics were not mutually exclusive categories.

CHAPTER II

PROSTITUTION

It is *men, men, men*, from the first to the last that
we have to do with! To please a man I did wrong
at first, then I was flung about from man to man,
then men police lay hands on us—by men we are
examined, handled, doctored and messed on with.
. . . We are had up before Magistrates who are
men, and we never get out of the hands of men till
we die!

A prostitute to Josephine Butler, circa 1870

Victorian ideology finally offered only two possible images for
women. They might be either the idealized wife and mother,
the angel in the house, or the debased, depraved, corrupt prostitute.[1] The image of the respectable, passionless middle-class
lady, in fact, depended upon a contrast with the other image of
the "fallen" woman. Whereas society and its main spokesmen
insisted that the two types of women operated in diametrically
opposed and separate spheres, feminists countered that, in the
end, they were not, in men's minds, distinct at all. Indeed,
feminists refused the terms of the contrast, insisting that prostitutes and women of the respectable classes received the very
same treatment from men.

The feminist critique, in fact, points to the interdependence
of the two images of women and their use in defining the terms
not only of female behavior but of male sexuality. In his discussion of pure women in *Functions and Disorders of the Reproductive Organs*, Acton asserted that motherhood provided the only
motivation for their sexual activity, whereas natural desire propelled men. "There are many females," he claimed, "who never

feel any sexual excitement whatever. . . . Many of the best mothers, wives, and managers of households, know little of or are careless about sexual indulgences. Love of home, of children, and of domestic duties are the only passions they feel." While desiring little or no sexual gratification for herself, the modest woman "submits to her husband's embraces, but principally to gratify him; and, were it not for the desire of maternity, would far rather be relieved from his attentions." Some women "evinced positive loathing for any marital familiarity whatever." In such cases "feeling has been sacrificed to duty, and the wife has endured, with all the self-martyrdom of womanhood, what was almost worse than death." Not all men were so fortunate as to have such a wife, Acton hinted. Some women, "who, either from ignorance or utter want of sympathy . . . not only evince no sexual feeling, but, on the contrary, scruple not to declare their aversion to the least manifestation of it." Sometimes this aversion to sex was due to disease, in which case the woman ought to have the problem looked into as soon as possible. "Much more frequently, however," he charged, "it depends upon apathy, selfish indifference to please, or unwillingness to overcome a natural repugnance for cohabitation."[2]

Many men found themselves in such a situation, Acton maintained. They complained to him, "and I think with reason," he empathized, "that they are debarred from the privileges of marriage, and that their sexual sufferings are almost greater than they can bear in consequence of their being mated to women who think and act as in the above-cited instances." He warned his readers that lack of a sexual outlet "might be . . . highly detrimental to the health of the husband," a problem "ultimately too often ending in impotence."[3]

Although nineteenth-century physicians preached the desirability of restricting or controlling the expenditure of male sexual energies, they believed the male sex drive to be "innate." One "expert" on prostitution, W. R. Greg, regarded sexual indulgence for men as natural; Acton believed that male sexual impulses could be controlled but not entirely repressed.[4] In fact, he counseled that repression of sexual energies could be quite dangerous for men. The equation of respectable, pure women with motherhood, and that of men with sexuality, required a construction of female sexuality that posited its dual nature. Masculinity and male sexuality rested on the twin pillars of motherhood and prostitution. For at a time when masturbation was perceived to be the agent of a whole slew of physical and mental pathologies, the only recourse for men in a society that separated maternity from sexuality was the creation of another class of women, existing exclusively for the gratification of male sexual desires. These women were "usually classed as prostitutes and were regarded as a necessary evil to protect the pure, who otherwise might unwittingly provoke the male to rape them."[5] William Lecky, in his 1869 *History of European Morals*, recognized that prostitution served as an essential sexual safety valve for Victorians. "Herself the supreme type of vice," he wrote of the prostitute,

> she is ultimately the most efficient guardian of virtue. But for her the unchallenged purity of countless happy homes would be polluted, and not a few who, in the pride of their untempted chastity, think of her with an indignant shudder, would have known the agony of remorse or despair. On that degraded and ignoble form are concentrated the passions that might have filled the world with shame.[6]

Through discussions of the dual nature of female sexuality—that of mother and of whore—theorists constructed a single sexuality for men that acknowledged the urgency of male drives and the necessity of relieving them. The general and pervasive acceptance of male sexual license in Britain required the official recognition and institutionalization of prostitution. Prostitution, O. R. McGregor pointed out, "operated through the double standard of morality to accommodate both the recognized waywardness of men and the purity of the middle-class wife and home. . . . The system of prostitution was the squalid basis of much Victorian rectitude and respectability. It must be understood and interpreted as an essential element in Victorian sexual morality."[7]

Contemporaries perceived the interdependence of constructions of male and female sexuality. The acceptance of a rapacious male sexuality made prostitution indispensable to the maintenance of a respectable class of women. Ellice Hopkins, a leader in the social purity movement, suggested in the 1880s, with pointed sarcasm, that "since prostitutes were martyrs of purity, brothels should be put next to churches."[8] "Our marriage system is buttressed with prostitution," Catherine Gasquoine Hartley argued in 1913.

> Without the assistance of the prostitution of one class of women and the enforced celibacy of another class our marriage in its present form could not stand. It is no use shirking it; if marriage cannot be made more moral—and by this I mean more able to meet the sex needs of all men and all women—then we must accept prostitution . . . we must give our consent to this sacrifice of women as necessary to the welfare and stability of society.[9]

These comments were made after the Contagious Diseases Acts and the campaign for their repeal brought into the open the discussion of prostitution and the double standard. Butler's campaign took the wraps off a subject that had been shrouded in secrecy, at least for female members of society. The double standard operated not simply to render respectable women passionless, it also encouraged complete ignorance of sexual and reproductive functions. Victorians believed, as Banks and Banks have written, that "the very knowledge of sexual immorality was harmful to their womenfolk"; they "banished sexual topics from their drawing rooms and exerted a stern censorship on those publications which were for mixed reading."[10] Butler recalled the outraged discussions among academics who had gathered in her home over the publication of a novel by Elizabeth Gaskell that dealt openly with prostitution. They insisted that "a pure woman . . . should be absolutely ignorant of a certain class of evils in the world."[11]

The "conspiracy of silence" surrounding sexual matters was more than the simple equation of ignorance and innocence, feminists charged. Ignorance about sexual matters among women facilitated the recourse of men to prostitutes and enabled them to cover up, with the help of physicians, any venereal diseases they might bring home to their wives. "It cannot be denied that women have been vastly to blame in the past for the present state of affairs in the world of morals," Ethel Snowdon acknowledged. "Their one substantial excuse is that they were kept ignorant, and taught to endure what they were led to believe was in the natural order of Providence."[12] The passage of the Contagious Diseases Acts, a sobriquet normally utilized in legislation dealing with animals, in the middle of the night with little debate, underscores the importance of silence and secrecy in maintaining the system of prostitution.[13]

Secrecy and silence were shattered by Butler's fiery sixteen-year campaign for the repeal of the Contagious Diseases Acts. The acts were originally intended to decrease the incidence of venereal disease among soldiers and sailors in port and garrison towns by requiring any woman in those towns suspected of being a prostitute to be examined for venereal disease. If found to be infected, the woman was required to stay in a lock hospital (a hospital treating venereal disease) until she was deemed to be disease-free, at which time she would be given a certificate verifying her status. Butler and the LNA became active in the repeal campaign when controversy surrounding the proposed extension of the acts to the civilian population brought the existence of the acts into public view.

State regulation of prostitution contained an implicit construction of male sexuality. The CD Acts gave institutional validation to "an unthinking acceptance of male sexual license," as

Walkowitz has asserted. They "represented a 'high water mark' of an officially sanctioned double standard of sexual morality, one that upheld different standards of chastity for men and women and carefully tried to demarcate pure women from the impure."[14] Having segregated one segment of the female population and ensconced them safely within the fortress of home, family, and domesticity, the construction of male sexuality required that Victorians target another class of women, the "fallen," as the proper outlet for male sexual drives. But prostitutes were more than a sexual safety valve for Victorian men, as Gordon Rattray Taylor noted. "The Victorians needed prostitutes as objects on whom to project all the negative part of their feelings for women. Prostitutes were to the Victorians what witches were to the mediaevals [sic]."[15] In Freudian terms, the prostitute served as the degraded creature with whom men could be sexual and avoid the symbolic incest of intercourse with pure women, whom they identified with their own mothers.[16] The prostitute was perceived to be a depraved individual, lacking all self-respect and decency, and therefore deserving of all the iniquities heaped upon her person by the exigencies of male sexuality, including the compulsory examination by that "instrument of hell," the speculum. Indeed, when the army attempted to institute periodic examinations among its soldiers, they "objected violently," and the practice was shortly discontinued lest it demoralize the enlisted men. Army brass then turned to the periodic examination of women, declaring that "such objections could not apply to prostitutes."[17]

The attempts to create two classes of women, the pure and the impure, and in effect to legalize prostitution by means of the Contagious Diseases Acts, in many ways paralleled the conception of separate spheres for men and women. Pure women remained within the private sphere of home and family, where sexual relations between men and women assumed the existence of love, companionship, and above all, procreation, all consistent with the ideology of a woman as the angel in the house.

The impure woman operated in the public sphere, where she sold sex for material gain. The one realm had no relation to or connection with the other, the argument went. Victorians regarded the prostitute as the seducer of young men, the corrupter of morals, and the carrier and personification of disease, who entered her profession out of vanity, pleasure-seeking, and greed. In 1882, the author of a pamphlet titled *The Social Evil with Suggestions for Its Suppression* maintained that the instinct for promiscuous intercourse among public women was "inherent." "In every large town without exception," this author asserted, "where a woman has a chance of this course and runs no danger of serious loss or inconvenience, and possesses the means of deluding her friends, she will embrace it."[18] The private woman, whose sexual feelings could be aroused, if at all, only in anticipation of motherhood, would have nothing to fear from the institutionalization of prostitution and would continue to enjoy the respect and chivalry of all good and true men, women were assured.

Butler and the LNA refused to accept the dual concept of womanhood. They objected instead that the prostitute implied social acceptance of an insistent male sexuality. The safety and dignity of respectable women rested upon the existence of "a slave class of women for the supposed benefit of licentious men," as Butler expressed it.[19] They opposed the acts not simply because they singled out one sex for punishment and obloquy, but because they sanctioned the notion of woman as the acceptable object for male use and abuse. The repeal campaign provided feminists with an opportunity to attack ideas about male sexuality, for state-regulated prostitution effectively constructed a particular vision of a natural, uncontrollable male sex drive.

By separating motherhood and sexuality, the ideology of separate spheres presented a single view of male sexuality as natural and a double view of female sexuality. Feminists insisted that if there existed one male sexuality, there was also one female sexuality. This insistence, however, contained a seemingly unresolvable tension. On the one hand, feminists asserted an equality with men, demanding a legal and social acknowledgment of equal rights. On the other, they appealed to the rights of women to maintain their special moral qualities. Olive Schreiner, for example, believing wholeheartedly in equality between men and women, also claimed that because they carried, gave birth to, and reared children, women had different experiences, perceptions, emotions, and knowledge than men. Thus they often held divergent attitudes toward "that particular body of human concerns which directly is connected with the sexual reproduction of the race," concerns such as prostitution, the double standard of morality, and equal custody rights to children.[20] "The horns of this particular dilemma," Barbara Taylor has observed,

> are ones on which feminists have always been caught. Minimizing distinctions between the sexes . . . gave coherence to demands for egalitarian treatment, but at the expense of ignoring those aspects of women's existence which simply could not be lived in the male mode. But to admit the particularity of women's lives and needs appeared to undercut the egalitarian argument. The dilemma could only be resolved . . . by postulating the simultaneous transformation of *both* sexes—the critique of socially-defined femininity must become a critique of masculinity as well.[21]

This tension was exhibited within the repeal camp itself, where divisions of interest and attitude existed. By and large these divisions broke down along lines of gender. Whereas most of the men advocating repeal, Walkowitz has noted, adopted it as simply one of many political "anti-causes" that attracted them, women committed themselves to the cause for personal and emotional reasons. "Women often expressed an identity of interest with inscribed prostitutes," she has stated, "and intense anger at the police and medical domination of their 'fallen sisters.' They perceived the acts as a direct threat to their own status and self-respect." In fact, Butler suspected that male re-

– 67 –

pealers had a prurient interest in prostitution and the compulsory examination. She noticed that although they objected to women's presence during parliamentary debates over the CD Acts, they evinced great pleasure at being there themselves. Butler also complained of the tactics used by some of these men, citing the case of a Dr. Hoopell as particularly offensive. "At meetings he has held in the North," she explained, "he is in the habit of displaying . . . the instruments used at the examination and describing minutely their use. I protest against this as needlessly and grossly indecent."[22]

At the heart of the LNA's campaign lay the argument by the leadership that the creation of a slave class of women, while ostensibly protecting the purity and chastity of respectable middle-class women, made every woman the potential victim of male sexual abuse. Feminists refused to accept the men's argument that modest, respectable women had nothing to fear from the acts. They regarded prostitution as the product of male lust, fueled by hatred of and contempt for women. In a society that forced women into a position of economic dependence upon men, only an accident of birth prevented women of the middle classes from resorting to prostitution to support themselves and their children. Their analysis of the causes of prostitution and the purposes it served led them to identify with the prostitute as a victim of patriarchal society. Respectable women were vulnerable to the same forces that were responsible for the existence of prostitution: "the unrestrained passions of men"—as the *Shield*, the official newspaper of the LNA, charged in 1872—and the lack of employment opportunities for women.[23] "[S]o long as men are vicious and women have no employment," Butler announced to the Royal Commission investigating the operation of the Contagious Diseases Acts in 1871, "this evil will go on."[24]

Feminists insisted that prostitutes entered the profession out of economic necessity, not out of sin or pleasure. They claimed that any woman in a society that made women the dependent or possession of men might be forced by circumstances beyond

her control to "fall." In 1870, Mary Taylor supported her demand for better education and training for women by alluding
to the fact that without it respectable women might be forced to
resort to prostitution to support themselves.[25] Lady Amberley,
the object of Queen Victoria's wrath and disdain for having actually gotten up on a public platform to speak in favor of wom-
en's suffrage, argued in 1871 that for women the lack of education, training, and opportunity to work was a major underlying
reason for prostitution.[26] Mary Hume-Rothery disclosed to
Gladstone that

> there is not one of us—no, Gentlemen, there is not one of
> the mothers, wives, sisters, or daughters whom you cherish
> with proud affection—who dare safely assert that, had she
> been born in the same unprotected, unfenced position, in
> the very jaws of poverty and vice . . . she, too, in the in-
> nocent ignorance of her unfledged girlhood, might not have
> slipped, like them, into that awful gulf from which society
> at large has long done its best to make escape hopeless.[27]

Butler lamented that "the absolute dependance [sic] on men to
which so many women are reduced, means either beggary or
shame," and she accused the government of conspiring to force
large numbers of women into the trade of prostitution by pro-
hibiting them from factories and the professions.[28] She noted
that prostitution was "the one trade or profession which our
Government appears anxious to throw open freely to women."[29]

State-sanctioned prostitution and the Contagious Diseases
Acts, feminists claimed, encouraged the notion of all women as
sexual objects, as fair game, as "prey," as Frances Swiney put
it.[30] Moreover, as O'Neill has suggested, prostitution served as a
paradigm for the status of women in general, and the prostitute
as "only a more deeply wounded version of themselves," a
"kindred victim of masculine depravity."[31] Walkowitz has stated
that feminists deemed prostitution "the end result of the artificial constraints placed on women's social and economic activ-

ity"; it represented "the archetypal relationship between men and women, repeated in perhaps a more veiled and subtle manner within the confines of genteel society."[32] Reduced to the producer of children by separate sphere ideology and ultimately to status object by the pressures of gentility and conspicuous consumption, and lacking the means by which to escape a marriage in which husbands were legally entitled to possess them by force, women might find themselves in a situation that some feminists described as "prostitution within the marriage bond."[33] Hume-Rothery, in her open letter to Gladstone regarding the proposed extension of the CD Acts to the civilian population, argued that marriage was not at all unlike prostitution, and she hoped that in the near future "women shall dare poverty, loneliness, contempt, starvation itself rather than sell themselves, whether to wealthy husbands, or less eligible purchasers."[34]

Feminists viewed the Contagious Diseases Acts and other efforts to regulate prostitution as a conspiracy to degrade women and to protect the real culprits, namely, men. Women in a desperate economic situation created the supply of prostitutes, but it was men who created the demand, without which there could be no possibility of women selling their sex. Feminists regarded prostitutes—and potentially all women—as victims of male lust, which men seemed unwilling to control and which the government appeared to encourage through the passage of the CD Acts. Feminists sought to overturn the image of the prostitute as the seducer of men and the personification of disease, and to assign to men the role of destroyer of women.

Butler argued that any attempt to eliminate prostitution that focused solely on the prostitute herself, such as the repression of solicitation, was certainly bound to fail, for "the root is there as firmly planted as ever, so long as you leave MEN as they are."[35] Not the inherent promiscuity of the female but "the low moral standard of men is itself the principal cause of the evil," she maintained.[36] Elizabeth Blackwell, whose exposure to female syphilitic wards "moulded the whole of my future life," observed that "without male chastity, female chastity is impossible."[37] "Who is guilty of this appalling conversion of women into demons," she demanded, "this contagion of evil which in ever-widening circles is destroying our moral health, and injuring the modesty, freedom, and dignity of all womanhood? The immediate cause is man, whether prince or peasant, who purchases a woman for the gratification of lust."[38]

Feminists believed that men could control their sexual urges, that natural impulse did not automatically mean license to act, and that acceptable sexual behavior was the product of social rules or definitions. Men's apparent refusal to acknowledge these considerations constituted proof, according to Butler, that they regarded women as objects upon which to gratify their "brutal appetite"[39]—that they intended to keep women in a position of dependence in order to guarantee the continuation of "this conspiracy of greed and lust which is destroying the daughters of the people."[40] Butler wrote to her sister, Harriet Meuricoffre, of the single-mindedness of the extensionists, telling her that "our opponents are . . . moving heaven and earth to . . . create & maintain a *slave* class of women to minister to lust."[41] "[M]en will have their victims," she told the Royal Commission, citing as examples the girls she took into her home. "I can tell you of these girls, none of whom were prostitutes by any means, though they were not chaste, that it was a common thing that their own fathers, in a fit of intoxication, had violated them." She spoke of women who had been "reduced to the level of brutes" by the regulation of prostitution, adding "which I suppose is what certain gentlemen desire they should be."[42] Butler's wrath was not limited to those men who indulged in extramarital sex but extended to any man who condoned the double standard. "[W]e shall regard all men," she insisted, "(however pure in their own conduct) as depravers of society, who hold the loathsome and deadly doctrine that God has made man for unchastity and woman for his degraded slave."[43] Butler's perception of men as "lustful destroyers" of women ultimately led her to a position of general mistrust of and hostility toward men, despite her own very happy marriage to George Butler. In 1872, she admitted privately to Henry Wilson that she had "a great lack of reverence for men. If the holiest man on earth were to tell me that black is white, I should find no difficulty in deciding for myself whether he was a liar or not!"[44]

In the course of their campaign to repeal the CD Acts, feminists aroused intense male hostility and often exposed themselves to physical as well as verbal abuse. In 1872, during the election for Pontefract, Butler and Charlotte Wilson held a meeting in a hayloft to campaign against a candidate who supported the CD Acts. While the police looked on, local men set fire to the hayloft and threatened the women with bodily harm and rape. "It was not so much personal violence that we feared," Butler wrote later,

> as what would have been to any of us *worse than death*; for the indecencies of the men, their gestures, and threats, were what I prefer not to describe. Their language was hideous. They shook fists in our faces with volleys of oaths. This continued for some time, and we had no defence or means of escape . . . half-a-dozen fists were at my face at once, and the epithets applied were such as one only hears of in brothels. They filled their foul talk with allusions to the visits under the Contagious Diseases Acts.[45]

In Manchester Butler was attacked by a mob. "She was covered with flour and excrement, her clothes had been torn off her body, her face was discoloured and stiff with dried blood and she was so bruised that she could hardly move."[46] The conviction of women who persevered in the face of such hostility and potential harm did not arise from an altruistic desire to see justice served or an abstract sense of the Constitution violated. It arose from an identity with the victimized prostitute herself, from a personalized understanding of the injustices done to all women, in all walks of life, by laws and customs made by men alone. Moreover, the incidents at Pontefract and Manchester suggest that women who left the private sphere and ventured into the public arena were perceived by men to be public women—prostitutes—and deserving of the same treatment.

In refusing to accept the distinction between pure and impure women, feminists also challenged the notion that respectable ladies need have nothing to do with a subject as distasteful as prostitution. They recognized that the very existence of two classes of women depended in part on the convention that preached ignorance of sex matters on the part of women. They set out to subvert that convention, which they regarded as a conspiracy of silence, insisting that prostitution was an issue of great importance to all women. But their demand for knowledge was also a demand for power in their private relationships with men.[47]

Butler angrily decried the notion that respectable women should remain unsullied by any knowledge of prostitution. While addressing a Dublin crowd, she announced, "The State . . . has now legalised prostitution in our midst. And women are not to speak! . . . women, to whom the question is one of life and death?"[48] At Croyden she told the crowd that "men have demanded of [women] . . . an affectation at least of ignorance on the subject, albeit it is one which more intimately and terribly concerns the whole of womankind than any other. Can the soul of my sister be defiled and my own soul not be the worse for it? It cannot."[49] When the House of Commons was debating whether to repeal the CD Acts, Butler wrote to an M.P. demanding the right of women to be present. "At the very base of the Acts," she declared, "lies the false and poisonous idea that women (i.e. Ladies) have 'nothing to do with this question,' & ought not to hear of it, much less meddle with it." Such "propriety & modesty," insisted upon by the ideology of the angel in the house, had been "the cause of outrage and destruction to so many of our poorer fellow women. . . . I cannot forget the misery, the injustice & the outrage wh. [sic] have fallen upon women, simply because we stood aside when men felt our presence to be painful."[50] Her letter demanded, in effect, the end of separate spheres for the sexes that made possible this attack upon women in the first place.

Feminists often expressed their identity with prostitutes in a somewhat removed way, as members of a group that had been singled out for particularly iniquitous legislation and outrage. Annette Meakin noted in 1907 that "for every honest wife, mother, sister or daughter, someone else's wife, mother, sister or daughter must be victimised."[51] Hale declared in 1914 that respectable women "are beginning to be unwilling to tolerate the theory of a personal exemption [from sex] based upon the annihilation of other women's daughters."[52] Zoë Fairfield, responding to the suggestion of "some who tell us that our own safety depends" upon the existence of prostitutes, proclaimed in 1914, "we will not have safety at that price."[53] The LNA leadership referred to themselves as "the representatives of the women actually oppressed & insulted by the Acts."[54] Their identity was most often circumscribed by issues of class to a spiritual level, or to one of sisterhood. Butler confided to her sister in 1875 that "we have not only *remembered* those that are in bonds, as being bound with them, but actually *suffered with them* in spirit for long, long years."[55] "Womanhood is *solidaire*," she insisted.

> We cannot successfully elevate the standard of public opinion in the matter of justice to women, and of equality in all its truest sense, if we are content that a practical, hideous, calculated, manufactured and legally maintained degradation of a portion of womanhood is allowed to go on before the eyes of all. 'Remember them that are in bonds, as being bound with them.' Even if we lack the sympathy which makes us feel that the chains which bind our enslaved sisters are pressing on us also, we cannot escape the fact that we are one womanhood, *solidaire*, and that so long as they are bound, we cannot be wholly and truly free.[56]

Prostitutes may be criminals or slaves, one feminist told the Twelfth Annual Meeting of the LNA in 1881, but "they are still women, and we also are women, and that is why we are here to-night in their defence."[57] Butler asserted that the CD Acts had evoked "a deeply awakened common womanhood. Distinctions are levelled. We no more covet the name of ladies; we are all *women*."[58] In reply to the verdict of the New York Medical Board that "in the case of prostitution there is no aggrieved person," she declared that "the verdict of the women of England in this matter is, 'we are *all* aggrieved.' "

> We have cast in our lot with the outcast, determined to know no rest until this wrong be avenged, determined to probe this matter to its foundation, determined to declare in the face of parliaments, and of insolently-proclaimed masculine necessities—'she is my sister, and you shall not use her so;' determined to prove that it is not a law of nature, though these men have declared it and ratified it by act of parliament, that women must be preyed upon by men.[59]

The identification of respectable middle-class ladies with women who were perceived by society to be the lowest, most degraded forms of life, however removed by circumstances of class and experience, was a remarkable phenomenon in the late nineteenth century. Sometimes feminists went further and expressed their identification more immediately and personally. They intimated that what men could do to fallen women they were perfectly capable of doing to respectable women as well, that the demarcation between pure and impure was false. "Sirs," Butler declared flatly, "you *cannot* hold *us* in honour as long as you drag our sisters in the mire. As you are unjust and cruel to them, you will become unjust and cruel to us."[60] The women of England, she maintained, "are conscious that in fighting for the injured class they are fighting for themselves, their own liberties, and their own honour." She pointed out that by the Contagious Diseases Acts, every woman is legally placed beyond the pale of the Constitution, and . . . only the accidental circumstances of her birth and surroundings prevent this expulsion from taking a practical form for her . . . the women of England . . . have refused to exchange the protection of their liberties, guaranteed to them by the 'Bible of the Constitution,' for the miserable protection afforded by the caprice or favour of a beaurocracy [sic].[61]

Women had united in a common womanhood to oppose the institutionalization of prostitution so that they "will have the power to say, 'You shall not slay us or our sisters.' "[62] Butler more explicitly drew the immediate connection between the treatment of prostitutes and that of respectable ladies when she warned, "this is no time in the world in which we can relapse into inactivity, or affected ignorance of the profligacy of men and the degradation of women, unless we are prepared to meet the consequences to ourselves and to our children."[63] Frances Swiney observed a direct correlation between the situation of women of the brothels and streets and those of the family and home. "There is no neutral ground," she insisted. "We fight for our sisters' liberty, and through them for the emancipation of our sex; or for their continued bondage and our perpetual disgrace."[64]

For these feminists, the double standard, prostitution, and especially the CD Acts encouraged the view that all women were the chattel, slaves, and playthings of men and legitimate outlets for male sexual urges; they made a mockery of the notion of the angel in the house and negated ultimately both the separation of spheres and the demarcation of pure and impure women. Prostitution served as a metaphor for the predicament of women under patriarchy, carried only to a more extreme degree. "Feminists realized that the popular sentimentalization of 'female influence' and motherhood only thinly masked," Walkowitz has maintained, "the view of women as 'the Sex,' as sexual objects to be bought and sold by men."[65] The Eighth Annual Report of the LNA in 1877[66] observed that

> the Acts were but the expression of the spirit of the time about women; they were no miraculous growth; they had not sprung out of nothing; they could not have been planned, or carried, or maintained, if there had not been amongst us, amongst women as well as men, an acceptance of the doctrine that women are inferior to men, that men's interests are paramount, and that, where necessary, women must be entirely sacrificed to those interests, that women are unfit and unentitled to regulate their own lives, which must be ordered by men in the interests of men.

The report attributed prostitution to the "dependent position of women,"

> that enforced dependence and inferiority of position which resulted from laws, customs, and public opinion, which affirmed and created inequality between the sexes, which made it difficult for a woman to live without being beholden to some man, impossible for her to attain the same measure of comfort and prosperity with the same expenditure of effort.

What society had defined as women's natural sphere—the home—feminists regarded as a training ground for dependence and subservience, eventually leading to prostitution in the case of those more unfortunate women. "That dependence of women upon men," declared the LNA leadership,

> was taught and maintained by early training in the family, by unequal means of education, by the limited field of industry, whether of brain or hand, yet open to women . . . by every fresh law which assumed or implied the inferior fitness or right of a woman to order her own life; by unequal laws between the sexes as to marriage, property, and

other matters; by the acceptance of that unequal moral standard which pardons vice in a man, but almost shuts the door of hope on a woman who has erred; and lastly, by political subjection or extinction of women, which deprives them of any direct means of altering the laws which affect them unjustly.

Feminists insisted that the belief that women were inferior to men and must be confined to a separate sphere meant in actuality that "women exist for men," and that this doctrine "first produced profligacy, and then organised it and established it."

The Contagious Diseases Acts, feminists charged, institutionalized the notion that "women are mere bits of flesh made for man's basest convenience."[67] Mrs. Ormiston Chant observed in 1886 that "these terrible laws . . . said, 'Women are helpless, feeble chattel in our hands; they are but women, and we may legislate for them as we like.' "[68] One LNA leader insisted that "the very existence of such laws encourages men to believe women are their playthings, or slaves, born to minister to their pleasures or their wants."[69] Butler claimed that because of the CD Acts there had been "an increase from year to year of offences against the person, of disregard for the claims of womanhood" to respect from men.[70] She argued that prostitution was a "question which *directly strikes* at the physical and moral life of tens of thousands of women . . . which threatens the purity and stability of our homes, which stabs at the very heart of pure affection, which degrades all womanhood through foul associations of thought and feeling, and which murders chivalry and generosity towards women in the hearts of our sons and brothers."[71]

"The happiness and character of all virtuous women throughout the land must eventually suffer from the consequences of such measures [as the CD Acts]," Butler protested.[72] She tried to explain her position to a Select Committee in Parliament in 1882, telling them that

there is nothing in the physical being of a man answering
to the sacredness of the maternal function of a woman, and
. . . these functions and every organ connected with them
ought to be held in reverence by man. Where this reverence ceases to be felt through the habitual outrage of any
class of women, however degraded that class might be, the
demoralisation of society is sure to follow. I am not here to
represent the virtuous women: I plead for the rights of the
most virtuous and the most vicious equally.[73]

Butler knew that the situation of the woman of the public sphere
and that of the woman of the private sphere were inseparable,
and that both served to support the construction of male sexuality. Having knocked down the first of these pillars by attacking state-regulated prostitution, feminists then, beginning in the
1880s, turned their attention to the other by chipping away at
the structure of marriage.

CHAPTER III

MARRIAGE

Marriage is itself in many cases a legalised form of prostitution.

CATHERINE GASQUOINE HARTLEY, 1913

The prostitute exemplified one aspect of female sexuality; the mother, pure and untainted by sexual motives, exemplified the other. Victorian ideology imbued marriage and motherhood with an element of the divine. The family and the home constituted for Victorians "a central fact of the greatest importance," as W. L. Burn described it;[1] the integrity of family life and the guardianship of all the comforts and benefits to be accrued therefrom rested with the wife and mother. Marriage and motherhood were the crowning achievements of a woman's life, her "natural destiny" and "best earthly happiness."[2] Reverence and awe surrounded her position and function. She was worshiped and exalted in literature; poets conferred upon her praise of the highest order. The "angel in the house" enjoyed a degree of respect and adoration second to none.

Victorians viewed marriage as "the equal yoking together of the man and the woman for the performance of high and sacred duties."[3] Notions of companionate marriage had raised the relations of the sexes to a loving partnership. "Love knows no superior or inferior," eulogized Defoe in the early eighteenth century, "no imperious command on the one hand, no reluctant subjection on the other."[4] Marriage was the sphere in which the relations between men and women were said to be inspired by love, purity, and altruism, in marked contrast to the institution of prostitution, where greed, base sensuality, and corruption characterized male and female interaction.

Examples abound to illustrate that marriage and family life produced a "vast amount of happiness and interest, a vivid sense of comfort, security and affectionate companionship."[5] In the late 1880s, in response to Mona Caird's attack on marriage in the *Westminster Review*, 27,000 letters poured into the offices of the *Daily Telegraph* before the paper closed off discussion in its columns. The overwhelming majority of the correspondents came down on the side of marriage.[6] But marriage and the home could also be "a prison governed by a drunkard or a gambler or a sexual monomaniac," as Burn noted, and it was buttressed by a system of family law that belied its altruistic and egalitarian connotations.[7]

Historians have usually argued that the feminist movement focused almost exclusively on the plight of single women and the needs of married women whose marriages had broken up through death or separation.[8] This interpretation holds only for the earliest period, for starting in the 1880s, the assault on marriage constituted a fundamental element of the women's attempts to gain freedom, equality, dignity, respect, and power. Most pioneers, like Josephine Butler and Millicent Garrett Fawcett, never questioned the institution of marriage. But for many feminists, even during the earliest years of suffrage agitation, marriage epitomized and helped to perpetuate the notion of the meek, submissive, powerless woman. It appeared to be "incompatible with freedom & with an independent career," Elizabeth Garrett wrote to her sister Millicent in 1870 upon becoming engaged to J.G.S. Anderson. She felt defensive about her impending marriage, hoping that Millicent and others would not "think I have meanly deserted my post." She justified her decision by suggesting that she and her husband might "be able to do something to discourage this notion" that marriage and freedom for women were at variance with one another. She took great pains to reassure her sister that the plans for the wedding ceremony would "end in our using the Scotch form & bargaining beforehand for no catechism as to obedience."[9]

Some pioneers went further. Frances Power Cobbe, who lived for thirty years with her companion, Mary Lloyd, in 1868 published a pamphlet in which she pointed up the hypocrisy surrounding the "honourable state of matrimony" for women.[10] Elizabeth Wolstenholme defied all convention when she and Ben Elmy decided to live together without benefit of clergy. Her feminist colleagues—Butler, Lydia Becker, and Emily Davies among them—seem to have tolerated this situation, at least at first. Then, according to Sylvia Pankhurst, "when it was obvious that she was pregnant, there was much fluttering in the suffrage dovecotes, and eventually Mrs. Jacob [Ursula] Bright induced the two to marry, on the plea that their continued refusal would be harmful to the suffrage cause."[11]

Elizabeth Wolstenholme Elmy was clearly exceptional among her generation. But by the 1880s and 1890s, "New Women" were expressing attitudes and demonstrating behavior that diverged significantly from conventional Victorian ways. Cobbe, in *The Duties of Women* (1881), warned against

> that neglect of social *bienseances*, that adoption of looser and more "Bohemian" manners, and, worst of all, that fatal laxity of judgement regarding grave moral transgressions, which have appeared of late years amongst us as the inevitable extravagance of reaction from earlier strictness (and which) constitute, I conceive, deadly perils to the whole movement for the advancement of women. There are women who call themselves "emancipated" now, who are leading lives if not absolutely vicious, yet loose, unseemly, trespassing always on the borders of vice; women who treat lightly, and as if of small account, the heinous and abominable sins of unchastity and adultery.[12]

Cobbe's alarm was undoubtedly excessive, but feminists were, indeed, challenging Victorian norms, especially in the realm of marriage. By the 1880s, because employment and educational opportunities for women had increased so impressively, spinsterhood was no longer regarded as a woman's failure but could, in fact, be embraced out of choice as a positive, beneficial experience. As the *Englishwoman's Review* noted in 1889, "whatever may be said by narrow-minded biologists, who apparently cannot regard a woman except as a female animal, we maintain that facts reveal to us the existence of a certain number of women who, in their own estimation at least, are happier and better as spinsters than wives."[13] More significant, because their impact on the general public was greater, were the "New Woman" novels that surfaced in the 1890s. The "New Woman" fiction, A. R. Cunningham has pointed out, consisted of "a series of novels, mainly by women, which deliberately set out to attack marriage, to break the bonds of censorship which tacitly forbade the treatment of sexuality in fiction, and above all to argue, from various points of view, the feminist case."[14]

Sarah Grand and Mona Caird counted prominently among the "New Woman" novelists. Their heroines rejected at least some aspects of the feminine role defined by Victorians and were involved in situations that clearly demonstrated that marriage was not the haven depicted in conventional popular literature. Grand and Caird, to quote Cunningham, "wrote of sexual behaviour with a frankness which had previously been unthinkable; [they] employed as mouthpieces women unusually independent, intelligent and free from convention. In the 1890s the woman question became linked with the demand for a more open approach to sexuality."[15]

The "New Woman" novelists can be divided into two schools, described as "purity" and "bachelor girl" by Cunningham. The purity school, represented by Sarah Grand, focused on the institution of marriage in order to expose its hypocrisy. Accepting the ideal of monogamous relationships within legal marriage, these writers "aimed for a frankness and honesty in relationships between the sexes."[16] Their characters spoke candidly and without guile about venereal disease, prostitution, and adultery, rejecting the stereotype of feminine delicacy; Grand's Ideala, for example, read Huxley's *Elementary Physiology*.[17] She wished to strengthen the institution of marriage by shattering the barriers between husbands and wives, not to destroy the "traditional structure of sexual relationships." The bachelor-girl authors treated the theme of female sexuality more radically than did the purity school. They included in the development of their characters, such as Caird's Hadria, in *Daughters of Danaus*, a greater awareness of "the sexual motivation of women."[18]

Freedom for women, insisted Caird, was impossible "without the marriage-relation, as at present understood, being called in question." The demand for a modified marriage, whether or not intended by all those women who claimed freedom, was inherent in the feminist movement, she insisted. At present, marriage constituted a "mere mouldering branch of the patriarchal tree," Caird contended, but with the emancipation of women it would be required to "alter its nature and its form." "[T]he spirit of liberty among women is increasing rapidly," she claimed, "and as soon as an approach to economic independence gives them the power to refuse, without harsh penalty, the terms which men have hitherto been able to dictate to them, in and out of marriage, we shall have some just right to call ourselves a free people."[19] By the twentieth century, feminist attacks on marriage had become commonplace. Teresa Billington-Greig alleged that Emmeline Pankhurst, head of the WSPU, placed a taboo on marriage for her followers, that she regarded marriage as "undesirable. . . . It was a fraternising with the enemy."[20] Christabel Pankhurst warned against marriage on the grounds that it rendered women vulnerable to venereal disease; she explicitly linked the possession of the vote with a more moral, dignified, and safe situation for women within marriage.[21]

Feminist critics did not object to marriage in the abstract. Most of them believed that a good marriage offered opportunities for happiness that could not be found elsewhere. They condemned marriage in its present, corrupt state, arguing that the private sphere, where women's purity and special moral nature supposedly prevailed, had in fact been invaded and conquered by the destructive values and behavior of the public sphere, presided over by men. Social constructions of male sexuality created tensions within the ideology of separate spheres, rendering it inherently contradictory and hypocritical.

In their discourse on marriage, feminists borrowed terms and concepts utilized in discussions about the political economy of Victorian England. The dominant metaphors of their critique consisted of notions of "contract," "production," "labor," and "class," terms most apposite to the public sphere of men and industrial commerce. Feminists analyzed the terms of the marriage contract, the meaning of the contract for the parties involved, the relative strength of each party in determining it, and the conditions of marriage for women as determined by the contract. Their appropriation of the language of the public sphere to present their reverse discourse served two purposes. First, if their critique was to have meaning and significance, it had to be heard. Jean Elshtain has suggested that the existence of separate spheres has made it literally impossible for men and women to "speak" to each other. Nineteenth-century feminists used the language of the public sphere to "speak" to men, in order to have their position heard and understood. Moreover, the language of fact and concrete reality was meant to expose, by contrast, the emptiness of idealized depictions of womanhood and the marital state. Second, the adoption of a commercial idiom was designed to demonstrate that the private sphere of women— the realm of generosity, compassion, kindness, and decency[22]— had been corrupted by the intrusion of the public, male sphere, symbolized for Victorians by greed, competition, exploitation, and lust. Use of this idiom dispelled the notion of a clear separation between public and private, demonstrating instead the public nature of all domestic life, even the most intimate aspects of the marital bond.

Feminist demands for a transformation of the institution of marriage contained the same seemingly unresolvable tension that was evident in the critique of prostitution and that permeated every aspect of the feminist movement. The tension between the special moral needs of women and their demands for equality with men gave the suffrage campaign, for instance, its distinct and radical character, perhaps most succinctly summed up in one suffragette slogan, "Votes for Women, Chastity for Men." Feminists attacked male sexuality and asserted their special differences from men in the realm of morals and values not in order to perpetuate the existence of separate spheres but in order to eliminate those spheres and to extend the qualities associated with women to society at large.

CHALLENGING the prevalent ideas about marriage as "connubial bliss," feminists posited that marriage resembled nothing more closely than a commercial contract, in which women exchanged themselves—their legal rights, their property, their bodies, and the fruits of their labor—for a wage paid in the form of material subsistence. Barred by law and custom from entering trades and professions by which they could support themselves, and restricted in the possession of property, women had only one means of livelihood, that of marriage. Those who controlled the means of production demanded of the woman as payment "that she should enkindle and satisfy the desire of the male," Cicely Hamilton declared in 1909, "who would thereupon admit her to such share of the property he possessed or earned as should seem good to him. In other words, she exchanged, by the ordinary process of barter, possession of her person for the means of existence." This state of affairs, Hamilton concluded, "justifies us in regarding marriage as essentially (from the woman's point of view) a commercial or trade undertaking."[23] Sanctification of marriage by the Church, custom, and public opinion obscured the motives of women who sought marriage; feminists emphasized that the underpinning of marriage was material. Gasquoine Hartley pointed out in 1913 that "the price the woman asks from the man for her favours is marriage as the only means of gaining permanent maintenance for herself and her children."[24] Woman "frequently obtains a husband only in order to support life," Hamilton claimed. "The housekeeping trade is the only one open to us—so we enter the housekeeping trade in order to live. This is not always the same as entering the housekeeping trade in order to love."[25]

Coerced into marriage by a social system that denied them other means of material support, women were yet hampered and constrained in obtaining and conducting that trade. "The man who has his bread to earn," Hamilton ruminated, "goes out to seek for the work to which he is trained; his livelihood depending on it, he offers his skills and services without shame or thought of reproach." The woman who would earn her bread, by contrast,

> is expected to express unwillingness for the very work for which she has been taught and trained. She has been brought up in the belief that her profession is marriage and motherhood; yet though poverty may be pressing upon her—though she may be faced with the actual lack of necessities of life—she must not openly express her desire to enter that profession, and earn her bread in the only way for which she is fitted. She must stand aside and wait— indefinitely; and attain to her destined livelihood by appearing to despise it.[26]

Hamilton claimed for woman the right to cry her wares, "since by her wares she lives," observing that "this freedom of bargaining to the best advantage, permitted as a matter of course to every other worker, is denied to her." The great irony for feminists was that wives, restricted in their freedom of bargaining, had less negotiating power than prostitutes, a class who claimed and exercised openly their freedom to haggle over terms, "a class which has pushed to its logical conclusion that principle that woman exists by virtue of a wage paid her in return for the possession of her person."[27] Feminists charged that the conditions of the marriage contract in fact made them prostitutes. Marriage was very simply a legalized and mystified prostitution, they insisted; it was the direct opposite of that institution represented in separate sphere ideology.

Having only one profession open to her, and limited in the possibility of making the best deal for herself, the respectable woman found herself a seller in a buyer's market. The laws of supply and demand favored the buyer in the determination of the terms of the contract. Although, in affixing his seal to the contract, a man pledged to a woman, "with this ring, I thee wed, with my body I thee worship, and with all my worldly goods I thee endow," the terms of marriage, critics pointed out, bore inequitably upon the respective parties to it.[28] Under English law, wives became the property of their husbands, ceding to them their rights to own property and to earn money; apart from a limited custody over infants, mothers had no rights to their children; husbands could sue their wives for restitution of conjugal rights and have them imprisoned if they refused sexual intercourse; they might rape their wives with impunity under the law; and they were free to indulge in extramarital sex without fear of a divorce action against them. Such a breach on the part of married women, however, constituted grounds for invalidating the contract. Feminists argued that this one-sidedness made marriage for women akin to "a state of slavery." Within it, Caird observed acidly, "father and mother are to share pleasantly between them the rights and duties of parenthood—the father having the rights, the mother the duties."[29] "Marriage is the formal repudiation of freedom," editorialized *The Freewoman* in 1912, "a repudiation which a very complete code of penal law protects against subsequent recantation."[30] "If one marries," submitted Caird's character, Hadria, "one gives to another person rights and powers over one's life that are practically boundless. . . . I have little enough freedom now, heaven knows; but if I married, why my very thoughts would become the property of another. Thought, emotion, love itself, must pass under the yoke!"[31]

Asserting their rights to equality in marriage, feminists demanded for women the possibility of bargaining freely and fairly with men. This necessitated economic independence for women—the ability to support themselves before marriage without loss of status or respectability, making marriage an option rather than an imperative; and the right to retain the property and earnings they brought to and accumulated during marriage. Feminists demanded a single standard of divorce, but most sought divorce reform that would raise the level of men's moral standards. They did not wish to see the law liberalized, for, because they were dependent economically upon their husbands, "women had material cause to defend the integrity of the family unit."[32] Divorce reform, custody rights to children, and an end to laws that made wife-beating and rape legal—these were fundamental demands for women who would ameliorate the condition of slavery within marriage. Equal rights in marriage would help raise the institution to a level approaching that touted by Victorian ideologists; at least it would be a step toward a "thought-out rational system of sex relationships," rather than "a lineal descendant of barbarian usages, cruel and absurd." "Is it conceivable," asked Caird, "that when there are, in good sooth, really two to the marriage bargain, one of the parties to it will consent to fetter herself by bonds which the other repudiates?"[33]

Votes for women offered the means by which marital equality was to be attained. "[W]hen women have some say in the making of laws which they have to obey," Caird averred, "the 'contract' can no longer remain unequal." The vote, too, would empower women to extend the special moral qualities associated with them to society as a whole by enabling them to pass legislation that bore with equal severity on men as on women. "All men who are eloquent about the 'sacred institution' will know that it rests upon them to sustain the sacredness which they will then, perhaps, talk less glibly about," Caird predicted. "They can no longer depute that office to their wives."[34] The vote would transform the elevating "influence" of women into an instrument of power with which to create a greater and truer morality among men by eliminating the distinctions between public and private spheres.

THE PRODUCTIVE function of women underwent a transformation in the course of the nineteenth century. Domestic management involved a great deal of work, and women contributed heavily to the economy of the household. Housecleaning, the provision of food and clothing, the daily care and education of children, the anticipation and meeting of the needs of husband and father—the myriad details of keeping a family in comfort and security—required of women much planning, foresight, and physical activity. The division of labor that placed women in a domestic role and men in a public role did not eliminate the economic function of women; " 'the prudent management' of the wife," Banks and Banks have argued, was "as necessary as the honest toil of the husband."[35]

Increasingly throughout the century, however, as Banks and Banks have demonstrated, household labor in middle-class homes, including the care and training of children, became transferred to a host of domestic servants recruited from working-class families.[36] Ideally, though not always in practice, the middle-class woman had become "for ever elevated above the still-room and the kitchen," as the *Saturday Review* put it. Mid-Victorian prosperity among the middle classes displayed itself not only in greater luxury for those classes but also in a compulsion for social status. One criteria of social status was the ability of a married man to afford enough domestic servants to keep his wife and daughters in expensive leisure. As Banks and Banks have pointed out, the middle-class wife theoretically no longer "engaged in the practical side of housekeeping. . . . In-

stead she demonstrated, by her talents as hostess, her arrange-
ment of little dinners and 'at homes,' and her success at conspicuous consumption, the ability of her husband to maintain
his wife and family in luxurious idleness." One contemporary
gave exquisite expression to the position of the perfect wife when
he remarked in a letter to a friend, "of course at a certain age,
when you have a house and so on, you get a wife as part of its
furniture." The pressures of gentility required that the "perfect
wife" become also the "perfect lady"—"leisured, elegant, and
above all expensive."[37]

This development was seen by some contemporaries (and by
some recent historians) as an emancipatory process for women,
freeing them from domestic labor. But others regarded it criti-
cally as a furthering of their inferiority to men. Feminists decried
this transformation of the domestic sphere from one of productivity to a showcase of the "frivolity, vulgar display, and helplessness" of women.[38] They came increasingly to regard the prescribed role of women as providers of material and spiritual
comforts to be one in which, in reality, they were exclusively to
provide for the sexual comforts and needs of men. In this critique of the reproductive role of women, feminists again betrayed the tensions between their aspirations for the acknowledgment of women's special morality and of their equality with
men. Utilizing the language of the public sphere, of industry
and commerce, they railed against a marriage contract that ob-
ligated them to perform, literally and figuratively, slave labor—
they called it compulsory motherhood. Drawing upon the language and imagery of the private, domestic sphere, they urged
that the "Law of the Mother"—the feminine qualities of love,
caring, nurturance, respect for life, and morality—dominate the
relations, especially the sexual relations, between men and
women.[39] Equality in the public sphere, epitomized by the vote,
would enable women to realize their special needs by so transforming the laws and morals of society that it would no longer
be possible for men to subjugate and abuse them. In short, a

"feminization" of society would bring a morality to both public and private realms, which could no longer be maintained as separate and distinct spheres.

The marriage contract, buttressed by the laws of England, gave husbands complete possession of their wives' bodies. Feminists charged that the rights of husbands to force sexual intercourse and compulsory childbearing on their wives established a condition of "sex-slavery."[40] For many, this issue stood at the center of the feminist movement. "Foremost of all the wrongs from which women suffer," declared Elizabeth Wolstenholme Elmy in 1888, "and in itself creative of many of them, is the inequality and injustice of their position in the marriage relation, and the legal denial to wives of that personal freedom, which is the most sacred right of humanity." Laws that taught men to regard women as their property, she asserted, permitted and encouraged "outrages upon women, especially upon wives."[41] Marion Leslie wrote to the *Women's Penny Paper* in 1890 that "so long as in the eyes of the law a woman is the property of her husband, and can be lawfully chastised by him, men will be brutal and overbearing to women, despite the most energetically conducted palliative schemes."[42]

Here again we find male sexuality under attack. Couched in rather vague terms, the issue that so inflamed the passions of feminists was marital rape. Elmy, for one, was not reluctant to address the situation head on. In a paper read before the Dialectical Society in 1880 titled *The Criminal Code in its Relation to Women*, she brought to the attention of the audience a decision handed down by one Judge Hale, whose dictum was proposed to be included in the Criminal Code Bill of 1880. Hale ruled that "the husband cannot be guilty of a rape committed by himself upon his lawful wife," Elmy told the Society, "for by their *mutual matrimonial consent and contract* the wife hath given up herself in this kind unto her husband, which she cannot retract." Section 200 of the proposed Criminal Code Bill, Elmy went on, defined rape as "the act of a man, not under the age of 14 years, having carnal knowledge of a woman, *who is not his wife*, without her consent." Confiding to her listeners that rape was a point on which it was "impossible for [women] to speak at all without expressing strong feeling," she protested heatedly that

> being a violation of a primary natural right, [rape] is, and ought to be by law declared to be, wholly independent of any legal or other artificially created relationship between the parties, and . . . it would be a gross immorality to en-act, as the section I have just quoted proposes implicitly to do, that any such act by a husband, however base and cruel it may be, is justified by the matrimonial consent of the wife once given and never to be retracted.[43]

A husband's right to sexual intercourse with his wife was absolute, superseding even the right of a woman to protect herself or her unborn children from disease. In the ruling handed down in *Regina v. Clarence*, the judge established the precedent that a husband could not be found guilty of raping his wife even if she had refused intercourse because he had venereal disease. Elmy denounced "this infamy in the name of the wife, the mother, the child, the race, and the higher humanity to which we aspire."[44] She believed ardently in the power of the vote to transform women's lives, writing to Harriet McIlquham in 1897 that "the making criminal in a husband the communication of foul disease to his wife" and the overturning of *Regina v. Clarence* were "two of the first things at which we shall have to work when once we win the Suffrage, and they will carry us very far indeed."[45] But Elmy also urged a special right for women based on their unique role as mothers and conservators of the race. "The only absolute right I should claim for a woman as against a man," she announced to McIlquham in 1896, "is that she should never be made a mother against her will."[46]

The legalization of marital rape implicit in the marriage con-tract made a mockery of the ideology of domestic bliss. "Inhuman and degrading chains" rather than ties of affection and love bound women to marriage, Kathlyn Oliver argued in 1912. "We will have no compulsion or coercion in marriage," she protested, adding, "personally, I regard rape as a far worse evil than prostitution."[47] F. W. Stella Browne in 1915 held that the existence of "conjugal rights," or rape in marriage, was an "outrage on decency and freedom alike," attributing its prevalence to and describing it as the ultimate expression of the "view of women as vessels . . . for men's use and as automatic breeding machines."[48] By appealing to the rights of women to "decency" and "freedom," she, too, illustrates the dilemma for women inherent in separate sphere ideology.

Browne's adoption of the term "breeding machines" reflects the feminist appropriation of language of the public sphere to demonstrate that women's private sphere had been corrupted by men. Motherhood, the highest, the most revered, the most subjective function of a woman, had become debased and depersonalized to the level of mere service and commodity production. Mother, the pure, adored angel, had been reduced to a machine. She had become alienated from the fruits of her labor; having lost control to so great a degree over the means of production, she had become, in effect, a slave laborer.

While Victorian theorists praised the moral, spiritual qualities of women, feminists emphasized that patriarchal society valued women only for their capacity to satisfy male sexual needs and to reproduce the race. This "Physical" theory of women, according to Frances Power Cobbe, writing in 1869, held that

> the whole meaning and reason of her existence is, that she may form a link in the chain of generations, and fulfill the functions of wife to one man and mother to another. . . . In a word, everything which enables a woman to attract conjugal love, and to become the parent of a numerous and healthy progeny, must be reckoned as constituting her proper endowment. Everything which distracts her atten-

tion or turns her faculties in other directions than these must be treated as mischievous, and as detracting from her merits.[49]

The male design for women, Caird contended, no matter how well camouflaged and sanctified by marriage, remained "that a woman's main duty and privilege was to bear children without limit; that death and suffering were not to be considered for a moment, in the performance of this duty; that for this end she had been created, and for this end . . . she must live and die." "Tender-hearted divines of the present era" might essay valiantly to exalt motherhood, but their attitude remained consistent with that of sixteenth-century Protestant reformers such as Melancthon, Caird maintained, who advised, "If a woman becomes weary of bearing children, that matters not: let her only die from bearing, she is there to do it."[50] Hamilton proclaimed that "women have been trained to be unintelligent breeding-machines until they have become unintelligent breeding-machines." So pervasively had the private sphere of women been taken over by men and the values of the public sphere that the terms "woman" and "breeding machine" had become indistinguishable, she lamented.[51]

Constraints on a woman's ability to secure a livelihood outside marriage, a legal system that gave husbands absolute control over their wives' bodies, and an ideology that insisted upon the primacy of the sexual functions of women engendered a situation in which motherhood reflected not "the mighty creative power which more than any other human faculty seems to bring womanhood nearer the Divine," but compulsory, forced labor.[52] Hamilton argued that childbearing was "an involuntary consequence of a compulsory trade."[53] Children "are born of women who are not free," Caird declared, "not free even to refuse to bear them." Again recruiting the language of men to make her point, she asserted that "unwilling motherhood is worse than unwilling military service."[54] Both women appealed to women's rights to equality in the public sphere in order to ameliorate the conditions in the private sphere. The rights of women to work outside the home, to own property, to enjoy equal opportunity of education, to make and enforce laws, to control their own bodies and destinies, to secure custody of their children—all would aid in the creation of a just, rational system of relations between men and women.

But the particularities of women's lives in a male-defined and male-controlled society necessitated more than equality of treatment with men. Feminists' arguments for the recognition of women's special needs grew out of their understanding of male sexual behavior as conflicting sharply and dangerously with the safety, integrity, and dignity of women and with that of the race in general. In effect they offered a critique of masculinity that encompassed the entire society, private and public sphere alike. The grounds for the critique came from appeals to the real experience of women in marriage. The juxtaposition of reality with the ideal was meant to underline the hypocrisy of separate sphere ideology.

The sexual experiences of women in marriage were necessarily colored by their socialization as pure, passionless, sexless beings. As Hadria, Caird's heroine, pointed out, "Think of what it means for a girl to have been taught to connect the idea of something low and evil with that which nevertheless is to lie at the foundation of all her after life."[55] Often ignorant of the most basic fundamentals of sex, inculcated with a conviction of sex as immoral, debased, and sinful, women were often shocked and horrified upon discovering what married life entailed for them. In reference to her initiation to intercourse, a respectable woman commented to W. R. Greg, "It is not that a quarter-of-an-hour's ceremony in a church can make *that* welcome or tolerable to pure and delicate feelings, which would otherwise outrage their whole previous notions, and their whole natural and moral sense."[56] "A Lost Life" informed readers of the *Daily Telegraph* that she was a born celibate. "I had not been married a week before I discovered that I was quite unfit for marriage," she revealed. "I had insuperable objections to it. In the years that have gone by I have heard of many similar cases amongst girls."[57] The distinctions between men and women in sexual matters, as prescribed by Victorian ideology, practically ensured that "there are few wives, high or low, but could bear testimony to incidentally distasteful or painful approach, silently suffered at the husband's insistence," posited the Elmys in 1896.[58]

Masculinity, especially as manifested in sexual behavior, constituted for feminists a selfish, destructive, uncontrolled, brutalizing force. The Elmys viewed the quintessential man as indulging in "an *inordinate* exercise of sexual functions; to a degree demanded neither by the physical nor intellectual economy of himself or of the race." He possessed "an exaggerated and abnormal amount of sensual desire; the reckless gratification of which has been the main incentive to the excess which has brought about an expectable outcome in woman's resultant suffering."[59] Men were obsessed by sex, announced Frances Swiney, observing that "there is no living organism so completely under the tyranny of sex as the human male. The majority of men are utterly incapable of freeing themselves from the limitations of masculinity."[60] Male sexuality, characterized by "restless adventure, aggression, rapine, and conquest of the weak by the strong," was responsible for outrageous sexual abuse of women in marriage.[61] "No female animal has been so ruthlessly, so brutally, so generally mercilessly exploited by the man, as woman," Swiney charged. "She stands the martyr of organised and systematic sexual wrong-doing on the part of the man who should be her mate."[62] Teresa Billington-Greig's mother described her marital relations as "Calvary." "Poor little victims," she called her children. "If all men are so driven, God help them! They need help."[63]

Caird, Hamilton, and Meakin, among many others, submitted that the exaltation of marriage and motherhood concealed the designs of patriarchy to confine women to a position of sexual slavery. "In sexual matters," Hamilton urged, "it would appear that the whole trend and tendency of man's relations to woman has been to make refusal impossible and to cut off every avenue of escape from the gratification of his desire."[64] Women's sense of their responsibilities for their children, Caird noted, their love for their children, often established insuperable barriers to any change for women. Children, she proclaimed, "have been the means, from time immemorial, of enslaving women." "Who could stand against them?" Hadria asked. "They had been able to force the most rebellious to their knees. An appeal to the maternal instinct had quenched the hardiest spirit of revolt. No wonder the instinct had been so trumpeted and exalted!"[65]

Some feminists went so far as to claim that patriarchal culture had "artificially fostered impulses" to motherhood to ensure the continual supply of compliant sexual partners.[66] Hamilton charged that men had "laid it down that woman finds instinctive and unending joy" in childbearing because of the "advantage . . . such a belief [gives] to a husband disinclined to self-control."[67] Caird's Hadria beleived that "female sexuality" was a male-defined entity. On the wedding day of a friend, she said to her companion, Lady Engleton, "Imagine . . . if Marion, on any day *previous* to this, had gone to her mother and expressed an overpowering maternal instinct—a deep desire to have a child!"

"Good heavens!" exclaimed Lady Engleton.

"Why so shocked, since it is so holy?"

"But that is different."

"Ah! then it is holy only when the social edict goes forth, and proclaims the previous evil good and the previous good evil," Hadria observed. "So we are all to be horribly shocked at the presence of an instinct to-day, and then equally shocked and indignant at its absence to-morrow. . . . It really shows a touching confidence in the swift adaptability of the woman's sentimental organisation."[68]

I. D. Pearce contended in 1911 that "contemptuous diatribes

against childless women" by men created a "subtle compulsion of a distorted public opinion upon all mothers to bear children." Contrary to their "professed concern for the continuance of the race," she declared, men's "true attitude . . . toward motherhood" was that of a "mere breeding machine" with which they might indulge in "the uncontrolled excesses . . . of sex."[69]

AS DETERMINED by the terms of the marriage contract, the relative strength of the parties to it, and the exclusively sexual character of women's productive role within it, the conditions of marriage for women, feminists contended, revealed the hypocrisy of separate sphere ideology. The private sphere of marriage and motherhood did not constitute for women their best earthly happiness or reflect their most divine function. The invasion of the private sphere by masculine—or public—values and behavior reduced respectable middle-class women to the position of that figure who best exemplified exploitation, indignity, degradation, and disease in Victorian society: the prostitute. "The beloved 'sphere' of woman," Caird raged, "where she was thought so safe and happy, has, in fact, been a very seed-bed of disease and misery and wrong, whose horrors will perhaps never be fully realised." The purported distinctions between two classes of women—the public, degraded prostitute, and the angel in the house—were a complete sham, feminists urged. In a society ordered along masculine lines, both classes of women existed for the gratification of male sexual desires. As a result, wrote Caird, "year after year, women are ruined, in body and soul, inside and outside the pale of society, the ruin in both cases being essentially the same in nature, and springing from the same cause."[70]

The ruin was moral, spiritual, intellectual, and physical; the cause was the reduction of women to a purely sexual level by men. Masculinity had so asserted its sexual prerogatives in the private sphere that the "present relation of the sexes is barbarous," not the embodiment of all that was held holy and sacred.

Marriage in the nineteenth century was not very different from the custom of "woman-purchase" that had prevailed thousands of years ago, Caird protested. It might bring women into "respectable" wedlock, but it still involved

> wives being bought and sold as if they were cattle, and educated at the same time, with what can only be called ferocity, to do their "duty" patiently, silently, devotedly, and to remain thus meek and submissive under the severest provocation. Carried off by the highest bidder, they were solemnly exhorted to obedience and purity, to a life of God-fearing service, and untiring devotion to their lords, in life and in death.

Wives were not valued or desired for the love and companionship they could bring to husbands but for the sexual services they could perform. Like prostitutes, they

> were to wear out their lives in a bitter service, but this service, as their masters were pleased to consider, was suited beyond all others to the inborn "nature" of women—a service, in fact, that good women must regard as the most blessed and sacred; epithets, by the way, which seem to be always employed when something peculiarly degrading is to be recommended, and when there really is absolutely nothing else that *can* be said to recommend it.

Women continued to marry, Caird suggested, because there was nothing else for them, and they put the best face on it. "While marriage remained practically the only means of livelihood for women," she held,

> there was little danger of their seeing too clearly the seamy side of the arrangement; for to see *that* would be to stand helpless and open-eyed between the alternatives of selling themselves for a livelihood, and starvation. . . . If the position was to remain tolerable at all, obviously it must not

be looked in the face. Therefore the pretence must be cherished that the mere form of marriage makes the purchased condition an honourable one. Thousands of respectable women feel in their heart of hearts its real nature, but for that very reason, they try to buttress their self-respect by angry denial.

Caird described marriage in its present state as "the worst, because the most hypocritical form of women-purchase."[71]

One of Sarah Grand's fictional characters, Ideala, naive and idealistic about marriage, lost her innocence one night upon seeing her husband with a woman of the streets. She later protested to a friend,

the marriage oath is farcical. A woman is made to swear love to a man who will probably prove unloveable [sic], to honour a man who is as likely as not to be undeserving of honour, and to obey a man who may be incapable of judging what is best either for himself or her. . . . There was never any need to bind us with an oath. If men were all they ought to be, wouldn't we obey them gladly? To be able to do so is all we ask.

From that night on, Ideala "saw in every woman's face a hopeless degradation, and in every man's eyes a loathsome sin."[72] Sarah Grand was an enthusiastic proponent of women's equality with men; the obvious tension between appeals to equality and to special morality may have been so unresolvable for her that she employed fictional characters to voice the one demand while she herself voiced the other.

In response to Caird's attack on marriage in the *Westminster Review* in the late 1880s, a good number of women wrote to the *Daily Telegraph* to support her contentions. "She is not afraid to expose the wretched marriage tie in all its mockery," wrote Edith Maxwell. "I agreed with her on all points . . . marriage . . . should be a free contract." Maxwell may have been speaking of her own experience when she protested that the marriage contract, buttressed by the Church, "compels an unhappy woman to live with a man who has repulsed and outraged her with his infidelity and cruelty." "A Widow" expressed bewilderment over "how any sagacious woman can think to better herself by the tie matrimonial. . . . [The man's] marriage oath lies lightly on his conscience as he calmly enters with his latch-key about two in he morning. . . . I entreat you, sisters," she pleaded, "to be slaves no longer, and to think well before taking on ties that may mean endless misery to you."[73]

Marriage, finally, was only a legal form of prostitution, feminists claimed. "[A] woman who has sold herself, even for a ring and a new home," advised Lyndall, Olive Schreiner's character in *The Story of an African Farm*, "need hold her skirt aside for no creature in the street. They both earn their bread in one way."[74] Caird's Hadria, commenting on the creation of two classes of women, good and bad, remarked, "the two kinds are substance and shadow. We shall never get out of the difficulty till they frankly shake hands, and admit that they are all playing the same game." "It is such insolence to talk to us—good heavens, to *us*!—about holiness and sacredness" when the only difference between wives and prostitutes was the treatment of "one class as private and the other as public property," she cried indignantly. The marriage vow was but an attempt to clothe a private form of prostitution in respectable garb, but "it is so feeble, so futile, to try to ornament an essentially degrading fact." Try as society might to put a good face on it, to endow maternity with an element of the divine, "motherhood . . . represents a prostitution of the reproductive powers, which precisely corresponds to that other abuse, which seems to most of us so infinitely more shocking," Hadria averred.[75] Women more conservative in their beliefs, even anti-feminists, decried the state of marriage in Victorian society. Dr. Mary Scharlieb, an ardent upholder of the sanctity of marriage, admitted in 1914 that "it too often seems as if the man were seeking someone to amuse him and to minister to his desires rather than one who would be his equal, his yoke-fellow, and the satisfactory mother of his children."[76] Eliza Lynn Linton, anti-feminist par excellence, in 1888 spoke out against marriage in its present form, noting, "in the streets it goes by an ugly name; but society and the Church call it marriage."[77]

Many other anti-feminist women responded to the feminist attacks on marriage with something resembling panic. In a statement remarkable for its revelations of women's understanding of male sexuality and their fear of male brutality to women, Lady Emily Acland in 1902 warned women of what might befall them if the marriage tie were to lose its inviolability through easier divorce. "Remember," she cautioned, "that if it comes simply to a physical struggle the men will always have the best of it. It is the Christian religion which has raised women to the position they now occupy. GOD had protected women by His law of marriage. We do not want to become simply the slave and plaything of men's passions."[78] Ethel Harrison, an ardent anti-suffragist, insisted in 1911 that "in any loosening of the marriage tie women must lose infinitely more than they can gain, and immeasurably more than men. The marriage laws, with all their shortcomings and defects, have been designed and instituted in the interests of Woman: to give her protection, materially, and raise her to a position of dignity in the family." Harrison, like Lady Acland, feared that greater facility of divorce would result in physical danger to women. "Increased divorce," she advanced, "must jeopardise the position of woman as wife and mother. . . . Woe betide the weaker partner—woman."[79] As these statements indicate, anti-feminist women shared the feminist belief that the relations between men and women were barbarous and constituted a "sex war." As will be demonstrated in a later chapter, these women differed from feminists only in their belief that masculinity was a biologically determined phenomenon and therefore unalterable. Their proposed solutions to the problems created for women in patriarchal society consequently differed markedly from those of feminists.

Feminists attempted to point out what they considered to be the absurdity of the anti-feminist position on marriage. Caird noted that because women feared that the removal of the bonds of marriage would result in a lower moral standard for men, "we consent to degrade that relationship lest it should be delivered over to our tyrants to be degraded still more terribly."[80] Sarah Grand acknowledged that with marriage, women were "constantly assured that their restricted liberty would be balanced by a sense of chivalry towards them which could not exist if they were free." The problem, she pointed out, was that "what this chivalry turned out to be in fact is a laughing matter."[81] "M. S.," writing to the *Daily Telegraph*, indicated just how far her husband's chivalry extended in her case.

> I am one of those who have most unhappily found marriage a most dismal failure. Married when only a girl, after a few years I am practically only a widow, having been obliged, from my husband's brutality, to seek a separation. This was not until, through his brutality, I lost an eye, principally owing to the very merciful law which compelled me to live with a man until I was maimed for life.[82]

"A Matrimonial Failure" asked readers of the newspaper to contemplate the fate of a woman who had to endure the "enforced and degrading companionship of a man brutalised by drink or bestialised by incipient softening of the brain. . . . Think of a sensitive, refined, or even a decent woman subjected to the horrors of such a matrimonial tie," she urged.[83]

Marriage, feminists claimed, entailed real physical dangers for women. One of the more common was that of too-frequent childbirth and the diseases and conditions consequent to it. Artificial means of birth control were anathema to feminists, who believed that they would simply allow men easier and more frequent access to their wives by eliminating the fear of pregnancy.

When Charles Bradlaugh and Annie Besant were prosecuted in 1877 for disseminating information about contraception, feminists remained conspicuously silent. In fact, when called upon to testify for the defendants, Millicent Fawcett refused and warned that "if we were called as witnesses, we could effectively damage your case." Elizabeth Blackwell referred to contraception as "a national danger."[84] Feminists certainly favored "voluntary motherhood"—the right to abstain from sexual intercourse. Indeed, it constituted one of their most important demands, as will be discussed below. But contraceptive knowledge did not become an explicit feminist demand until after the turn of the century, and then only rarely did it find its way into print until after the war.

Feminists opposed contraception because they feared it would "give men greater sexual license."[85] But abstinence from sexual intercourse was possible only if men agreed to it. Feminists doubted the willingness of most husbands to safeguard their wives from physical ruin if it meant continence on their part. "One of the most revolting spectacles still extant in our 'civilization,'" lamented the Elmys in 1896, was "that of a husband wearing out (i.e., literally killing) his wife with child-births . . . with sheer licentiousness. . . . Scarcely less appalling is the fact that of the further manifold feminine ailments, specifically classed as 'the diseases of women,' the large majority are but the various results in her of sexual wrong-doing on the part of men."[86] The fact that "one fortnight after confinement some men will insist on resuming sexual relations with their wives" compelled Swiney to conclude in 1912 that "men have sought in woman only a body. They have possessed that body. They have made it the refuseheap of sexual pathology." She quoted Dr. T. L. Nichol's *Human Physiology* to support her claim that "the so-called Diseases of Women" are due "directly or collaterally to one form or another of *masculine* excess or abuse."[87]

One not improbable consequence of matrimony was the transmission of venereal disease to wives and newborn children by errant husbands. Christabel Pankhurst's infamous diatribes against sexual disease were only a later and more dramatic manifestation of concern among feminists about the dangers women faced. Butler, as early as 1870, expressed indignation that supporters of the CD Acts completely ignored the fact that it was men who transmitted infection from "fallen and contagious women" to "pure women and children." She wished, she said, to expose the existence of "that most important link, the adulterous husbands and fathers, who are dispensing disease and death in their families."[88] Venereal disease among men, she believed, "is almost universal at one time or another."[89] Hamilton referred to the "risks [to wives] attaching to the profession of marriage other than the natural ones of childbirth," of the "tangible, physical consequence of loose living" on the part of husbands, of "quite unnecessary risks from which their unmarried sisters are exempt."[90] Lily Waring, in a 1910 article in *Common Cause*, warned of the probable consequences to a woman who married a man with "a past": "a wife branded with disease or children branded with disease, perhaps both." Men have "been content to let women enter blindly upon matrimony without knowing the possible results," she charged, "matters that may make the difference between life-long misery and happiness. Women have been wilfully blindfolded, agonised for men's badness, without being allowed to suspect the why and the wherefore of it."[91] As a matter of course, the literature department of the NUWSS stocked Dr. Louisa Martindale's *Beneath the Surface*— a treatise on the dangers of venereal disease—and "placed its title in the list of books and pamphlets they were prepared to supply." Fawcett defended the book and the NUWSS's holding of it in Parliament, describing it as a necessary "warning to men and women of the physical risks connected with promiscuous sexual intercourse."[92]

The ground was well prepared by the time Christabel Pankhurst unleashed her fury at a society that permitted and encouraged the infection of women with venereal disease. Gonorrhea, she insisted, "is acquired before marriage by 75 per cent. or 85 per cent. of men, and it is very often contracted after marriage by such men as are not entirely faithful to their wives." As a result, "a very large number of women are infected by their husbands with gonorrhoea," she maintained, but very little was done to prevent this from occurring because "to men the disease gives comparatively little trouble," though to women "it is one of the gravest of all diseases."[93] Few women knew of the menace of venereal disease to themselves or to their children, she claimed, because men and their doctors had entered into a conspiracy of silence. Men and doctors "keep them in ignorance so that they cannot even protect themselves from future danger," she protested.[94]

As a result of venereal disease, Pankhurst asserted, "an enormous percentage of the operations upon women are necessitated." In many cases, venereal disease "so affects the organs of maternity as to necessitate their complete removal." She offered the apocryphal example of a "bride struck down by illness within a few days, or within a few weeks, of her wedding day [who] is told by her husband and the doctor that she is suffering from appendicitis and under the cover of this lie her sex organs are removed without her knowledge." In fact, she declared, "the female ailments which are urged by some ignoble men as a reason against the enfranchisement of women are not due to natural weakness, but—to gonorrhoea. Women—and there are so many of them—who 'have never been well since they married,' are victims of gonorrhoea."[95]

Historians who have dismissed Christabel Pankhurst on the basis of her data have ignored the fact that she relied on the figures used by medical men of her time; as Walkowitz has noted, "later statistics would suggest that syphilis was endemic to the civilian population in Great Britain in the Victorian and Edwardian periods." The "Report of the Royal Commission on Venereal Diseases" estimated that "the number of persons who have been infected with syphilis, acquired or congenital, cannot fall below 10 percent of the whole population in the large cities, and the percentage affected with gonorrhea must greatly exceed this proportion."[96]

Nor were Pankhurst's accusations of cover-up by doctors entirely groundless. Dr. William Sinclair, in *On Gonorrheal Infection in Women* (1886), admitted that "British doctors frequently acted as willing accomplices for errant husbands, helping them to camouflage their gonorrheal discharge." He cited the case of a French venereologist, a physician greatly respected in Britain, who treated a young man for venereal disease just before his marriage. The imminence of the wedding date left no time for a cure; hence,

> in these embarrassing circumstances one sovereign remedy remains, only one—injections of nitrate of silver. . . . Suppose one employs a medium dose of the solution, in an hour and a half or two hours after the injection there appears a discharge, the simple effect of traumatism; accompanied by a little smarting in micturition. This slight inflammation lasts five or six hours. But then, precious result, the canal becomes dry; all morbid secretion is arrested, and this condition persists for eighteen or twenty-four hours—quite sufficient time for the bridegroom to seek his nuptial couch in a healthy or, at least, non-contagious state. In exact figures, if the newly-wedded pair ought to retire to their room on Friday morning at one o'clock, the preservative injection ought to be made about nine o'-clock on Thursday afternoon.[97]

Nor did Pankhurst invent the idea that gonorrhea caused many female diseases; rather she echoed a view shared by many others in the women's movement. In an address to a meeting of medical women in 1897, Dr. Elizabeth Blackwell, citing the works of Drs. T. More Madden, J. W. Sinclair, T. Gaillard Thomas, Lawson Tait, and others, reported that "many of the female complaints which have so largely increased . . . are now considered by experienced and clear-headed physicians to be often due to gonorrhoeal infection derived from husbands of former loose life; infection conveyed either directly, or from recrudescent and insidious forms of trouble, hitherto unsuspected."[98] Dr. Mary Scharlieb, in *What It Means to Marry* (1914), warned her readers that venereal disease "takes a terrible toll of health and life from women. . . . It has been calculated that probably half of the serious cases of pelvic disease leading to major operations are due to this trouble." She maintained that "this infection is the cause of the great majority of still-births and miscarriages."[99] Pankhurst's warnings to women of the dangers of marriage, her exhortations to women to remain single, and thereby protect themselves from disease or injury, followed logically from the writings of Blackwell and others.

Feminist revelations and denunciations of disease transmitted by men served a purpose beyond that of cautioning women about the dangers of male sexuality. They constituted an attempt to dispel the myth of the woman as polluted, as the personification and purveyor of disease. Anthropological works demonstrate that an "emphasis on the polluting, dirty, dangerous and thus anti-social character of women's sexuality" pervade primitive cultures[100]—we need look no farther than the Contagious Diseases Acts to see that such beliefs maintained a firm grip on Victorians. As Douglas has observed, "pollution beliefs can be used in a dialogue of claims and counter-claims to status . . . some pollutions are used as analogies for expressing a general view of the social order." More specifically, sex pollution is likely to flourish "when the principle of male dominance is applied to the ordering of social life but is contradicted by other principles such as that of female independence, or the inherent right of women as the weaker sex to be more protected from violence than men."[101] Such a situation certainly existed in the nineteenth century, when patriarchal rights to property in women faced challenges from both feminism on the one hand and the ideology of the angel in the house on the other. In attempting to reassert sexual hierarchy, domestic ideologists utilized the belief that women were polluting and diseased. "A polluting person is always in the wrong," Douglas has written. "He [sic] has developed some wrong condition or simply crossed some line which should not have been crossed and this displacement unleashes danger for someone."[102]

In reversing the pollution belief, in declaring men to be the agents of danger and disease for women, Butler, Elmy, Swiney, and Pankhurst demonstrated their intentions to overturn the sexual order in England. They made a "counter-claim to status" for their sex as not merely equal with men but morally superior to them, a claim they hoped would help to effect a recreation of society and culture consonant with values characteristically assigned to women.

A fascinating little book by Elmy and her husband serves as a classic example of pollution reversal and the ends toward which it aimed. In *Life to Woman* (1896), the Elmys took up the issue of menstruation—its causes and effects, and how its elimination could both be secured by and would help to secure the emancipation of women. Woman experienced not merely political and social subjection and deprivation, they argued, "but is still in bondage, in varying degree, to a physical infirmity or incommodity which is, as we assert, abnormal,—both needless and useless in the strict economy of Nature." They believed menstruation to be "an acquired and inherited bodily result of ages of corporal subjugation and ill treatment by her quondam brute companion and master; an ailment peculiar to [the human female], and which indubitably has the characteristics of being the outcome of persistent and inconsiderate excess and wrong usage by the male portion of the race." Because of the sexual brutality of men, menstruation, "the periodic 'spontaneous ovulation,' which is in other female animals a painless and inconspicuous operation of Nature, has in woman developed an attending wearisome and sometimes hazardous infirmity." In other words, menstruation was not a natural function but the consequence of centuries of sexual abuse by men. At times describing it as a wound, at others an abortion, the Elmys theorized that periodic pathological hemorrhaging (as opposed to ovulation, which they viewed as natural) had become an acquired hereditary trait. Men had consented to this unhealthy development in woman and withheld knowledge as to its true nature in order to maintain her in "a slave condition of mental ignorance and bodily incapacity, thus to achieve her non-resistance to inordinate masculine passion." Ideological prescriptions as to the constitutional inferiority of women, "all the honeyed cant about the tender weakness of femininity," were in fact designed to keep women in "the vilest of servile bondage."[103]

Menstruation could be cured, the Elmys insisted, by a new sexual ordering of society. Votes for women would compel society to recognize the right of women to regulate sexual intercourse, thereby limiting men's access to them. The ascendancy of "psychic love"—as taught by women to men—over brute passion would be secured when women held their rightful place in society. Finally, the emancipation of women would allow more women to enter the medical profession and thereby discredit the "scientific" view that menstruation was natural and inevitable. "Can one doubt," they demanded, "that had men suffered analogous 'pain and discomfort,' the evil—despite its being 'periodic' and 'physiological' (?) [sic]—would long ago have been recognised, enquired [sic] into, and intelligently treated with a view to its amelioration and permanent remedy?"[104] Menstruation would become a thing of the past with the emancipation of women.

APPEALING simultaneously to women's rights to equality with men and to their right to maintain a special morality, the feminist critique of marriage necessarily involved a critique of masculinity such as that put forth by Butler, the Elmys, Swiney, and Christabel Pankhurst. Male sexuality, exemplified in microcosm by the institution of marriage, was, they believed, destructive not only to women but to the whole of humanity. Feminists asserted the need for women's values to transcend those of men in the ordering of society. They made that assertion first in the domestic sphere, in the form of the woman's right to control her body and her fertility.

The experience of women in marriage, where they were subject—in the Elmys' words—to "the excess of sexual proclivity and indulgence general on the part of man," led feminists to demand the right to control their bodies.[105] For some, the right to refuse intercourse stood at the core of their movement. "The maternal instinct" constituted for Caird "the red-hot heart of the battle."[106] The *Englishwoman's Review* in 1889 claimed that "the woman has as much right to live her individual life before God as the man . . . no man is a good husband who does not respect the individuality of his wife, body, soul, and spirit, as much as his own."[107] Lady Florence Dixie announced in the *Woman's Herald* in 1891 that the feminist "Plan of Campaign" for women prominently included "rights over their own person and the control of the birth of children."[108] The Elmys insisted that "the functions of wifehood and motherhood must remain solely and entirely within the wife's own option."[109] Ethel Snowdon spoke of "the equality in sex-relations for which the collective sense of women yearns" and described "a woman's absolute right over herself after marriage" as the

> greatest demand which the thorough-going feminist will make, and which she will probably achieve last, since it is the one which apparently flies most deliberately in the face of all established order. . . . The old idea taught from the cradle, that it is a woman's part unquestioningly to obey, must be exploded if a sacred companionship between husband and wife—which is what the feminist desires—is to take the place of the ancient relationship; the latest, newest, finest chivalry will admit this unalienable right, and will take nothing that is not yielded in love and confidence.[110]

Female doctors lent their expertise and prestige to the feminist assertion that control over the incidence of sexual intercourse belonged to the woman. Elizabeth Blackwell argued that physiological laws demanded that a woman be the "regulator of sexual intercourse," that her "constitution . . . must determine the times of the special act of physical union." To date, men had maintained control over women's reproductive functions, but the truth of Christianity, as demonstrated through physiology, would triumph with the "regulation of sexual intercourse in the best interests of womanhood."[111] Dr. Alice Ker insisted that "wives have rights towards themselves and their children as well as duties toward their husbands." She advised mothers that

> the girl must be taught that her body is her own, subject only to her Maker, and that she has no right to make the undue ownership of it over to her husband. This is the great law that needs to be fully understood and acted upon, if the next generation is to be better and purer than this one. . . . In the marriage relation, the choice of time and frequency is the right of the woman, by reason of the periodicity which characterises her being, and the violation of this law injures not only herself, physically and morally, but also her husband and her children.[112]

"If a wife has not got the control of her own person," Ker asked, "in what respect is she better than those most unhappy members of our sisterhood who are pathetically defined as 'unfortunates?' " Ker claimed that "the proper adjustment of this one question would be the beginning of the Millennium."[113]

CHAPTER IV

THE DOCTORS

But for Miss Garrett I must say of her that I gained
more from her than any other doctor . . . *because* I
was able to *tell* her so much more than I ever could
or would tell to any *man*. . . . This is a subject on
which I feel very, very much, for I have suffered
so long. O, if men knew what women have to endure, and how every good woman has prayed for
the coming of a change, a change in this . . . believe me, the best and the purest feelings of women
have been torn and harrowed and shamefully
wounded for centuries, just to please a wicked *custom*.

JOSEPHINE BUTLER, 1868

The medical profession had lent its considerable authority to
scientific definitions of the female as "the Sex" in the course of
the nineteenth century. This identity had been evolved both to
justify women's exclusion from the public sphere and political
power and to make them the proper complement to the "inherent" sexual drives of men. Confidence in science as the basis for
virtually all knowledge permeated Victorian mentality; physicians enveloped themselves in the scientific mantle as they
sought to establish themselves as the "supreme authority" in
sexual matters. Doctors mobilized "the truth of sex," as Foucault
termed it, in a bid for power based upon their monopoly on
"knowledge."[1]

Because science, and especially medicine, served as the legit-
imizing discourse on sexuality, suffragists regarded the admission of women to the medical profession as a necessary and

integral component of their campaign. Female physicians would bring a degree of comfort and security to their patients not available to them with male attendants and would help to eliminate the abuses they suffered at the hands of male doctors and surgeons. But more important, through their understanding of biology and physiology, female physicians would play a leading role in the reconstruction of notions of femininity and masculinity. Female doctors became for the women's movement a source of scientific legitimacy as they sought a redefinition of sexual identity for women that would justify their political inclusion. For this reason, the movement to admit women to the medical profession must be seen as integral to the campaign for enfranchisement.

The women's movement first sought to discredit the men who had appointed themselves the sole legitimate spokesmen for the health and welfare of society, who claimed expertise and "truth," and whose "science" had determined the identity of women to be an exclusively sexual one. Gynecologists and obstetricians in particular, as Seymour Haden observed in 1867,

> in choosing the particular branch of medicine which we follow, practising as we do among women particularly . . . have constituted ourselves the true guardians of their interests, and in many cases in spite of ourselves we become the custodians of their honour. We are, in fact, the stronger, and they the weaker. They are obliged to believe all that we tell them. . . . We, therefore, may be said to have them at our mercy.[2]

Feminists insisted that this situation was not simply unjust but hypocritical. They charged that the medical profession had created a mystifying ideology that, far from promoting health, allowed the "custodians of their honour" to violate women in the name of science and medical expertise. "The true guardians of their interests," in fact, offended women by their practices; they carried out procedures that demonstrated brutal, aggressive, and sexual rather than altruistic motivations and intentions. Feminists marshaled evidence of especially horrible cases to show that doctors were sexually perverse, and that women's extreme reluctance to consult with male physicians was entirely justified by reality. The effects of this situation, the women protested, ran counter to health and to the doctors' ability to know about women's bodies or their sexual identity. They argued that what purported to be scientific knowledge and expertise was in fact medical ignorance, and that medical practice served as a cloak for male sexual abuse. The mystifying ideology surrounding the medical profession was a lie, they concluded, for it was the very opposite of what it claimed to be.

Feminists cited evidence of a particularly gruesome nature to support their contention that "scientific" expertise could be used to justify the abuse of women. In 1867, Isaac Baker Brown (see Chapter I) was ousted from the Obstetrical Society of London for malpractice. His practice and the circumstances of his ouster from the Society illustrate in lurid detail just what feminists sought to eliminate through their discourses of resistance and in opening the medical profession to women.

The Fellows of the Obstetrical Society expelled Brown from their number because of his proclivity to perform clitoridectomies upon women without the knowledge of their husbands, their friends, or themselves. The issue was not clitoridectomy as such, but the dishonor Brown brought to the medical profession. As the *Lancet* of 6 April 1867, editorialized, "the verdict which was pronounced on Wednesday evening bore no direct relation to the utility or uselessness of a particular operation."[3] Rather, as Dr. Barnes stated during the hearings, "our opposition is directed against a gross infringement of professional honour."[4] The *Lancet* protested "indignantly" against the operation of clitoridectomy upon "married women without the knowledge and consent of their husbands, and upon married or unmarried women without their own knowledge of the nature of the operation."[5] The point to be noted here is the injury done to the medical profession, which presumably suffered great harm to its reputation by the injury done to husbands. The patients upon whom this operation was performed were given the last, and least, consideration by the Society. This was because many members themselves were accustomed to performing clitoridectomies and ovariotomies; they, presumably, took the precaution of informing their patients' husbands and friends of the procedure, whether or not they told the patients themselves of its nature. Brown, to the dismay of the Obstetrical Society, did not.[6]

The proceedings against Brown reveal that gynecological surgery was commonplace. In his defense, Brown stated that clitoridectomy "is an operation, as Dr. Aveling has shown, that has been performed from the time of Hippocrates again and again." "There are many in this room that often perform the operation of clitoridectomy," he argued. Dr. Savage concurred. "Others . . . have performed the operation of clitoridectomy, at least of clitorotomy," he stated. "They were cases which seemed to require it, and they did well under it." The President of the Society interrupted the proceedings several times to remind those members who tended to defend Brown on the grounds of the success of his procedure that "it is the manner in which the operation is performed, not the operation itself, which we have met to consider."[7]

Brown received some support for his operations even under the conditions in which he performed them. Dr. Routh defended the practice of clitoridectomy without informed consent, demanding of his colleagues, "when we are about to operate upon a patient (I do not care what the operation is), is it customary to enter into the exact minutiae of the operation? Because, if it is the custom, I think there are very few surgeons who observe it."[8]

The testimony of Dr. Locking, who was present for one of the clitoridectomies performed by Brown, and who resigned his appointment "in consequence of what he considered the breach of faith towards the profession," illustrates just what some women, at least, endured at the hands of physicians who professed to be the "true guardians of their interests," the "custodians of their honour." "[T]he whole of the organ was removed," he told the Society,

> and in the following manner. Two instruments were used,—the pair of hooked forceps which Mr. Brown always uses in clitoridectomy and a cautery iron. . . . This iron . . . is somewhat hatchet-shaped. The clitoris was seized by the forceps in the usual manner. The thin edge of the red-hot iron was then passed round and round its base until the organ was severed from its attachments, being partly burnt, partly cut or sawn, and partly torn away. After the clitoris was removed, the nymphae on each side were severed in a similar way by a sawing motion of the hot iron. After the clitoris and nymphae were got rid of, the operation was brought to a close by taking the back of the iron and searing the surfaces of the labia and the other parts of the vulva which had escaped the cautery, and the instrument was rubbed down backwards and forwards till the parts were more effectively destroyed.

Locking reported to the Society that "on interrogating the patient subsequently, she told me she did not know what had been done to her, nor had she been asked if she would consent to the operation."[9]

The statement of Dr. Barnes reveals whose interests and honor were being protected in the case of Mr. Isaac Baker Brown versus the Obstetrical Society of London. "The great reason why the Council placed this in the published matter was this," intoned the prestigious London physician, "that it got before a public court of law, it got into all the daily papers . . . [it] had become a matter of public scandal . . . we were compelled, in vindication of the honour of the Society, to bring it forward."[10] As will be discussed further below, it is just this self-serving attitude of the medical profession—to say nothing of the abuse involved—that feminists raged against in the course of their critique of male doctors.

WOMEN'S INTENSE ANGER against the medical profession surfaced as a result of the Contagious Diseases Acts. The efficacy of the acts in reducing venereal disease rested upon the compulsory examination of suspected prostitutes. Ironically, examination by the speculum also acted as the motive force behind the feminist repeal campaign by allowing middle-class women to identify with the subject women. The speculum examination enabled respectable women "to bridge the social and moral gulf between 'pure' and 'impure' women," Walkowitz has noted. It also helped to focus hostility toward those "terrible aristocratic doctors" who lent their prestige and professional offices to the violation of women under the acts.[11] The examination itself and the doctors' central role in the administration of the acts represented for feminists the ultimate indignity of their inferiority and subservience. The physical violation of their bodies was the logical outcome of an ideology that defined women in terms of sex and in relation only to male sexuality.

Defenders of the acts repeatedly insisted that the surgical examination of prostitutes could have no deleterious effect on such degraded creatures. In fact, according to Glen Petrie, "military and naval surgeons testified readily enough that, while they would object profoundly to inspecting soldiers and sailors for symptoms of venereal infection as being degrading both to themselves and the Service to which they belonged, they saw nothing degrading in inspecting queues of young girls for signs of the same disease."[12] The LNA leadership countered that however degraded the woman involved, men had no right to violate her. Butler explicitly refused male constructions of a dual female sexuality that justified the outrage of one class of women. "Unchastity in a woman can never give you a right to forget the sanctity of her person," she declared. "The man—be he a debauché, a drunkard, or a high-class physician well paid by the State for the execution of this outrage—who violates any woman whatsoever, violates his own mother in her."[13] Butler regarded the speculum examination as

> the concrete expression of the will and determination of a certain portion of male humanity to subject womanhood to be an instrument to the convenience and lust of men. It is the concrete expression of this desire—unconscious perhaps to most of them—to make a certain number of women things, vessels of dishonour, chattels, slaves, but not women; and our task is to restore them to womanhood, to deny that upon the very vilest of our sex this outrage may be perpetrated.[14]

The doctors' role in establishing and administering the Contagious Diseases Acts demonstrated to feminists the hypocrisy of the mystique surrounding their profession. It was not the search for scientific "truth" or the desire to heal and cure that motivated medical men, but "the medical love of power . . . the medical lust of handling and dominating women," as one repeal advocate put it.[15] For Butler, the violation of women under the CD Acts was merely the first step in a campaign by doctors to translate their "tendency . . . to despotism" into concrete expressions and forms of power.[16] In 1872, she wrote to Joseph Edmondson, a prominent repealer,

> perhaps you know that there was a meeting held in London last Thursday of MPs and doctors, and that they agreed to ask that a "Medical Council" should be attached to the "Local Government Board." You will at once see what an awful power this will be. . . . No words can tell what I and other women suffer at the sight of this violent desire on the part of certain powerful men to legalise by one means or another this hideous personal outrage. . . . It is coming to be more & more a deadly fight for *our bodies*. If these

doctors could be forced to keep their hateful hands off us,
there would be *an end* to laws which protect vice & to
many other evils, for this indecent outrage is surrounded
& connected on every side with fraud & hurtful purposes.[17]

As Butler indicated here, feminists believed that the male monopoly on medicine, most especially that branch pertaining to
women, had prepared the ground for the Contagious Diseases
Acts in the first place. Mary Hume-Rothery, in *Women and Doctors: or Medical Despotism in England* (1871), insisted that the
practice of "man-mid-wifery" had made it possible for the state
to institute the CD Acts. "To what course of study and practice
by the medical profession are we indebted for the devising of
that diabolical outrage on all the sanctities of the female organism," she demanded,

> by which it has flattered the State authorities into believing
> that it has the power to render women the safe playthings
> for men's vices which the aforesaid State authorities desi-
> derate [sic]? I answer unhesitatingly, to the indecent and
> unnatural study and practice of male practitioners of ob-
> stetric medicine . . . but for this practice, the very means
> for perpetrating that outrage could never have been de-
> vised.[18]

Male physicians, Hume-Rothery charged, had developed a
mystifying ideology that camouflaged their true intentions—the
degradation and sexual abuse of women. Through the practice
of obstetrics and gynecology, she explained, "medical men have
obtained that ascendancy over the minds of women . . . which
has over-ridden, if not absolutely extinguished, feminine instincts of modesty and self-respect, till women . . . till ladies of
the highest character and position submit themselves, of their
own free will, to similar 'examinations' at the hands of their
medical attendants." Noting that defenders of the CD Acts cited
the speculum examination of respectable women to justify its

use for prostitutes, Hume-Rothery insisted that doctors had terrorized and duped women into accepting the necessity of the procedure. The very opposite of skilled professionals, physicians had taken "advantage of the fears and sufferings of weak women, carefully trained in profound ignorance of all that it most deeply concerns them, as women, to know, have played upon that ignorance and established their despotic sway over that weakness, till when they were pleased to inform them such outrage was necessary, their victims ventured not to dispute the fiat." Denying that their profession rendered them any less immune to lust than other men, Hume-Rothery argued that "the placing of a large body of men . . . in a position of the utmost temptation, with complete practical irresponsibility," had "produced its legitimate harvest of unspeakable abuse and corruption." The exposure of "parish surgeons' apprentices and raw medical students" to "sickrooms where male doctors do what they like with women" could not help but break down their reverence for all womanhood. "The whole relation between the sexes is affected, their proper mutual reverence, their fitting self-respect, is tainted and blunted at the best by this unnatural custom of placing women and girls in the absolute physical custody, and at the sole mercy, of male attendants."[19]

For Hume-Rothery, Butler, and other feminists, the speculum examination under the Contagious Diseases Acts was but a mere tip of the iceberg, only one manifestation of terrible wrongs perpetrated against women by male doctors every day and in all classes of society, wrongs made possible by acceptance of a male monopoly on the profession of medicine, which had branded women sexual objects. They cited the "medical lust of indecently handling women" and the "legislative lust of ruling them with an iron hand for the purpose of gratifying vicious propensities in men"[20] as proof that, as the *Shield* proclaimed, "we must have a share in the work of legislation, and we must have medical attendants of our own sex."[21]

Opponents of women's entry into medicine most often cited

their desire to preserve the "innocence, purity, and modesty of the ladies" as the reason for their opposition.[22] Feminists responded that the argument for separate spheres, especially in the case of medical attendance by men, was inherently contradictory and hypocritical, that it in fact exposed women to the very corruption from which it was designed to protect them. As a woman wrote in the *Examiner* in 1871, "every young woman has to go through the ordeal of being shocked over and over again, before she is able to bear her fate with resignation. . . . The cruelty of denying to women the ministry of their own sex is enhanced by the great pains taken to develope [sic] their native modesty to the most extreme degree."[23] Frances Power Cobbe pointed out in 1878 that

> to propose deliberately to teach girls to set those sacred feelings [of delicacy] aside on one point, and that point the one where they are necessarily touched immeasurably more closely than anywhere else, is simply absurd. They could not do it if they would, and they ought not to do it if they could. . . . Violence must be done to [a young woman's] natural instincts, either by the pressure of the mother's persuasion (who has undergone the same *peine forte et dure* before her), or else by unendurable anguish, before she will have recourse to aid which she thinks worse than disease, or even death.[24]

Feminists offered their own experiences at the hands of male physicians to demonstrate that separate sphere ideology was hypocritical in practice. The hegemony of those "terrible aristocratic doctors"—who, having defined women as sexual beings, were seeking to gain complete control over women's bodies—established a situation in which women were vulnerable not simply to intrusion but to abuse in many cases. Feminists often expressed their objections to male medical attendance in terms of injury to their modesty, but they were able at times to articulate their concerns about a far more pervasive and dangerous wrong—the actual violation of women by male doctors.

Butler described the internal examination as a procedure "which is so intolerable to womanhood, violence done to the deepest and most indelible instincts of her nature," that there were few women "who would not rather endure any amount of bodily pain than that."[25] She declared that "not a few of us *choose to die*" rather than submit to male attendance, especially during childbirth, when the presence of a male physician defiled "the finest most sensitive part of a woman . . . with such a wound as no proud and gentle nature ever recovers from."[26] She became incensed when doctors who were associated with the CD Acts defended their actions on the grounds that "it is nothing more than what virtuous women of the better classes constantly go through," as one physician told the War Office. Butler countered that

> it is useless to defend *one evil* by citing *another evil*. It is a distinct evil, if not an immorality, that virtuous women should ever have been driven to such extremities [sic]. But he exaggerates; for they do not *constantly* do so. There have been thousands (unknown, of course, to the doctors) who have endured anything rather than go through such a process.[27]

Women testified repeatedly and publicly about the "agonies of shame and outraged modesty" they experienced "when submitting to male medical and surgical treatment," even at the hands of "a long-known and valued medical man." "An Englishwoman" wrote to the *Scotsman* in 1872 of her experience as "a patient under a very eminent doctor of Edinburgh." Her trauma was such that "nothing would again induce me to do what I did then, in ignorance of what was before me. The anguish of mind suffered silently by women in such circumstances is not to be described."[28] One member of the LNA leadership announced that examination by male physicians, especially that by speculum, was "the deepest humiliation a woman can be called upon to subject herself to."[29]

Women sometimes testified that their profound objection to male medical attendance arose from more than injured modesty. Many felt that they had been violated by doctors who had prurient interests in them. In 1851, an American woman demanded, "what motive, but a lustful or mercenary one, can induce Physicians to make frequent examinations with the finger, or the speculum, when the highest medical authorities have declared such examinations generally *unnecessary*, and often hurtful?"[30] Elizabeth Blackwell wrote in 1858 to her sister Emily, also a physician, of a "Madame ———— . . . She is seriously interested in the entrance of women into the medical profession, a wish founded in her case on the moral degradation which she has observed amongst her own acquaintance from the practice of being treated by men in female complaints."[31] J. J. Garth Wilkinson published a letter from "another lady," perhaps Blackwell, who described a case

> in which a lady had been accustomed for a length of time to submit to specular examination for some slight ailment connected with the womb. . . . She had believed in the necessity for examination as asserted by her medical attendant . . . until the feeling of real injury caused by the process grew unmistakeable, and to use her own words, 'It made me ask myself, *why* is the man always insisting upon it?' The conclusion she came to I will not give, but content myself with saying that she did *not* think her health had been the chief motive for the advice.

The letter writer charged that "many women in their weakness and ignorance, are persuaded or commanded into these examinations when not the slightest *necessity* exists."[32]

Women simply had no confidence that male members of the medical profession entered their practices with altruistic motives. Blackwell referred to "the painful doubt which certainly exists in many minds in relation to the high morality of the Medical Profession."[33] Cobbe reflected that while convention taught everyone to "look on a doctor as an old woman," "the members of the Royal Colleges of Physicians and Surgeons and of the Society of Apothecaries are *not* 'old women.' They are not even all old, nor all good men." She noted that

> a few months before they begin to practise . . . they are commonly supposed to be among the least steady or well-conducted of youths; and where a number of them congregate together—as in Edinburgh, for example—they are apt to obtain an unenviable notoriety for "rowdyism." I have more than once myself witnessed conduct on the part of these lads at public meetings which every man on the platform denounced as disgraceful. I could not but reflect as I watched them: "And *these* youths a year hence will be called to the bedsides of ladies to minister at hours of the uttermost trial when the extremest refinement of tact and delicacy must scarce make the presence of a man unendurable. Nay, they *now* attend in crowds the clinical instructions in the female wards of the hospital."[34]

In medical school, Blackwell witnessed the "horrible exposure" of women to students, shocked that any poor woman had to be "subjected to such a torture."[35] Edith Pechey, one of the first seven women enrolled in medicine at the University of Edinburgh, described an encounter with medical students there. One night in 1871 she was followed through the streets by "a knot of young men" who shouted at her "all the foulest epithets in their voluminous vocabulary of abuse . . . using medical terms to make the disgusting purport of their language more intelligible to me." "I should be very sorry," she lamented, "to see any poor girl under the care (!) of such men as those. . . . When a man can put his scientific knowledge to such degraded use, it seems to me he cannot sink much lower." Pechey's determination to study medicine was redoubled by her experience, "by the desire to remove women from the care of such young ruffians."[36]

The inclusion of women in medical courses might "refine and restrain the manners of those who certainly seem now a good deal in need of restraint," argued the *Englishwoman's Review* in April 1873.[37] Blackwell noted that just at the age at which a man should begin the study of medicine—nineteen or so—

> the passions are strong, the judgment is unformed, and the discipline of self-control . . . is unattained. . . . The indispensable foundation of all medical study—anatomy—when it fails to create reverence for the instrument of life, tends to destroy reverence . . . it is especially necessary that elevating influences be brought to bear upon the period of medical study . . . [the student] should be imperatively required to bring the self-control and pure association of true manhood into his confidential post of advisor of women and youth.[38]

Blackwell associated the lack of reverence for the female patient with the "common resort to sexual examination," "an evil" that had "grown up in medical practice of comparatively modern date." She charged that the use of the speculum was "reckless" and not limited to cases where it was "absolutely necessary." "I know from fifty years' medical experience," she wrote, "that this custom is a real and growing evil. It should be a last resort of medical necessity."[39] Its unrestricted use by male physicians constituted a violation of women and an abuse of power on the part of those "trusted unreservedly by the father to guard wife and children."[40]

Sophia Jex-Blake, one of the driving forces behind the women's medical movement, was moved to express concern about the motives and behavior of some male physicans attending women after her experience with female patients. In the first edition of *Medical Women* (1872), Jex-Blake wrote that, based upon her association with upstanding medical men,

I am, indeed, far from pretending, as some have done, that it is morally wrong for men to be the medical attendants of women, and that grave mischiefs are the frequent and natural results of their being placed in that position. . . . I am very sure that in the vast majority of cases the motives and conduct of medical men in this respect are altogether above question, and that every physician *who is also a gentleman* is thoroughly able . . . to remember only the human suffering brought before him and the scientific bearing of its details.[41]

Her qualification is noteworthy, as is her reference to a London surgeon who remarked, "Whoever is not able, in the course of practice, to put the idea of sex out of his mind, is not fit for the medical profession at all." Jex-Blake apparently became aware of physicians who had not also been gentlemen, for in the second edition of her book (1886) she amended her statement of confidence in medical men. "I feel obliged to say frankly," she wrote, "that, with greater experience, I have come to see more rather than less reason for the attendance of women on women in all the special ailments relating exclusively to their sex." She supported her contention with the statement by a Professor Laycock that he knew "from experience that a proportion of the students have prurient thoughts, and are apt to express them."[42]

Jex-Blake also included in the second edition of *Medical Women* a letter to the *Pall Mall Gazette* from a male physician. He told of a meeting of the Obstetrical Society that he had attended, a meeting called to oust a member for malpractice. The writer noted that the report of the meeting, published in the *Lancet* of 6 April 1867, was "toned down for publication, as any one who was present will admit." He revealed that "some of the statements made, and the bursts of laughter—*hilarité*—which were elicited by certain portions of the discussion, created a most painful and disagreeable impression on my mind. I could not help thinking that any woman reading that report would be

glad to have at least the choice allowed her of employing one of
her own sex as a medical attendant in case she preferred to do
so." The physician referred to in the letter included in Jex-
Blake's book was Isaac Baker Brown, Fellow of the Obstetrical
Society of London. Jex-Blake did not reveal to her readers the
reasons for his ouster, perhaps because she feared the repercus-
sions from her male colleagues that such disclosure might entail.
She did, however—citing the words of Sir William Gull—hint
that the case was a particularly horrible one. "I consider," Gull
had written in 1875,

> that there are some parts of the medical profession that a
> highly-trained woman could do better than a man. There
> are certain sex relations which might be avoided in that
> way with great advantage to the public. I need not say that
> there is a quiet scandal in certain parts of our profession
> about women's diseases, which will be gotten rid of by
> introducing high-minded well-trained women into the
> practice of Medicine.[43]

The reluctance of women to seek help from male doctors—
stemming not from prudery or false modesty but from their
experience of violation—had serious ramifications. As Cobbe
noted in 1878, the "little health of ladies" was a prominent fea-
ture of the Victorian period. "No one is ignorant," she wrote,
"[of] how often the most agonising diseases to which female
nature is liable follow from the neglect of early premonitory
symptoms, and how often, likewise, lifelong invalidism results
from disregard of the ailments of youth." She attributed these
"deplorable catastrophes" to the woman's "modest shrinking
from disclosing her troubles to a male advisor."[44] Ethel Snowdon believed that "tens of thousands of women have neglected
to consult a physician when there was real need for such a con-
sultation because of their natural shrinking from exposing their
weaknesses to a male doctor."[45] Jex-Blake described cases in
which "ladies have habitually gone through one confinement

after another without proper attendance, because the idea of employing a man was so repugnant to them." Even when overcoming their hesitation and finally seeking help, women often could not discuss the nature of their complaints, nor could doctors bring themselves to ask about them. A male physician and surgeon of fifty years' practice disclosed in a letter to the *Inverness Courier* in 1871 that "every medical man must confess that he is often merely able to hint as to information he required from his female patients, and consequently, for want of plain questions and answers, which a lady M.D. [sic] would at once ask and receive, frequently mistakes and mistreats a case . . . great numbers of women are sickly for life, and die, simply because they shrink from speaking of their ailments to men."[46]

Separate sphere ideology barred women from attending their own sex, a situation, feminists charged, that limited male physicians' capabilities to truly understand women's bodies or their sexuality. Cobbe protested that the doctors had "failed . . . as the guardians of the health of women."[47] More ominously, women had no confidence that male physicians gave proper attention to the diseases of women—precisely because they *were* diseases of women. In 1865, the Female Medical Society pointed out that the great number of cases of puerperal fever were caused by "doctors passing straight from the dissecting-room or post-mortem theatre to the lying-in room." The *Lancet*, in outrage, called the Society's accusations "all erroneous," though the women were entirely correct.[48] Some medical men conceded that their profession had neglected, with grave consequences, the study of the diseases of women. Edward J. Tilt, in the *Handbook of Uterine Therapeutics*, wrote that "the principal reason why the knowledge of diseases of women has so little advanced, is the hitherto undisturbed belief that one sex only is qualified by education and powers of mind to investigate and to cure what the other sex alone has to suffer."[49] As late as 1912, Dr. Agnes Savill could state with conviction that with regard to women, male doctors were fifty years behind the times.[50]

The medical profession's handling of venereal disease, particularly gonorrhea, encouraged the belief among women that male doctors were not simply indifferent to women's health but actively engaged in a conspiracy of silence about venereal disease that was literally destroying them. Feminists, as noted in an earlier chapter, accused male physicians of helping their male patients to cover up venereal diseases; in fact, doctors regularly advised men as to how they might camouflage their gonorrheal discharge and continue to cohabit with their wives.[51] Whether or not male doctors were consciously helping to spread venereal diseases to women, the feminists' conviction that they were doing so strengthened the women's argument that medical practice in the hands of men had resulted not in a body of scientific knowledge but in medical ignorance. Separate sphere ideology as it pertained to medicine was hypocritical, feminists insisted; instead of providing health and protection, it promoted disease and permitted sexual abuse. Male doctors were not skilled, objective professionals but corrupters of morality. In demanding women's entry into medicine, feminists sought a corps of female doctors who would develop a "true" body of scientific knowledge and expertise and create a medical practice that would aid women, not exploit them.

LIKE THE CAMPAIGN to repeal the CD Acts, the movement to open the medical profession to women was regarded by many of its advocates as a great moral crusade. The pioneers in the movement, Elizabeth Blackwell, Elizabeth Garrett (later Garrett Anderson), and Sophia Jex-Blake, sought to practice medicine not because of any absorbing personal interest but because it provided, as Blackwell wrote to her mother in 1849, an opportunity for "the redemption of mankind." "Do you think I care about medicine?" she asked. "Nay, verily, it's just to kill the devil, whom I hate so heartily."[52] Jex-Blake attributed the perseverance of the early medical women to "the conviction . . . that we were fighting a true battle for liberty against tyranny, for the powers of light against the powers of darkness."[53] These references to satanic forces were more than attempts to dramatize the women's struggles. They served as a metaphor to characterize the sexual relations between the sexes as determined by current medical prescriptions of male and female sexuality. The arrival of the forces of light promised the end of male domination of women in the medical field and the undermining of those justifications for male domination in society at large. "The study of human nature by women as well as men, commences that new and hopeful era of the intelligent co-operation of the sexes through which alone real progress can be attained and secured," Blackwell asserted. It was "especially incumbent upon women physicians," she believed, to raise up a moral race.[54] Garrett regarded it as her duty to become "a great physician. Nothing else I cd [sic] do wd [sic] help women so much as this."[55]

Medical women and their supporters hoped to help women in many ways. First, attendance by physicians of their own sex would provide women with opportunities for greater autonomy and personal control. Examination by a woman would not be experienced as an oppressive, indecent intrusion, as it was at the hands of men. Cases of actual sexual abuse by male doctors would be eliminated altogether. Women believed that they could more comfortably and readily impart to female physicians information of a delicate nature that they might withhold from men, thereby improving their chances for good health, though as Brian Harrison has pointed out, better health for women resulted from the general advance of science, not from the introduction of women into the medical profession.[56] But for contemporary feminists such as Jex-Blake, the female physician, by virtue of her sex, could better understand and sympathize with the patient, "far more fully appreciate her state, both of mind and body, than any medical man would be likely to do."[57] She was able, on the basis of her personal experience with or understanding of the ills suffered by women, to give counsel "to which many attribute the preservation of life and health,"[58] Cobbe insisted.

In the same vein, women suspected that male physicians simply were not interested in advancing their knowledge of the ills that bore heavily upon women, especially venereal disease. They looked to medical women to bring to the attention of their patients at least an awareness that their husbands' extramarital activity could have severe consequences for them and for their unborn children. Lily Waring asserted in *Common Cause* in 1910 that "chiefly through the agency of women doctors, women now know the truth, and this knowledge will probably cause more of a revolution in England than any scientific discovery of the age." Explicitly making the connection between the campaigns for women in medicine and the suffrage, she added, "it is a significant fact that there are over 500 medical women who are Suffragists, against fifteen who are not."[59] Hale noted in 1914 that "until within the last few years the mass of women . . . remained ignorant of the hideous danger to themselves and their children of venereal disease. . . . Now . . . they give credit to the women doctors for their own enlightenment, and for that forewarning which is forearming."[60] Ethel Snowdon agreed, stating that "medical science in the hands of women has taught them many sad and sorry things, unrevealed before, of the grave damage to children which comes of moral laxity in either sex."[61]

Second, the women doctors expected to be educators of women in the matter of health, hygiene, and sex. An understanding of the functioning of their bodies would enable women to take better care of themselves and to assert some control over their reproductive processes—allow them a degree of reproductive freedom. Blackwell et al. hoped to impart to women a sense of themselves as autonomous individuals with needs and rights in the matter of sex, not the mere slaves and playthings of men, or mere breeding machines. The feminist demand for knowledge—for the power of self-definition that such knowledge would bring to women—constituted a powerfully subversive form of resistance against male domination of women, within both the medical profession and society at large.

Third, and most important, the medical women insisted upon the need for studying human nature and the physiological laws governing the sexes. They understood that what purported to be "facts" about the nature of masculinity and femininity were nothing more than male bias couched in the language of science, and that those "facts" formed a body of opinion that justified the subjection and degradation of women. As Blackwell wrote in 1854 to her sister Emily, a physician studying the diseases of women in England at the time, "Pray bear in mind to collect all the information you can about maternity, the relation between the sexes, and kindred subjects. We have a vast field to work in this direction, for reliable information is desperately needed in the world on these topics. I feel as if it were peculiarly our duty to meet this want."[62] Blackwell and her female colleagues hoped that the truly scientific study of human nature would, in the case of men, undermine the pervasive acceptance of their "inherent" need to find sexual release, and in the case of women, help to develop a fuller and more comprehensive definition of femininity, one that would mitigate against their characterization as "the Sex." A truer, more moral relationship between the sexes, a sex peace, if you will, depended upon the reconstruction of gender and sexual identity. It was incumbent upon the female physicians, whose education and knowledge of science placed them in a singularly strong position to refute the "science" of male physicians that had such destructive effects for women, to undertake this reconstruction. As Blackwell exhorted her colleagues in 1897, "the redemption of our sexual relations from evil to good, rests more imperatively upon [you], than upon any other single class of society."[63]

The first task of female physicians was to challenge "one of the greatest fallacies that ever existed," as Dr. Louisa Martindale put it, "the idea that sexual indulgence is a necessity to [men's] health."[64] Blackwell described this doctrine as "an audacious insult to the nature of men, a slander upon their human constitution." This notion of masculine "necessity" maintained that "men are not capable of self-control, that they are so inevitably dominated by overwhelming physical instincts, that they can neither resist nor control the animal nature, and that they would destroy their mental or physical health by the practice of self-control." Societal acceptance of this doctrine implied that "women must recognize this fact, and unbridled lust must be accepted and provided for." Blackwell called such a belief "blasphemy."[65]

Blackwell's arguments rested upon her unshakable conviction that "no physiological truth is more firmly established than the fact that we can modify the action of our physical organs toward the special objects related to them, by the way in which we use our organs." Sexual urges were not uncontrollable; sexual release was not imperative to a man's health. "Physiological facts" contradicted the assertion that "one human being is dependent on the degradation of another human being for the maintenance of personal health." Because "Nature never allows the male, any more than the female, to become impotent through abeyance of function," and because human beings were infinitely capable of controlling their sexual drives, sexual continence among men was both possible and desirable.[66]

Men and women were not controlled by sexual drives, Blackwell asserted, because in human beings, unlike in animals, "procreation . . . is not limited to any special season." Human reason "as to the time and circumstances" of sexual intercourse governed the relations between men and women. Nor would continence destroy the capability of the sexual organs to function effectively when the time came, for "the physical organs are maintained in fit condition for reproduction by [the] functions of ovulation and spermation, as servants ready to obey at any time the superior intelligence of the master will." Ovulation and "spermation" served as natural release valves for sexual energy: menstruation served to accommodate "the constant formation of ova," and the "natural function of sperm-emission" (nocturnal emission, not masturbation) allowed for "the slower secretion of semen" in men. Through these processes, the sexual functions were subordinated to "the needs of individual freedom and to the power of mental self-government," Blackwell advised.[67]

Blackwell insisted that the degenerate state of society had its roots in "errors in relation to sex," "errors as to human physiology and neglect in education with regard to the most important functions."[68] Medical women, "the special guardians of home life," by virtue of their "scientific medical knowledge," possessed the tools to recast society along lines that would reflect the needs, interests, and special morality of women, and thereby preserve the future of humanity.[69]

Female physicians also challenged the identity of women as "the Sex." This identity rested on the twin assertions that women were governed by their sexual and reproductive organs and that they experienced no sexual feelings, that they were sexless. Elizabeth Garrett Anderson addressed the first issue in 1874, in response to Maudsley's article on "Sex in Mind and Education" (see Chapter I) in which he had argued that menstruation made women unfit for intellectual activity. Garrett Anderson replied that women advocating education for women were not rebelling against "the tyranny of their organization," were not choosing not to be women, for reproductive processes and functions did not control or determine their ability to pursue successfully other activities. "It is," she stated, "a great exaggeration to imply that women of average health are periodically incapacitated from serious work by the facts of their organization." Menstruation was not pathological or debilitating, she insisted; "the cases in which it seriously interferes with active work of mind or body are exceedingly rare; and . . . in the case of most women of good health, the natural recurrence of this function is not recognized as causing anything more than very temporary *malaise*, and frequently not even that." She conceded that puberty might be a time of weakness for young women, but that it was only a temporary phenomenon; moreover, the new schools for women imposed a regimen of exercise and diet that improved the girls' health. Lastly, Garrett Anderson pointed out that boys were not exempt from "difficulties which attend the period of rapid functional development. . . . Analogous changes take place in the constitution and organization of young men, and the period of immature manhood is frequently one of weakness."[70] Since puberty in boys obviously did not disqualify them from the pursuit of education, she implied, nor should it in young women. The reproductive functions of women bore no more heavily upon the identity of women than upon that of men.

Medical women offered specific evidence to undermine the view held by male doctors that during menstruation women were unfit for any mental or physical efforts, were almost temporarily insane, and thus challenged, as one feminist noted, the "underlying idea [that] has been an enormous barrier in the path of the woman seeking a career other than sex."[71] "Thanks largely to the woman doctors," echoed Hale, "we are beginning to recognize that the seasonal disturbance of the women's physique is a perfectly normal function which, if rightly observed and understood, need not detract from her full healthfulness and efficiency."[72]

The prescription of women as sexless devolved upon women a sexual definition. Blackwell, for one, believed that the view of women as sexless ensured that there could be "no healthy blending of the sexes," which in turn kept the relations between men and women in a state of "licentiousness."[73] The belief that women had far less sexual passion than men, she asserted, formed a "very sandy foundation" upon which an "enormous practical edifice of law and custom . . . has been built up." If the relations of men and women were to be placed on a truer footing, then "the facts of human nature" regarding sexuality must be acknowledged. One fact of human nature, Blackwell asserted, was that "the compound faculty of sex is as strong in woman as in man." "[T]he laws guiding the human sexual functions as established by Creative Power are as conducive to health, and as consistent with the freedom and perfection of human growth, in one sex as in the other." Sex and physical pleasure for either sex were not necessarily evil; on the contrary, they were "a legitimate part of our nature." The proper use of sex helped to bring "renewed and increasing satisfaction to the two made one in harmonious union."[74]

Blackwell sought for women a sexual identity that would reflect and protect their needs. She distinguished between sexual passion and sexual appetite, the former implying a "mental, moral, or emotional principle," whereas the latter connoted an instinct or physical impulse. Men tended to develop the merely physical side of their sexuality, women the emotional. The "unrighteous use" of sex by men, the mere satisfaction of physical impulses, Blackwell explained, repulsed women, producing "misery to the two remaining apart, through the abuse of a Divine gift." She noted that the act of coition, or "the special act of the male," was not the exclusive source of physical pleasure for women. "The affectionate husbands of refined women often remark," she revealed, "that their wives do not regard the distinctively sexual act with the same intoxicating physical enjoyment that they themselves feel, and they draw the conclusion that the wife possesses no sexual passion." If men approached their wives with "kisses and caresses," and took care to respect their needs, foremost among them being the "assent of the mother in the joint creation of . . . offspring," they would be rewarded by passionate response. For "terror or pain . . . will temporarily destroy all physical pleasure. In married life, injury from child-birth, or brutal or awkward conjugal approaches, may cause unavoidable shrinking from sexual congress, often wrongly attributed to absence of sexual passion." The righteous use of sex, on the contrary, the coupling of mental and emotional with physical passion, could bring untold happiness to the couple.

Although physical sexual pleasure is not attached exclusively, or in woman chiefly, to the act of coition, it is also a well-established fact that in healthy, loving women, uninjured by the too frequent lesions which result from childbirth, increasing physical satisfaction attaches to the ultimate physical expression of love. A repose and general well-being results from this natural occasional intercourse, whilst the total deprivation of it produces irritability.[75]

The reconstructions of gender and sexuality sought by these women doctors entailed "a truer development of character" for men and women.[76] They intended to enhance the identity of women as humans, and thereby confer upon them autonomy and rights, and to challenge the notion of "inherent" male sexual drives. It was a fundamental step, they realized, if the laws and customs that subjected women to men were to be overturned.

THE LAW

Why have we vicious laws? Because they have been
made and carried out by men alone.
MRS. SHELDON AMOS, N.D.

Laws made and administered by men constituted the focus of
women's intense anger during the entire period under study.
Nina Boyle of the Women's Freedom League raged in 1913
against "the open immorality of the Courts of Justice," where
the overt "sex bias" of magistrates manifested itself in "tenderness to male ruffians who inflict the 'reverberations of their
physiological emergencies' upon women and children." "We
have watched the treachery and dishonesty of politics and the
abuse and tyranny of the administration of the law until we are
sick and sore with the shame and vileness of it," she wrote fu-
riously. Commenting upon the reception of the Criminal Law
Amendment Act of 1912, Boyle noted

> the wild indignation of the male person when for the first
> time "soliciting" is under this Act made a male as well as
> a female offence. The callous admission of Mr. Huntley
> Jenkins that "thousands of men" annoy and molest women
> and that it is preposterous to consider it an offence; the
> contention that "two young officers" (police) must on no
> account be considered witnesses sufficient to bring home a
> charge like this to a man—although 9,000 women are con-
> victed every year on less; and the triumph of sex bias over
> even the police evidence ending in the acquittal of the ac-
> cused against the clearest evidence.

Nina Boyle and many other suffragists insisted that "these things are possible because women have no power."[1] The power of women, opponents of women's suffrage asserted over and over again, resided in the private sphere, in their influence in setting the moral tone of the nation. It was women, they claimed, who made the morals of the country. "That is not true," Butler fumed in the nineteenth century, "it cannot be true, so long as *men alone make the laws*. For the law is a mighty teacher of morality or immorality, justice or injustice."[2] Feminists argued that patriarchal attitudes that maintained and encouraged their degraded status in a separate sphere were legitimated by a body of law enacted by Parliament and interpreted in the courts. They understood law to be the expression and exercise of power in society. "Is it to be wondered at," asked the author of an NUWSS leaflet in 1913, "that little respect is paid to women when the law classes them with regard to their political status . . . with criminals, paupers, and lunatics?"[3] "[T]he unprotected position of our girls and women," asserted *Common Cause* in 1910, is a direct consequence of their unrepresented state."[4] Feminists insisted that a monopoly on power in the public sphere created a tyranny of power in every other sphere as well; that women's lack of power in the public sphere meant lack of power in any sphere; and that public and private were concepts of separation that had no basis in reality and had to be eliminated altogether.

The feminist critique of man-made and man-administered law demonstrates once again the tension between women's desire for equality with men and their need to maintain a special moral position. As in the case of their discourses on prostitution and marriage, they attempted to resolve this tension by including in their critique of legally defined femininity a critique of legally defined masculinity as well. Feminists challenged the double standard of law on two grounds, reflecting their desire for equality and morality respectively. Consonant with prevailing liberal tenets, they attacked laws that restricted or confined their scope of opportunity, demanding equality of education and em-

ployment, property rights, custody of children, and enfranchisement. In addition, laws that legitimated unequal standards of
behavior and imposed unequal penalties on the sexual transgressions of men and women were targets of furious feminist on-
slaught because they were perceived to encourage and perpetuate that male sexuality that abused and degraded women. Here
feminists demanded equality under the law—a raising up of the
moral standards applicable to men to those pertaining to
women—in order to protect and defend themselves and to punish the corruption implicit in the double standard. As Fawcett
testified before the Royal Commission on Divorce and Matrimonial Causes in 1912, "I urge most strongly that the difference
between the sexes which now exists in divorce law should be
put an end to. . . . If the law were equalised as between men
and women in the matter of divorce, it would tell in the direction of leveling up" in matters of morality.[5] By imposing on men
the same penalties for adultery that applied to women, a single
standard of divorce law would discourage men from resorting to
prostitutes or mistresses and would help protect wives from
adulterous and disease-carrying husbands. More important, a
single standard of divorce would end the hypocrisy and falseness
of the public/private divisions, distinctions that effected not the
protection of women but their violation.

Divorce law and the Contagious Diseases Acts were only two
examples of "evil laws" that victimized women and allowed men
to abuse women with impunity.[6] Chief among others was that
pertaining to seduction, which—until Stead's notorious exposé
of white slavery brought about the Criminal Law Amendment
Act of 1885—set the age of consent for women at twelve years.
"At present for the purpose of seduction," Butler raged at the
Commission investigating the acts in 1871, "and of seduction
only, our law declares every female child a woman at 12 years
of age. . . . I know from my experience amongst this class of
women, how many have become so from that cause."[7] The public outcry following Stead's revelations in the *Pall Mall Gazette*

forced Parliament to raise the age of consent to sixteen. Although an improvement, the Criminal Law Amendment Act of 1885 fell far short of the expectations and desires of many feminists. Fawcett protested in the *Contemporary Review* that "the evil state of the law . . . an outcome of the . . . notion that women are possessions or chattels, with whom men are fully justified in dealing as they please," remained essentially unchanged by the new act, for it contained every sort of loophole possible.[8] Unlike all other laws, she noted, the act included a three-month statute of limitations. Again exceptional to this law, the act incorporated provisions whereby a man brought up on charges of seduction could exonerate himself by swearing he thought the girl was over the age of sixteen. Particularly upsetting for Fawcett was the lack of any clause dealing with incest. "Hideous and loathsome as it is," she lamented in 1892, "it is by no means extremely uncommon." But because a Parliament composed entirely of men felt no pressure from an entirely male electorate, *"there is no law put in motion"* to protect children from sexual abuse by their fathers.[9] When a law against incest was finally placed on the statute books in 1907, feminists charged that it was "really of little avail in stopping this grievous, almost inconceivable, crime of fatherhood against childhood." Swiney noted that 37 percent of the cases of assault against children in Britain were incestuous, attributing this to the fact that "juries and magistrates invariably take a lenient view of this unnatural offence: being men they condone it."[10]

The bastardy law, ostensibly providing a mechanism whereby a woman might sue the father of her illegitimate child for maintenance, in practice made it so difficult for the woman to obtain support that it put "the full burden of responsibility on the mother."[11] This state of affairs, feminists charged, not only encouraged male sexual license, but also, by forcing a woman to secure a wage when her condition made it particularly difficult to find decent employment, provided "one of the most fertile sources from which the army of prostitutes is recruited."[12]

Inconsistencies in the law demonstrated to feminists patriarchy's intention of making women sexually available to men. The Women's Freedom League pointed out that "the *property* of girls and boys is protected up to the age of *21*, as until then they are not considered to have sufficient experience or knowledge of the world to protect it themselves, yet girls are protected by law from seduction up to the age of *16* only." Moreover, whereas the theft of goods valued over two pounds constituted a major offense under the law, "procuring young girls for an immoral life is only a misdemeanor."[13] Suffrage literature regularly charged that these laws, and those pertaining to marriage, were detrimental to the lives and well-being of women and served only to facilitate male sexual transgressions against them. As an NUWSS leaflet of 1913 urged, "our laws which deal with the relations between men and women set a low standard which puts great difficulties in the way of those who are working for health and purity in social life, and which in some cases actually gives support to evildoers."[14] The law served not to protect women but actually to harm them. Men in Parliament, ruling self-interestedly, would do nothing to ease the plight of women, the leaflet implied, because it would restrict their opportunity to indulge their sexual appetites. Swiney submitted the feminist case against man-made law in a nutshell when she asserted, "throughout the whole code affecting sexual relations, the conclusion must be unwillingly admitted, that male vice is safeguarded in every possible manner, and such condemnation as it is considered politic to observe, falls with unqualified severity on the weaker and more helpless accomplice."[15] The law gave aid and protection to the self-interested (and corrupt) man of the public sphere and hampered the selfless (and moral) woman of the private sphere in her attempt to preserve social purity and morality.

With the exception of women such as Josephine Butler, feminists frequently demanded that the coercive powers of the state be utilized in a policy of sexual control. Feminist historians have evinced some difficulty in reconciling the feminist position with social purity movements seeking to restrict or control sexual behavior—as well they might, given, as Walkowitz has pointed out, that repressive measures always fell much more heavily upon women than men.[16] They have, however, as Martha Vicinus has suggested, ignored the question of how "the demand for women's sexual self-actualization fits into a world where women's power over the economic, social, and political structures of society is minimal."[17]

For all their willingness to discuss sexual problems and sexual issues, the vast majority of even the "New Women" of the 1880s and 1890s did not raise the idea of sexual pleasure for women. Helena Swanwick, for instance, because of her mother's excessive shyness, found out what she could about sex "by such means as were available"—scientific and medical texts, the Bible, Shakespeare, and Chaucer. This research helped her to formulate in her adolescence a negative attitude toward (male) sexuality that precluded any notion of a positive female sexuality. "None of the girls I associated with at Notting Hill even so much as mentioned sex," she wrote, "and we dismissed as disgusting any evidences of schoolgirl flirtations and premature passions . . . the notion of any sex-element in a girl-and-boy friendship repelled me. Occasional acquaintances on the outskirts of our little society who hinted at such a thing were summarily cold-shouldered."[18]

Almost alone among the "New Women" of the 1880s and 1890s, Olive Schreiner acknowledged that women experienced sexual feelings.[19] She denied that their sexual drives were weaker than those of men, claiming that sexual abstinence was, in fact, "more terrible" for women than for men.[20] According to Havelock Ellis's biographer, Schreiner "would walk the floor for hours in a state of sexual frustration" and took bromide, prescribed by Ellis, to "diminish her sexual drive."[21] An immensely complex figure, she found it almost impossible to reconcile her intellectual stance toward sexuality with her own personal experience. She could write to Ellis of the "beauty and sacredness and importance of sex" and yet suffer her whole life from asthma, possibly a somatic manifestation of the guilt she felt at violating Victorian sexual mores. In their biography of Schreiner, Ruth First and Ann Scott have pointed out that she scorned those who held that men and women should have sexual intercourse only for procreation and yet "withdrew, wounded, when she was suspected, or when she suspected herself, of asserting sexual demands."[22]

Schreiner advocated monogamous marriage as the ideal form of male/female relationships but remained unconvinced that men and women could ever truly establish a harmony between them, ever truly "escape from the suffering which sexual relationships now inflict." As First and Scott have suggested, Schreiner's candor about sex might have shocked her contemporaries, but she herself "typified, to the point of neurosis, the condition of the Victorian woman seeking a sort of sexual freedom by denying her sexuality . . . she seemed to want freedom from sex or the risk of being considered and treated as a sexual object." The difficulties created by the view of women as "the Sex" were given poignant expression in Schreiner's letters to men with whom she sought friendship. In a postscript to Karl Pearson, to whom she wished to appear as a scientifically minded researcher, she penned, "I am not a woman, I'm a man, and you are to regard me as such." She signed another letter to him, "Your man-friend O.S." To Edward Carpenter she wrote, "I wish I was a man that I might be friends with all of you, but you know my sex must always divide. I only feel like a man but to you all I seem a woman." Referring to her approaching menopause, she noted, "I won't be a woman in a couple of years . . . and then you'll think I'm a man, all of you, won't you?" At that time, she believed, they could all be comrades.[23]

Schreiner's interpretation of the state of male and female sexual relations, articulated in *Woman and Labour* (1911), found an appreciative audience among the feminists of the early twentieth century. In the book, described by Vera Brittain as the "Bible of the Woman's Movement," Schreiner sought to dissect the "problems connected with marriage and the personal relations of men and women in the modern world."[24] "More than any one other author," according to Lady Constance Lytton, a suffragette, Schreiner identified the source of feminism: the economic dependence of women upon men, which made all women prostitutes, whether married or single, at home or in the streets.[25] With the success of the women's movement, once women were freed from this position of sexual serfdom, the social and sexual relationships of men and women could be transformed for the better. The suffrage movement, Schreiner insisted, was leading "not towards a greater laxity, or promiscuity, or to an increased self-indulgence, but toward a higher appreciation of the sacredness of all sex relations, and a clearer perception of the sex relations between man and woman as the basis of human society."[26]

Victorian and Edwardian society offered only a male-defined model of sexual liberation, one in which women's social, economic, and political powerlessness rendered them vulnerable to sexual depredation. Sexual freedom, in the context of nineteenth- and early twentieth-century society, meant for most feminists the freedom of men to inflict the "reverberations of their physiological emergencies" upon women and children.[27] Legal double standards reflected the accepted beliefs in an inexorable, uncontrollable sexual drive in a man and institutionalized the notion of a woman as the legitimate outlet for and victim of that drive. Though feminists hoped finally to develop a society in which a positive paradigm of female sexuality might be constructed, they were compelled by the realities of their position first to criticize and attack the sexual culture designed and perpetuated by men, to attempt through law to protect the victims of that sexual culture, and to punish the offenders that enjoyed the protection of the law. On a more profound level, feminists sought to use the law to challenge male sexuality. What is more important, laws that protected women from men also refused the interdependence of definitions of male and female sexuality.

Some women, such as Boyle, Fawcett, and Sylvia Pankhurst, recognized that repressive sexual measures did not effect the protection of women but imposed greater hardships upon them. Boyle attributed this to the fact that men alone interpreted and enforced the law, noting that "all this shows us how much satisfaction the new law[s] will give us when administered by men only."[28] Fawcett objected to the prosecution of victims of vice and urged the authorities to go after the customers and owners of brothels.[29] That women bore the brunt of coercive laws was not intended by feminists, and they believed the situation to be amenable to change through the participation of women in Parliament, "on Bench, at Bar, in the jury box."[30] The legal repression of women only increased feminists' determination to gain for women access to positions of power in order to create and administer law that reflected and protected their own interests rather than those of men exclusively.

Feminist arguments for representation in Parliament resembled those of liberal theorists such as James Mill, Jeremy Bentham, and William Gladstone. During debate over the Second Reform Act in 1867, Gladstone asserted that "the unreformed Parliament [prior to 1832] used to job for individuals, while the reformed Parliament jobs for classes . . . I think that the influence of separate classes is too strong, and that the influence of the public interest properly so called, as distinguished from the interests of sets, groups, and classes of men, is too weak." Mill and Bentham had directed their attacks on the "sinister interest" of the landed, aristocratic elites; Gladstone at that of the upper and middle classes. Feminists railed against the "sinister interest" of men. For male liberals, greater representation served to mitigate against the corruption of wealth; feminists sought representation to destroy what they perceived to be the sexual corruption. Gladstone called for Members of Parliament "who would look not to the interests of classes, but to the public interest."[31] Feminists called for a Parliament that would look not to the interests of men but to those of the public, of which they formed a preponderant part. They protested against the hypocrisy of a system of representation and law that was designed to advance a monopoly of male interest while refusing to acknowledge that that was the case.

Here again we see the insistence on the part of feminists that private and public spheres could not be maintained as separate and distinct if the interests of women were to be protected. Anti-suffragists claimed that separate spheres for men and women were in the nature of things and God-given. Men in their natural, public sphere looked after the interests of women in a legislative system founded upon a body of disinterested law. Feminists countered that the reality of their situation demonstrated that men did not understand their needs and desires, let alone legislate and administer law in such a way as to meet them. Emmeline Pethick Lawrence of the WSPU challenged the patriarchal assumption of disinterested law based on principles of abstract justice that served men and women equally. She argued that the world is "man-made . . . in the deepest sense of the word; it is a man-made and man-ruled world. Its laws are men's laws; its rules of commerce and every-day business are men's laws. Its moral standard, its public opinion, is formed by men." The concentration of power in the hands of men, the confining of women to the private sphere, she insisted, had resulted in a society in which "there is nothing that expresses the woman's point of view. There is nothing that tallies with the woman's soul . . . everything is arranged upon a plan different from their own, and upon a system which has taken no account of their point of view."[32] This was most especially true in the case of sexual relations. "[I]t is impossible," argued Lady Chance in 1912, "for men to see quite with the same eyes as women, especially in the matter of sex morality."[33]

Feminists attacked M.P.s and magistrates to expose the hypocrisy of a legal system purported to be based on abstract principles of justice. They sought to demonstrate that self-interest, rather than disinterestedness, characterized laws made and administered by men: Parliament "jobbed" for the "sinister interest" of men. Reflecting the interests and aims of that class alone, law gave free rein to the destructive sexual nature of the male at the tragic expense of the female members of society.

The male point of view as reflected in law was not that of woman as the object of men's protection but woman as sexual object. Frances Power Cobbe held this belief as early as 1878, maintaining that "man, who has lost the spontaneous chivalry of the lion and the dog, needs to be provided with laws which may do whatever it lies with laws to effect to form a substitute for such chivalry. Alas! instead of such, he has only made for himself laws which add legal to natural disabilities, and give artificial strength to ready-constituted prepotence." To the physical superiority of men over women, men had added the power of the law to own and assault their wives. "Every brutal-minded man, and many a man who in other relations of life is not brutal," Cobbe asserted, "entertains more or less vaguely the notion that his wife is his *thing*, and is ready to ask with indignation . . . , 'May I not do what I will with my own?' " Laws that prevented women from divorcing brutal or rapacious husbands belied the notion that an all-male Parliament protected the interests of women. When women were refused representation, "and told year after year by smiling senators that we have no need whatever of it," she stated, "that we form no 'class,' and that we may absolutely and always rely on men to prove the deepest and tenderest concern for everything which concerns the welfare of women, shall we not point to these long-neglected wrongs of our trampled sisters, and denounce that boast of the equal concern of men for women as—a falsehood?"[34]

"Men have made their laws to fit in and give licence to their stimulated predilections," stormed Swiney.[35] Women were dependent on men for their laws, those same men, Martindale pointed out, "who have . . . demanded that a whole class of women shall be set aside to exercise for gain those functions which Nature had given to them for the propagation of the race only . . . these men who have instilled into their womenfolk the idea that sexual indulgence is a necessity to their health."[36] Man-made laws, "bred of sexual perversion," Swiney wrote, demonstrated for feminists the state's "underlying intention to permit the man free access to pleasure . . . at the cost of the woman."[37]

Since man had made laws "for the gratification of his desire," as Constance Smedley put it,[38] it was "not at all surprising" to feminists "that we should find the way of the male transgressor made very much easier than that of the female."[39] The administration of the law, as much as the deficiencies in the law itself, showed just how little protection and security women could expect from a system in which all power rested with men. The *Women's Herald* in 1891 reported in an article titled "Wife Beating Made Easy" the statistics for assaults against women for the year 1889. Citing a report to Parliament, the paper noted that for assaults against women, including rape, bodily assault, and murder, the vast majority of offenders received less than one year's imprisonment. Most of those offenders were given fines in lieu of a jail sentence. The *Women's Herald* concluded that "clearly[,] assaulting women is an offence which need have no legal terrors for most men."[40] Eunice Murray of the WFL compared the case of an Edinburgh man who received six months for stealing clothes with that of another who was given six weeks for criminally assaulting a young girl of eight.[41] The *Englishwoman's Review* of 1875 noted, under its heading "Brutal Assaults," that "at Clerkenwell a man was convicted of brutal and murderous attack upon his wife. He had previously been imprisoned for assaulting her, and yet he was sentenced to one month's imprisonment only."[42] Mrs. Sheldon Amos expressed great alarm at the "growing and most dangerous tendency to make light of sexual offenses against women and children" among magistrates. "They are the echo of the military tone of mind about the unimportance of women," she urged, "the unchecked licence to be conceded to organised groups of men in relation to women."[43]

Common Cause, in an editorial of 27 October 1910, railed against magistrates who gave lenient sentences to child molesters, purportedly so that the men might have another chance. "Another chance of what?" the editorial demanded. "Of doing the same thing? And what other chance was there for this unhappy child?" The state had the responsibility to safeguard the weak from predators, for "a man will do what he desires to do, unless his desire conflicts with his own conscience, or the consciences of others or the fear of legal penalties. A considerable number of men desire that which will cause fearful suffering and injury to innocent little children." Acquittal or light sentences for child molesting only encouraged their vicious and destructive behavior.[44] The paper publicized the dismissal of two cases of indecent assault upon children—one because "no damage had been done to the child," and the other because it was a matter of incest, where the jury found the father not guilty but "guilty of very foolish conduct"—to demonstrate the dangers of a system that "jobbed" for men.[45] The *Vote*, the organ of the Women's Freedom League, regularly ran a column titled "How Men Protect Women." As an example of how the law ignored or covered up the brutality of masculinity, it reported the case of a man who received three months for indecent assault on a semi-paralyzed girl. The Recorder of the case, by way of explanation, observed blandly that assault on little girls was a crime "which the most respectable man might fall into."[46]

This attitude validated feminists' suspicions that individual M.P.s and magistrates, whose integrity was presumably unimpeachable, had a direct, personal stake in maintaining laws that rendered women so vulnerable to degradation and sexual assault. In the course of the CD Acts repeal campaign, Butler had come to identify "gentlemen," particularly those in Parliament, with the abuse of women. She protested that M.P.s, following the dictates of their sexual drives, had enacted and were now obstacles to the repeal of the Contagious Diseases Acts and to the elimination of the double standard of the law regarding so-licitation. "Parliament would not endure that men should be put in prison for solicitation on such slight evidence before a summary court, as is the case with women," she claimed, "for the men of the upper classes would be laid hold of by the Bill, and it would be a terrible thing indeed to the hearts of our present legislators to think that one of themselves or their sons might be touched." She told the Commission investigating the acts that she was greatly troubled "at the sight of so many men with so base and low a moral character as you seem to have."[47] Butler frequently charged, as Walkowitz has written, that the persons administering the acts against women were the "same men who also bought their sexual services."[48] Men in Parlia-ment, "whose very presence there is a block to all good and pure measures," were directly responsible for the "miseries, the wrongs, the soul murders, and the destruction of young lives which have been going on for years past," she cried. It was impossible, she insisted, for "a man who was corrupt in his private life to be a useful, just, or beneficent ruler."[49]

Fawcett suspected that the "low position of women generally" under the law was sustained at least in part by those who "pros-ecute the street walker with the one hand, and with the other elevate to the place of chief magistrate in the town a man who is living in adultery."[50] Motivated by this belief, Fawcett in 1894 embarked upon a semi-public campaign to expose the "ghastly" private behavior of Henry Cust, M.P. for Lancashire, who, with the support of the Conservative leadership, proposed to stand for election to Parliament at North Manchester. According to Fawcett, Cust had seduced a young woman of good Lincolnshire family, a Miss Welby. She had become "*enceinte*," and he de-serted her, subsequently offering marriage to another woman. "Miss Welby wrote Cust a despairing, imploring letter," Fawcett explained, "which he spoke of, or showed to other men at the country house where he was staying, with odious remarks in-

tended to be facetious. The other men did not take these observations in the spirit in which they were made: they told Cust he
was a cur." They also informed the father and family of the
woman to whom Cust was engaged of his actions, and after a
bitter dispute, "Cust was told that unless he married Miss Welby
at once (whom he said he particularly disliked) the whole thing
would be made public." Powerful Conservatives refused to allow
Cust to stand again for Lincolnshire, "but he is thought good
enough for North Manchester," Fawcett noted acidly.[51]

She informed well-placed people in Manchester of this state
of affairs because she "considered that Cust's conduct struck at
the root of everything that makes home and marriage sacred,
and that to place such a man in a position of public honour and
responsibility would have a very bad effect." She told Cust that
"as a woman I have naturally the strongest feeling against men
of known bad character being elected to the House of Commons." Eventually, A. J. Balfour, the leader of the Conservative
Party in the House of Commons, involved himself in the controversy, chastising Fawcett for making the scandal known to
influential people in Manchester. He advised her that "as the
duties of a Member of Parliament are public ones, the capacity
of a Candidate to perform those duties should in most cases be
the sole ground of his selection. . . . Private life—the doings of
a man in his own home—ought not . . . to be dragged gratui-
tously before the public." In response to his assertion that the
matter was "of no public concern," Fawcett asked, "Is a man
who, in private life, can be suitably described by his intimates
as an 'infernal scoundrel' a fit and proper person to be brought
forward by his party as a Parliamentary Candidate? I would
answer this in the negative."[52] She felt that the private behavior
of men like Cust reflected attitudes toward women that found
their way into law and contributed heavily to "the utter rottenness of the whole of public opinion on morals," public opinion
that necessarily affected women adversely.[53] "Up to our own
generation," she wrote to Balfour,

the whole of the social punishment in these cases has fallen on the woman, and none, or next to none, on the man. But now whether we like it or not, a movement is making itself felt towards equality. If we don't level up we shall have to level down. I want to level up. . . . If for the last four or five generations the H. Custs of the world had been disciplined by a healthy "coercion" of law and public opinion, the whole of this pitiable business might have been prevented.[54]

The Piccadilly Flat case confirmed for many feminists their belief that the private behavior of M.P.s rendered them incapable of legislating or administering law disinterestedly. In the summer of 1913, police raided a brothel, "alleged to be of the luxurious type," run by Queenie Gerald. In the course of the investigation, "men prominent in social and political circles, whose names were kept out of the case, were said to be frequenters of the brothel." Parliament effectively squashed the prosecution of Gerald's influential clientele, said to be involved in "sadistic practices." She received three months imprisonment for living on the immoral earnings of other women, the charge having been reduced from that of procuring, which, under the Criminal Law Amendment Act of 1912, would have imposed a much stiffer sentence.[55] Christabel Pankhurst, among others, seized upon this incident to demonstrate that Parliament and the courts were determined to ensure men's access to women as "a subject sex created entirely for sex uses."[56] Her reporting of the case in the *Suffragette*, the testimony of Butler before the Commission investigating the CD Acts, and Fawcett's revelations of Cust's private behavior were all part of a discourse of resistance designed to reverse the stereotype of women as "the Sex" by accusing men of sexual perversion and of using the law to further and protect their perverted behavior.

The interests of women clashed so violently with those of men, most especially in sexual matters, that feminists believed that this constituted the fundamental basis for opposition to women's suffrage. Swiney identified anti-suffragists as "men whose private moral characters will not bear inspection."[57] Christabel Pankhurst charged that anti-suffrage men were best represented by "the men patrons of the Piccadilly Flat, [who] after their share in degrading young girls, after wading through physical and moral filth, went home, and doubtless forbade any 'meddling with the Suffrage question.' "[58] Emmeline Pankhurst feared that "unless women got inside the Constitution before the introduction of manhood suffrage, they would never get in at all; never! If manhood suffrage came, men would never agree to bring women in; they would be afraid of womanhood suffrage because it would place women in a majority."[59]

Feminists clearly intended—as their opponents realized—to use the vote to "fight masculine arrogance," to destroy the power of men to prey on women sexually, and to eliminate the distinction between private and public spheres that strengthened the position of men in what feminists perceived to be their war against women.[60] Power in the public sphere, exemplified by the vote, would arm women with the weapons necessary to defend themselves effectively and to bring about a condition of "sex peace." As Lady Chance observed, "the only weapons which women have are their prayers and their tears, and . . . it is pitiful to think of the waste of strength and time and money which this unarmed battle entails on them." Quoting Josephine Butler, Chance continued, "tears are good, prayers are better, but we should get on faster if behind every tear and every prayer there were a vote."[61]

CHAPTER VI

SEX WAR

Girls must remember that men hang together. It is
their habit to sacrifice women for their own or each
other's benefit.
SARAH GRAND, 1898

It is women, and women alone, who, by their combined and outspoken efforts, shall protect their sex
and vindicate the sorrows of the slain.
LAURA E. MORGAN-BROWN, 1891

Feminists conceived of their movement as a response to the
sexual degradation of women created by the ideology of separate
spheres and the double standard of morality for men and
women that it justified. By reducing women to a role composed
solely of sexual functions, by imposing upon them male definitions of sexuality, and by validating the belief in the inexorable
necessity of men to find release for their sexual drives, Victorian
ideology, they charged, stimulated the notion of woman as "a
creature of sex value only, created to fulfil the will, the pleasure
and the needs of men," as Emmeline Pethick Lawrence put it.[1]
State regulation of prostitution, the institution of marriage, the
male monopoly on medicine, and the exclusively male administration of laws that failed to protect and often endangered
women, constituted for feminists evidence that a state of war
rather than mutual cooperation for common goals characterized
the relations between the sexes. From the start, the feminist
campaign sought to attain for women opportunities with which
they might escape the role of victim and find scope for their
own agency in establishing the conditions of their lives. Educa-

tional and employment opportunities; the opening of medicine to women; the right to own property, to dissolve a brutal marriage, to obtain custody of children; and, above all, the vote, were the means by which feminists hoped to throw off their male-defined identity as sexual objects and to establish and receive acknowledgment of their individual humanity.

Despite the efforts of women like Fawcett to tone down the rhetoric so as to present the suffrage campaign as a picture of civic moderation, feminists repeatedly testified explicitly as to the purpose and meaning of their movement as a defensive strategy in an unprovoked "sex war." Pioneers of the feminist movement rarely spoke *publicly* of the sexual nature of their motives and aims, or what for later feminists such as Wilma Meikle was "part of the essential tissue of feminism."[2] Discreet hints occasionally appeared in the early feminist press, such as the references by Lady Amberley and the *Englishwoman's Review* that women required opportunities for education and occupations if they were to escape the fate of the prostitute (see Chapter II). Suffrage memoirs, however, suggest that in private the theme of sexual problems dominated feminist discussions. Meikle recalled in 1916 that "very frequent discussions with older suffragists of the more sordid problems of sex" took place in suffrage meetings, deputations, and lectures. "There were women," she recounted, "who pierced their veil of gentility with a disquieting hint, women who flung it aside to display a lamentable and astounding picture of their married life." One very old suffragist told her "that her wedding night had been a dreadful revelation to her, and that she would never have married if she had known the true meaning of marriage." These women, reported Meikle, "regarded the majority of men as conscious and wilful [sic] oppressors," and they "very sincerely believed that marriage must always be a sexual sacrifice for women." Despite their reticence to make their views known publicly, the early feminists, Meikle asserted, perceived the suffrage campaign as a means by which they would "win a political power which would secure, if not economic equality between the sexes, at least economic independence for women, and that this independence would establish in law and custom that sexual equality which Nature ordained."[3]

Butler's campaign for the repeal of the Contagious Diseases Acts destroyed the conspiracy of silence surrounding sex, helping to create an atmosphere in which women felt somewhat freer to speak about the issues that were central to their movement. By 1914, sexual issues permeated the literature and propaganda of virtually every suffrage organization. White slavery, prostitution, and venereal disease were the favored topics, serving as dramatic and powerful, albeit extreme, examples of the fate of women in a male-defined and male-controlled society. But the images of victimized women emphasized by suffragists had an additional function. They played deliberately on certain cultural stereotypes, reversing the age-old portrayals of woman as temptress and man as innocent victim. As Meikle pointed out,

> suffrage propaganda was a slashing revenge for the early Christian calumnies upon women. It was man now who was held to be of the earth earthy, tempting to destruction a sex naturally pure and spiritual. It was man who appeared as a wily serpent, luring women away from lofty thoughts and snaring her into carnal pleasures. Man was a white-slaver, a greedy, clutching, oppressive capitalist, a lover of bloodshed . . . and from the hell of his tyrannies and sensualities the new woman was at last freeing herself to redeem the world.[4]

Utilizing such imagery, feminists sought to subvert the beliefs about and fears of women that underlay arguments against women's enfranchisement.

Suffrage literature and propaganda did not, however, serve disingenuous purposes. Feminists believed the "sex war" to be very real and quite devastating in its consequences for women. The campaign for suffrage sustained itself, with occasional lulls

– 159 –

in activity, for over fifty years in the face of bitter and often violent opposition; such would not have been the case unless the issues motivating and informing the movement were of the most intense and personal nature, committing women for life to a cause they believed to be vital to the safety, well-being, and self-respect of all women. Fawcett, who eschewed all inflammatory rhetoric in the furthering of the Cause and sought to discourage feminist allusions to "sex war," nevertheless perceived the suffrage campaign as a way to eliminate forever "degrading and vulgar" images of women such as that put forth by an anti-suffragist who stated, "organized society . . . would go on quite comfortably if every woman retired to her own particular wigwam and did nothing but breed."[5] Charlotte Despard, leader of the Women's Freedom League, hoped the vote would help to break the chains "which woman has forged round her own consciousness from the moment she permitted herself to be the instrument of man's pleasure."[6] Billington-Greig attributed "much of the present unrest" to laws and customs that forced a woman to live with a man who degraded and infected her with disease.[7] Gasquoine Hartley claimed that women's "deep-lying dissatisfaction with the existing relations of the sexes" had compelled them to "revolt against the ignominious conditions of amatory life as bound by coercive monogamy."[8] Emmeline Pankhurst proclaimed in a speech on 5 August 1913, that prostitution, a metaphor for the position of all women, was "perhaps the main reason for militancy."[9] According to her daughter Sylvia, "far into the night she railed against the treachery of men, and bemoaned the impotence of women!"[10] Hale asserted that the knowledge of prostitution and venereal disease had more than any other single factor "contributed . . . recruits to the suffrage cause" because they demonstrated just what befell women who "left their fate in the hands of a sex who have signally failed to protect their most vital needs."[11] *Common Cause* urged all those who were uncommitted to votes for women to visit in hospital the victims of incest or child molestation, contending, "this alone would make any woman into a Suffragist."[12]

Though lacking the language and tools of analysis available to feminists today, nineteenth-century feminists incorporated in their critique of masculinity an understanding that masculinity was culturally, not biologically, constructed. They sometimes slipped into rhetoric suggesting belief in an instinctual sexual brutality in men; some feminists actually claimed as much. Frances Swiney, for instance, relying on the work of scientists such as Geddes and Thomson, geneticists Hurst and Castle, and sociologist Lester Ward, formulated a theory of natural law in which life began as female. All else evolved from the first female cell; because he received life from "the mother" in a process of parthenogenesis, the male was a secondary being. More precisely, the first male organism was a deficient female, the result of a failure, due to a chemical deficiency, of the maternal organism to reproduce itself. Genetically inferior to the female, the earliest men lived in a civilization directed and controlled by women—the "Matriarchate," as Swiney called it.[13]

This primitive society, in which "woman was the selector and controlled all sexual relations," wrote Swiney, provided men with the nurturance necessary to grow, to develop their faculties, and to progress toward a humanity characterized by the principles of the feminine natural law.[14] In particular, this was a civilization in which

> Woman . . . had, in harmony with the natural law governing all species in the reproductive processes, under control sensual desire except as an agent for designed use. Woman was, in concert with all females, virtuous through inherent virtue; chaste with an inborn chastity that keeps pure and undefiled all the mechanism of Life in its transmission. The idea of coercing the female or making her subservient to male desire never so much as occurs to the male mind in the sub-human species, and did not in man in the primitive gynaecratic state.[15]

But as men grew physically stronger under this regime, they began to transgress against the laws of nature. At that point,

Swiney theorized, quoting Ward, "when man wrested from woman her right of selection, 'man ceased to advance, and woman begin to decline under the depressing effects of male abuse.' "[16] Present-day society's ills—rampant sexual license, adultery, prostitution—resulted from this violation of natural law. "The social, moral and physical evils of mankind can be traced to that fatal divergence from nature's well-trodden path, wherein the feminine was the leader and the guide."[17]

Olive Schreiner, on the other hand, would not accept examples of sexual relations drawn from nature as exemplary of human beings, arguing that no one hard and fast rule of nature existed. "[S]ex relations may assume almost any form on earth as the conditions of life vary," she wrote in *Woman and Labour*. "[T]hose differences which we, conventionally, are apt to suppose are inherent in the paternal or maternal sex form, are not inherent."[18]

Most feminists attributed women's degraded, victimized position at the hands of men to a socialization process, reinforced by scientific and medical "proof" and legitimized by law, that encouraged a belief in the natural, biologically ordained sex drive of men. Their demand for the elimination of separate spheres embodied an attack on both the cultural construction of women as "the Sex" and of men as the sexual aggressors. For the most part, feminists believed that male behavior could be changed and that masculinity and male sexuality were not biologically determined but culturally constructed, implying that femininity and female sexuality, too, were a product of environment and socialization. Even Swiney, while insisting that female superiority was rooted in natural law, added that "in no sense . . . is the inference to be drawn that individually every woman is better than every man, other than physically as the most highly functioned organism."[19] Others might demand equal rights for women from a belief in the natural equality of men and women while still claiming for women greater moral qualities. Though not always consistent, these women, like Schreiner, tended to believe implicitly that this special moral position was the product not of their biological role as mothers but of their social role as mothers. Furthermore, like Swiney, they believed implicitly that men could be taught to assume the positive qualities associated with women. They aimed ultimately to transform the cultural constructions of femininity and masculinity so as to create a better society in which the "natural" equality and freedom of men and women might be realized.

Separate sphere ideology rested fundamentally on the notion of the chivalric intentions of men toward women as the product of an evolutionary process. In practice, having been denied legal, economic, and political rights, women's safety, well-being, dignity, and integrity did indeed depend on the "laws of chivalry." In individual instances, feminists conceded, chivalrous attitudes served to protect the interests of women. But on a broader, societal scale, they believed, men's "natural" respect and reverence for women was an illusion, an utter sham. Women were not, as ideology would have it, the revered, exalted angels in the house. Rather, they had been, in the words of Caird, the ugly ducklings of society,

> hunted, insulted, threatened or cajoled by [their] masters; scouted, scolded, admonished, betrayed; suffering all the evils of [their] age and country, while enjoying not a tithe of its compensating privileges; held in tutelage, yet punished for all sins and errors with a ferocity and a persistence specially reserved for the sex which is called weak; and specially directed against those who are held incapable of the responsibilities of freedom and citizenship.[20]

The "sex war," a conflict model that countered the notion of the complementarity of separate spheres, was one in which women lacked the basic weapons with which to defend themselves. The notion of women's "influence" was perceived by feminists to be cant, a device intended to keep women in sexual thraldom. " 'The softening influence of woman!' " scoffed Gasquoine Hartley. "It is not the purifying influence of women . . . but an unguided and therefore deteriorating sexual tyranny that regulates society. . . . It is only in obedience to man that woman has gained her power of life. She has borne children at his will and for his pleasure. She has received her very consciousness from man: this has been her womanhood, to feel herself under another's will."[21] The feminist movement, and more singularly the suffrage campaign, aimed to supply women with the weapons necessary to repulse male attacks and to establish a condition of "sex peace."

Politicians had appropriated science to justify the subjection of women to men: male superiority was rooted in biological principles. Feminists countered that men, encouraged by law and custom, tended not toward the establishment of impartial justice, or the advancement of civilization, but toward the destruction of the race; they were not higher political beings but animals. Spencer and Geddes and Thomson had maintained that the reservation or conservation of energy characterized the female organism, whereas the expenditure or dissipation of energy characterized the male. Feminists deftly twisted these concepts to demonstrate that man was an aggressive, selfish, brutal creature. They explicitly associated "the brute consciousness" of man with "sexual excess," with "violence and unbridled sensuality,"[22] emphasizing his "destructive power."[23] The image of man for feminists, and for many women who would be loathe to describe themselves as such, was not of the rational, justice-loving individual portrayed by Spencer et al. but of a being whose uncontrolled sexual impulses led him to prey upon the weak, especially women. Not only had men failed to protect the interests of women, they were almost incapable of it. Their lives, their laws, and the administration of justice, feminists declared, reflected deep-seated desires to debase women sexually.

"Self-centred masculine individualism" governed the behavior and thinking of men, Swiney asserted.[24] Annie Swan believed that "it is without a doubt a more arduous task for a man to cultivate the unselfish spirit, because the training of the race for centuries has rather tended to the fostering of selfishness in him."[25] "It is not the capability for pain or pleasure in others which arouses man's sense of responsibility," lamented Caird, "but the facts of belonging to his own division of creation" that determined his attitudes and conduct toward others.[26] A male friend of Ideala, Grand's unhappy heroine, advised her that she must put up with her husband's base and boorish behavior. "He behaves like a brute," conceded the high-minded Lorrimer, "but I dare say he can't help it. A man can't help his temperament."[27] Rejecting the image of men as defenders of female dignity, Swiney protested that "the only being in civilised life from whom the human female has to be protected is the male of her own species."[28]

The professed reverence of men for women, especially as wives and mothers, often revealed itself for what it was in surprisingly public forums. Commenting upon the hoots and jeers with which issues such as maternity and the welfare of mothers were greeted by M.P.s, Cobbe observed, "truly it is a gallant and gentlemanly sport, and one of which it appears that the Members of Parliament will not soon tire."[29] Fawcett was dismayed to discover that "it was the general habit of members of Parliament to receive any mention of women, or of childbirth, with roars of laughter."[30] George Bernard Shaw, not himself an advocate of women's suffrage per se, did believe that it would help to raise the tenor of debate within public bodies. "If you had sat," he stated, "as I have, for years,"

> on a health committee, trying to persuade a parcel of men who regarded women as angels and subjects for loose jests, and who burst into shouts of laughter when the doctor mentioned a maternity case . . . you would not press me for my reasons . . . how hopeless it is to get any sort of decent feeling concerning women in an exclusively male governing body.[31]

Some feminists suspected that chivalry served merely as camouflage to facilitate access of men to women. Priscilla Barker warned women of the true intentions lurking behind the chivalric facade of men. "Beware of men," she cautioned, "who will come to you with the appearance of honour, integrity, and love, but who in the secret of their hearts only hunt for women as the huntsman hunts for game. That gilded hero, that demigod of yours, that ideal man, is a sensual and heartless destroyer of female virtue for his own bestial, selfish gratification."[32] For others, the veneration of female purity masked base ulterior motives. In a statement that came close to accusing British men of delighting in the deflowering of virgins, Grand's Ideala charged, "I think that even their reverence for the purity of women is a sham. For why do they keep us pure? Is it not to make each morsel more delicious for themselves, that sense and sentiment may be satisfied together, and their own pleasure made more complete?"[33] Smedley suggested that the male insistence on female innocence, "towards which he must maintain the fiction of respect," only thinly disguised his need to protect himself from women's knowledge of his true attitudes and behavior. Men had decreed that women must "view the world as an exquisite flower garden, and believe all men to be immaculate, more especially the man they love," she urged. "No matter that this belief is a lie: that he knows it is a lie . . . he would have all girls educated to believe this lie." For if a woman knew of the thoughts and designs of men "she may criticise and reject" them.[34]

In response to politicians like Gladstone who asserted that the participation of women in politics would diminish men's respect for them, Smedley countered, "isn't Man's respect for Woman as a sex one of the most grotesque pictures the world has ever countenanced? . . . Man threatens to withdraw his respect: Has woman ever had it?" she demanded. "The idea of Man falling on his knees whenever Woman passes is a pretty one; the idea of his devoting his strength to the protection and upholding of her purity . . . is another charming theory; and with regard to the individual, idea and theory are sometimes true enough, but man's opinion of woman, as a sex, does not partake of reverence." In an open letter to "Certain M.P.'s," she stated, "when next you arise in the House and deliver an impassioned oration of your intentions of preserving the purity and dignity of Woman, and of not allowing her to cut her own throat by destroying your 'respect' for her—excuse us, gentlemen, if we in our turn smile in a gentle and feminine manner at you."[35]

Feminists asserted that in truth men despised and were contemptuous of women.[36] The Elmys described patriarchal institutions as "woman-reviling systems."[37] *The Freewoman* charged that the majority of men hated women.[38] Try as they might to conceal their feelings, hatred of women dominated male emotions and had led to antagonism and ultimately to war between the sexes. "However much they love the individual of their fancy," observed Maud Braby, "a kind of veiled distrust seems to obtain between the sexes collectively, but more especially on the part of men." Men had always found fault with women, she believed, but the revolt of women against the "old man-made conditions" had intensified their contempt and antagonism. Where formerly, men's diatribes against women had contained a certain good humor and were along the lines of genial chaff, they had taken on a "bitterness, a distinct animus," with the rise of the women's movement, Braby noted.[39] Writing in *Fraser's Magazine* in 1880, "M.O.W.O." explained why many women did not attend suffrage meetings, although they were in complete sympathy with the Cause. They were "offended deeply and wounded by the ridicule which has not yet ceased to be poured" on women who dared to assert their rights in the public sphere. Their demands for equality were met with "an insolent laugh, a storm of ridiculous epithets, and that coarse superiority of sex which a great many men think it not unbecoming to exhibit to women." The author explained that she meant by "coarse superiority of sex" the greater size and strength of men, hinting that women attending suffrage meetings had met with threats of violence from men, threats that often succeeded in frightening women away. She denied any moral or intellectual superiority to men and was contemptuous of those who stood upon that of force to keep women in their place, but she feared that physical superiority "must always tell. It will keep women in subjection as long as the race endures."[40]

The ideology of separate spheres, contended feminists, exaggerated the differences between men and women and confined women to an exclusively sexual role; it did not, as claimed, further notions of harmonious complementarity. It thus led to "sex-antagonism" between men and women. "[O]wing to the unnatural relations of the sexes," claimed Gasquoine Hartley, "which has unduly emphasised certain qualities of excessive femininity, sex-feeling has been at once over-accentuated and under-disciplined. Thus, an extreme outward sex attraction has come to veil but thinly a deep inward sex-antipathy, until it seems almost impossible that women and men can really understand one another." This development was responsible for "much of the brutal treatment of women by men and the contempt in which too often they are held," she asserted.[41] Olive Schreiner articulated what was perhaps a typical feminist opinion in writing to Havelock Ellis in 1884, "in that you are a man I am afraid of you and shrink from you."[42] Her statement reflects a profound fear—shared by many women in Victorian and Edwardian England, feminists and anti-feminists alike—that men could not be trusted not to assert their physical superiority over women if faced with a challenge to their prerogative to determine and direct the lives of women. As Hamilton noted in her article titled "Man,"

the appearance in woman of any characteristic that he considers unfitting or unpleasant, the attempt in woman to assert her own personality or needs, as distinct from his, is usually followed by a solemn and voluble warning that the [chivalric] courtesies are conditional, the perquisite only of the feminine, and that if she goes on like this the practices of masculine chivalry will be shortly and sternly discontinued.[43]

The extermination of women, charged Laura Morgan-Brown, extended logically from laws and customs that gave free rein to the destructive sexual nature of men; in fact, she noted, the campaign was well on its way. Reporting on the murder of a woman in Whitechapel in 1891, Morgan-Brown asserted that "it is the state of public opinion on questions of morality which is chiefly responsible for the death of Frances Coles." Men had taught women, she argued, that men *must* sin, that there must be a class of women available to service them—those "eternal priestesses," quoting Lecky, "blasted for the sins of the people." "By their laws, their institutions, their social, legal, and theological sanctions," she raged, "they try to convince us that God left one half of the human race with the possibility that each individual of that half might in herself (given certain conditions of accidental circumstances) become 'blasted' for the sins of the other half." The results of such teaching—exemplified by the murder of Frances Coles—demonstrated conclusively that "we may not [sic] longer allow men . . . to be our only teachers on this awful subject."[44] Snowdon noted that the destruction of women by soldiers in wartime was commonplace. "If the leaders of soldiers were not prevented by loyalty to their caste from making disclosures," she hinted darkly, "they could all tell stories of the deeds of men towards women which would make the civilian shudder with horror."[45] Instances and examples of male brutality toward women led Swiney to state baldly that "Woman's cruellest and most relentless foe is her brother, Man." "We are thus," she made outraged women cry, "because we are the sisters of *men*."[46]

Anti-suffragists frequently accused feminists of fomenting sex war. Feminists responded with the assertion that women's suffrage was "not the cause, but the consequence" of war instigated by patriarchal institutions, practices, and ideas. "[T]he war started long before Votes for Women was first whispered," maintained *The Freewoman*.[47] Louise Creighton of the NUWSS attributed the rise of women to "the cruel wrongs that women suffered because the sensual was dominant, because brute force ruled." If blame was to be ascribed, she contended, the fault was to be found with "men, whose weakness and wrongdoing is so clearly the cause of the degradation of numberless women, and of the suffering and disease which follows." Women, far from having conspired to carry out a war against men, were fighting rather to bring peace, to advance the cause of civilization, but such an outcome was "impossible if women are to be looked upon as existing solely for the pleasure and use of men," explained Creighton. For her, as for many other suffragists, the true and deepest meaning of the women's movement was contained in its efforts to eradicate the "sensual," the "brute force" that characterized patriarchy and that victimized women. It looked to "purify society by giving women their due place in society."[48] As Vera Laughton Matthews pointed out, the heart of the movement for women's emancipation consisted of "women's increased responsibility and knowledge in matters of public and private morality."[49] Put in other words by Hale, feminism demanded "a change in the status of the Englishwoman in her home." This change required reconstructing the "whole mental attitude of men towards women" through "education, sexual instruction, the equality of the sexes as citizens and before the law, the adequate safeguarding of maternity, and in a hundred other ways." In short, feminism was motivated by and intended to eliminate the notion of women as the proper and legitimate objects of a brutal and destructive male sexuality. An understanding of the true meaning of feminism and its goals, noted Hale, explained "the instinctive aversion of man . . . to Feminism . . . his instincts tell him that the way of love will be harder under the new regime."[50]

One of the criteria necessary for women to take up a defensible position vis-à-vis men and to establish the new regime was the creation of a united front. Caird's misogynist Professor Theobald, in *Daughters of Danaus*, reveled in the "obvious conveniences" a "lack of *esprit de corps*" among women held for men. Hadria, for her part, realized that "a spirit of sisterhood among women would have sadly upset the social scheme, as it has been hitherto conceived" by men; she also knew that the social system had been so conceived as to make "such a spirit well-nigh impossible."[51] Feminists hoped to form an unbroken phalanx of women by exposing the "true" nature of men's attitudes and behavior toward them. Through what amounted to a nineteenth-century version of consciousness-raising, they sought to establish a united sisterhood ready and willing to take up the battle against an enemy—the patriarchal system—that was intent on destroying them, and to neutralize the threat of men to women. The nonmilitant feminist campaign of patient and persistent exposé of the wrongs suffered by women at the hands of men on the streets, in the home, in the doctors' offices, and in Parliament and the magistrates' courts did bring many recruits into the movement. But it was with the advent of the militant suffragettes, whose "outrageous" but still nonviolent actions provoked furious physical assaults on them, that the "chivalry" of men was revealed as hypocrisy. As a result, thousands of women joined in the cry for "votes for women."

However one may evaluate the role of the WSPU in furthering or harming the Cause, there can be no question that militant tactics riveted the public gaze on women's suffrage. The militant campaign galvanized women, advocates and detractors alike, to take action where efforts by the nonmilitant suffrage societies had failed. Tactically, the campaign sought to force into the open what it deemed a hitherto covert sex war, or at least a war conducted by men from traditional positions using the subtle but effective weapons of law and public opinion. Militancy provoked "male sex-antagonism to open and candid expression," according to Rebecca West. Realizing, perhaps for the first time, just how men might behave toward them, women who had sat on the sidelines felt compelled to come out in support of women's rights.[52]

For anti-suffragist women, the open expression of male hostility confirmed their suspicions that this was exactly how men felt about them. The participation of women in politics would threaten men to such a degree that they would revert to their physical superiority to assert their authority. All legal and customary protections enjoyed by women would be destroyed, and then, woe betide the women of the nation. Eliza Lynn Linton warned that votes for women was "the sure precursor to the loss of men's personal consideration and to the letting loose the waters of strife; and . . . the sure precursor to a future regime of redoubled coercion and suppression." For Lynn Linton, as for so many anti-suffragists, male and female alike, the rule of law concealed only thinly the rule of force in society. "[A]fter all," she maintained, "the strong right arm is the *ultima ratio*, and God will have it so; and when men found, as they would, that they were outnumbered, outvoted, and politically nullified, they would soon have recourse to that ultimate appeal—and the last state of women would be worse than their first."[53] Anti-suffragism, as Brian Harrison has observed, "rests on the fact that there is a cross-cultural male tendency toward aggressiveness."[54] The militant campaign incited this latent male aggressiveness to flagrant manifestation, compelling one group of women to flock to the banner of women's rights to defend themselves and another group of women to the Women's National Anti-Suffrage League to prevent any further escalation of hostilities.

Militancy began in October 1905, when Christabel Pankhurst and Annie Kenney demanded of Sir Edward Grey his stand on women's suffrage. They refused to yield the floor when he did not respond. Their defiance resulted in their being bodily—and brutally, by some accounts—thrown out of the Free Trade Hall by Liberal stewards. Outside, wishing to commit an assault,

Pankhurst spit at a policeman and ended up in jail. Their treatment at the hands of men spurred many women to action. Helena Swanwick, not then associated with any suffrage organization but believing in the enfranchisement of women, identified
the Free Trade Hall melee as the stimulus to her activism. She
promptly joined the NUWSS branch in Manchester, explaining,
"my heart rose in support of their revolt. . . . I could not keep
out of this struggle at this time. It bludgeoned my conscience."
Swanwick maintained that "countless other women" reacted in
exactly the same way.[55]

Men often responded to nonviolent militant tactics with un-
repressed fury. When Helen Ogston heckled an Albert Hall
meeting in 1908, "a man put the lighted end of his cigar on my
wrist; another struck me in the chest. The stewards rushed into
the box and knocked me down. I said I would walk out quietly,
but I would not submit to their handling. They all struck at
me. I could not endure it. I do not think we should submit to
such violence. It is not a question of being thrown out; we are
set upon and beaten."[56]

An unprecedented display of male brutality occurred on 18
November 1910, a day ever after referred to in the annals of
suffrage history as "Black Friday." Three hundred suffragists
marching on Parliament Square were confronted by uniformed
and plain-clothed police, whose orders were to prevent the
women from reaching the Houses of Parliament. For six hours,
the women suffered "violent and indecent treatment" at the
hands of police and bystanders. Ada Wright was "knocked down
a dozen times in succession." Police "struck the women with
fists and knees, knocked them down, some even kicked them,
then dragged them up, carried them a few paces and flung them
into the crowd of sightseers." Victims and bystanders testified to
"deliberate acts of cruelty, such as twisting and wrenching of
arms, wrists, and thumbs; gripping the throat and forcing back
the head; pinching the arms; striking the face with fists, sticks,
helmets; throwing women down and kicking them; rubbing a

woman's face against the railings; pinching the breasts; squeezing the ribs." "An old woman of seventy was knocked down by a blow in the face, receiving a black eye and a wound on the back of the head." Cecilia Haig, alleged Sylvia Pankhurst, a generally reliable source, died in December 1911 from injuries sustained that day.[57] The attacks on the women on Black Friday were explicitly sexual. Whereas Sylvia Pankhurst only hints at sexual assault, David Mitchell, in *Queen Christabel*, has presented the incident more plainly. "Clothes were ripped, hands thrust into upper and middle-class bosoms and up expensive skirts. Hooligans, and occasionally policemen, fell gleefully upon prostrate forms from sheltered backgrounds."[58]

The incidents in 1912 at Llanystmdwy, in Wales, where suffragettes heckled David Lloyd George, rivaled the ferocity of Black Friday. According to Sylvia Pankhurst, "men and women were beaten, kicked and stripped almost naked. The hair of the women was torn out in handfuls." One of the women present described it as a "revelation of the latent beast in man."[59]

There is every reason to believe that Emmeline and Christabel Pankhurst welcomed, if they did not court, these displays of sexual violence against women, for they served as powerful recruiting agents to the suffrage cause. Militants and nonmilitants alike expressed appreciation that the "brute" sexuality in men had finally been exposed. Hale, critical of the militants, nonetheless credited them with shaking "some of us out of our easy acceptance of the ills about us." "[T]he resurgence of the male brute induced by militancy," she argued, must not "be counted wholly as an evil. If this brute exists among men of all classes, if the woman-hounding instinct is not yet bled out of any large section of British males, it is time that women knew the truth." Hale professed reluctance to describe "the tortures which have been inflicted on suffragettes by men of all classes maddened by the mob-spirit, because the truth is beyond printing, but there are women in England to-day who could tear themselves for having borne sons capable of such acts. Perhaps just such horrors were needed before women could be forced into seeing that their own weakness and compliance had rendered them possible." Suffragettes were to be applauded, she maintained, for "these women's sufferings have spurred hundreds of both men and women from apathy to activity."[60] Lucy Re-Bartlett, an ardent enthusiast of militancy, stated that only the militants were doing anything to eradicate from civilization the "brute consciousness" and "sexual excess" of men. Their "passion for sexual righteousness" had "brought to the surface the 'brute' in many men," thereby removing "the fetters of sentimentality and illusion from many thousands of women."[61]

For anti-suffrage women, the surfacing of the "brute" in many men served not to remove "fetters of sentimentality and illusion" but to confirm their very worst fears about the nature of men. Anti-suffrage women shared with feminists the belief in the destructive proclivities of men and the consequent victimization of women. They differed, however—and this difference formed the basis of their anti-suffrage stance—in perceiving the destructive characteristics of masculinity as natural, innate, biologically determined, and thus ineradicable. Whereas the feminist movement sustained its momentum with the confidence that notions of masculinity and femininity were culturally constructed, and thus subject to change, the anti-suffrage movement was informed by the conviction that the antagonistic relations between men and women were natural. Separate spheres for men and women formed a protective barrier around women, shielding them from the manifestations of the most primitive instincts of men. The elimination of culturally constructed categories of masculine and feminine—such as those determining political participation—would not enhance but wreck the status of women by placing them in direct competition with men, whose wrath would be provoked and whose physical superiority and innate brutality would result in women's decimation.

It is this fear of men that explains and makes comprehensible the participation of many educated, accomplished, and powerful women in the anti-suffrage cause, women who were often active in other reform movements advocating education, property rights, or guardianship over children for women.[62] Lynn Linton, for instance, went to work for the *Morning Chronicle* in 1848, the first woman to draw a salary for her journalistic efforts.[63] Mary (Mrs. Humphry) Ward, a respected novelist, was instrumental in promoting higher education for women at Oxford and chose the name for Somerville College.[64] Gertrude Bell served in an unofficial capacity as a distinguished diplomat, helping to found the state of Iraq.[65] Yet all three—and countless others who were equally active—organized, wrote, and lobbied against women's suffrage with a vengeance. Snowdon appreciated the irony of the situation, noting that "with a fine disdain of logic they have proclaimed that the sphere of woman is the home, and have come out of the home to prove it!"[66]

There was, however, a logic to their seemingly inconsistent activity. Education, property rights, and custody of children were perceived to be reforms that strengthened the role of the woman in the home and did not appreciably disturb, in Lynn Linton's words, the "grand fundamental fact of humanity, difference of sex, and consequent difference of functions, virtues, qualities, and qualifications."[67] Reforms such as enfranchisement took women out of their private sphere, diminishing the influence they enjoyed there and placing them in direct competition or rivalry with men, a contest they were bound to lose. Brian Harrison has likened many of the anti-suffrage women to those described by the psychologist Eysenck in 1953 as "tough-minded": women who espoused "a self-image of conventional femininity defined by subservience to and adulation of men, while at the same time showing evidence of an exploitative and hostile attitude toward them." They tended to rely on the stereotypical feminine qualities to influence and even manipulate men, using their purported weakness as a strength, a form of protection against men's rapacious, destructive qualities.[68]

Anti-suffragists such as Lynn Linton would have justified

such behavior because of what they regarded as the "destroying propensity" of men, whose "nature it is to seek and have where they can."[69] The connotation here is explicitly sexual, as Lynn Linton attempted to point out that female victims of seduction were themselves to be blamed, knowing what they knew about men.[70] Arabella Kenealy, responding to Olive Schreiner's *Woman and Labour* in a book pointedly titled *Feminism and Sex-Extinction*, flatly informed her readers that "sex-lawlessness . . . is an innate Male-trait."[71] "Even to-day," she warned,

> despite the evolution of the higher faculties . . . the male sex-instinct may be seen still in all its native tyranny and selfishness; seeking gratification in sensuality and cruelty, with callous disregard alike of the welfare as of the suffering of its victim. In the violation of women and children that occurs both in peace and in war, the instinct manifests as an impulse of aggression, and the sex-function as one of brutality or ruthless lust.

Masculinity was God-given and natural; there was little that could be done to alter its fundamental characteristics, and consequently, "the Plan sets most women at the mercy of most men, by reason of the greater physical strength of males, and by temptation of their more urgent sex-instincts."[72] Kenealy, a physician, marshaled her "scientific" knowledge in an attempt to restore the power of men in the economic sector following the end of World War I by urging women to leave their wartime jobs.

The inherent sexually destructive nature of men could not be eradicated, anti-suffragist women believed, but the possibility of its manifesting itself could be minimized by adhering to a policy of separate spheres. In Kenealy's words, the "highly specialised and inspiring disabilities" of woman, "her inspiring unfitnesses" to function outside of the home and family served as an "uplifting appeal to . . . manhood."[73] The disabilities of woman, Ellen Thorneycroft Fowler maintained, are "a source of power to her. It is in her weakness that her true strength is to be found. Because she is incapable of fighting for herself, men have always fought for her; because she is not strong enough to carry life's heaviest burdens, men have carried them for her; because she is not able to do things for herself, men have done them for her. There is no power so irresistible as the power of weakness."[74] The angel in the house gave man "something holier and weaker than himself to worship and protect," insisted Olive Parr. "Woman's strongest appeal is her dependence, especially her physical dependence, on man. It arouses all his fatherhood."[75] So powerful an influence was this feminine helplessness, asserted Kenealy, that man, "in the teeth of his inherent instincts, has chivalrously protected woman and the family." This development was not, however, to be taken for granted. The protection of women by men was not a "mere matter-of-course," cautioned Kenealy, but a "matter of chivalry." "Were it not that an advance-guard of higher and chivalrous men stand, by force of the laws they have made, between women and the lower and coarser masculine orders, no woman's life would be worth living because of perpetual affront."[76]

The entry of women into the public sphere of men undermined the precarious security they enjoyed. Lynn Linton discovered this personally, and the experience determined her antifeminist position. "I belong to the generation," she wrote to the *Daily News*,

> when women of a certain class were absolutely secure from insult, because the education of our brothers, as of our fathers, included that kind of chivalrous respect for the weaker sex which was then regarded as inseparable from true gentlehood and real civilisation. . . . I belong, too, to the generation which made the first steps for the emancipation of women; and I was one of the most ardent and enthusiastic of the advanced guard. I thought that the lives of women should be as free as those of men, and that community of pursuits would bring about a fine fraternal

condition of things, where all men would be like big brothers and no woman need fear. I have lived to see my mistake. Knowing in my own person all that women have to suffer when they fling themselves into the active fray, I would prevent with all my strength young girls from following my mistake, and guard them with my own body from such insults as you and your kind have showered on me when differing from you in opinion.[77]

Lynn Linton devoted the remainder of her professional life to exhorting women to remain in their private spheres and cultivate those qualities that men found acceptable, and to castigating viciously those "Wild Women" who persisted in social and political insurgency. To "the sweet girls still left among us who have no part in the new revolt but are content to be dutiful, innocent, and sheltered," she dedicated her compendious novels.[78] She took up her pen to warn the Wild Woman that by "her attempt to imitate, to rival, perhaps to surpass, man on his rightful ground she is not only destroying her distinctive charm of womanhood, but is perhaps digging her own grave, to be filled too surely as well as prematurely."[79]

The fear of male sexual violence provoked by women who insisted upon competing with men in the public sphere permeated the women's anti-suffrage movement. With "clamours for equality" on the part of women, "man's protecting instinct will dwindle and die," Parr intoned darkly. "Our judges complain that crimes of violence on women are becoming more common. Little children, lonely women are brutally done to death. This horror will increase as more women claim equality with men and deny his protectorship. 'She is my equal, she must take her chance against me,' says man taught by this type of woman."[80] As long as men remained men, in their public sphere, and women remained women, in their private sphere, the distinctions between the sexes would afford women protection and security; any blurring of the functions and roles of men and women would result in the destruction of the female sex. "[T]he moment that women cease to be women," warned Fowler, "and range themselves alongside of men in the arena of political life, then the days of chivalry and of the reign of womanhood will alike be numbered, and the actual and intolerable subjection of woman will begin."[81] "If women are to have scope and authority identical with men's," Kenealy echoed, "then they must forego all privileges; must come out from their fence behind strong arms and chivalry to meet masculine blows in the face, economic and ethical—if not actual. . . . And then, Heaven help them."[82]

The language of physical violence pervaded anti-suffrage literature, testimony to women's conscious and unconscious fear of male brutality, especially after militancy provoked overt manhandling of the suffragettes. "Shall we sacrifice our Womanhood to Politics?" asked Marie Corelli. "Shall we make a holocaust of maidens, wives, and mothers on the brazen altars of Party?"[83] The Women's National Anti-Suffrage League, later the National League for Opposing Woman Suffrage, was founded in 1908, the timing suggesting that women organized in response to men's reaction to militancy.[84] Its official publication, the *Anti-Suffrage Review*, published a letter in 1908 in which the author stated her belief that "the great mass of our countrywomen desire, I am convinced, to be counsellors, not combatants."[85]

The League based much of its opposition to women's suffrage on what became known as the "physical force" argument. The argument followed two lines of thought. The first held that because the security of the state rested on the ability of men to defend it physically, men were entitled, through their vote, to participate in matters of national concern. Women, by virtue of their physical incapacities, were not.[86] This reasoning, I suspect, was designed to counter the rather awkward fact that, as feminists persisted in pointing out, men of low class and limited education possessed the franchise where wealthy, well-educated, and well-connected women did not. The second line of argument was more subtle, but its meaning was unmistakably that of the threat of men using physical force against women. It also betrayed a prevalent lack of confidence in the rule of law as the fundamental guarantor of personal liberty.

Proponents of the physical-force argument such as Ethel Harrison maintained that "the vote is an expression of force. . . . Government rests ultimately on force. . . . Votes are not given according to value; your opinion may be of infinitely greater value than many coachmen's and gardeners'; but they have votes just because of that element of force behind consent."[87] Physiological facts, declared one anti-suffrage pamphlet, had determined that

> women could not undertake the physical responsibilities of enforcing any law, which, by their votes, they might cause to be enacted. . . . Any measure traceable to the votes of women would lack that physical sanction which is essential to the enforcement of law in the last resort. And if any law came to be popularly regarded as woman-made, not only might that law be treated with disregard and contempt, but it might drag down respect for law in general. The effectiveness therefore of the legislative power of women could not exceed the limits of the moral force exercised by their influence upon men. This influence is immense without the vote, and would naturally be lessened in proportion as women attempted to become competitors and rulers of men, rather than their companions and help-mates.[88]

The *Anti-Suffrage Review* of August 1909 insisted that the antics of the militant suffragettes demonstrated that women would undermine law and order, bringing the law into disrepute. If this were to happen on a large scale, women would be the victims. "Once let loose the wild beast, which the law holds in chains, and who are likely to fall the quickest and easiest prey?" demanded the author.[89]

The members of the Women's National Anti-Suffrage League

did not simply pull out of thin air these assumptions about men's readiness to resort to physical force to maintain their power. They enlarged upon and extended logically ideas that intelligent and influential men had put forth in justifying the disenfranchisement of women. Heber Hart, a doctor of laws, had argued in 1908 that "voting is at present the conventional mode of ascertaining who in fact have the power of enforcing their will upon the rest of the community." "Now, it is unnecessary," he stated, raising the threat of violence,

> to labour the point that the power of women to compel obedience of others by physical force is not only less than that of men, but is, comparatively speaking, almost negligible. It follows that, if the suffrage were granted to women, the majority of votes cast at an election would bear no ascertainable relation to physical power. . . . It would never be certain that the legal repositories of power were in actual possession of predominant force.

The "unnatural separation of legal right from physical power" that would result from enfranchising women would facilitate, in times of crisis, "the development of personal government and general disorder."[90] Hart left no question as to what the fate of women at the hands of those with superior physical power would be in such an event. Frederic Harrison, an ardent anti-suffragist, was satisfied that this confrontation would never come to pass, for he believed the possibility of women "obtaining a controlling voice in Parliament" to be nil. "Physical force would come into play long before such a point was reached," he threatened.[91] *Common Cause* reported that Hilaire Belloc, son of Bessie Raynor Parks, a pioneer of the women's movement, agreed with Harrison that "men would prevent women with violence from registering their votes."[92]

Feminists shared with anti-suffrage women the goal of protecting women from men. They differed in their beliefs as to how best to achieve their ends. Because they believed men's qualities to be formed socially, not naturally, feminists envisaged "a furthering evolution of the spiritual force in man."[93] Anti-suffragists, taking the "natural" position, despaired of any such possibility. As Hale pointed out, "the anti-feminist, unconsciously or not, holds men to as low a standard as the feminist holds them high."[94] Ethel Colquhoun validated her observation and suggested how profound was the pessimism that infused anti-suffragism with her statement that "there is . . . very little warrant for the feminist theory that we are on the eve of a period in which the fighting capacity of the male sex will cease to be flung into the scale of determining the social value of the sexes." Given this assumption, women could find security from men only in the private sphere. "The true woman's movement," insisted Colquhoun, "must be one which, recognising the principle of a natural division of duties between the sexes, aims at strengthening woman in her normal, natural sphere."[95] As that very private sphere, for feminists, justified oppression and abuse, they sought to eliminate separate spheres altogether and to bring the positive qualities associated with women to society as a whole.

SUFFRAGE

[A]t the bottom of that desire, underneath many
other good motives, there lies a bitterness of woe
which is the most powerful stimulus towards the
desire for representation in the legislature.

Common Cause, 1910

It is impossible to show the depth and moral passion of the women's liberation movement without
showing the root at once of woman's weakness and
woman's strength. Her sex is the ground of her
disability . . . . So long as women are in the degrading stultifying servitude of sex, you cannot
work for their liberation if you never name their
sex and all it implies.

Common Cause, 1910

Feminists struggled for over fifty years to obtain votes for
women. Their campaign, although a continuous one, was
marked by three distinct phases. During the pioneering phase,
from 1866 to 1870, suffrage agitation focused on the Reform Act
of 1867 and was characterized by great optimism and spirited
activity. The second phase, lasting from 1870 to 1905, has been
described as a period of "doldrums," when the movement became muted and diffused.[1] With the advent of militancy in 1905,
votes for women took on an intensity of purpose marked by "an
almost religious fervour," as Strachey described it. "It was the
flowering time of the Women's Movement," she wrote, "the long
years of preparation and slow growth were forgotten, and the
Cause seemed to be springing new born from the enthusiasm of
the time."[2] Although the issues and concerns of suffragists re-

mained fundamentally the same, each stage was characterized by different personalities, emphases, and tones; all three, therefore, must be given consideration.

THE WOMEN'S SUFFRAGE campaign as an organized movement began in April 1866, when Barbara Bodichon, Jessie Boucherette, Emily Davies, and Elizabeth Garrett set out on a petition drive to demand votes for women. By June they had collected 1,499 signatures. Prominent among the names were those of Florence Nightingale, Harriet Martineau, and Josephine Butler. John Stuart Mill, who had stood for election to Parliament from Westminster on a platform that had included the enfranchisement of women, presented the petition to the House of Commons.

In October 1866, Bodichon read a paper on women's suffrage before the National Association for the Promotion of Social Science in Manchester. In the audience that day sat Lydia Becker. Moved by Bodichon's words, Becker decided to act. In January 1867, she formed the Manchester Women's Suffrage Committee.[3] Elizabeth Wolstenholme, later Wolstenholme Elmy, and Mary Hume-Rothery were among those who attended the first meeting.

The significance of the Social Science Association goes beyond its support of women's suffrage and the opportunities it provided as a forum for the articulation of suffrage arguments. Founded in 1857, the Association boasted such members as Lord Brougham, Lord Shaftesbury, Lord John Russell, and Charles Kingsley.[4] Reflecting the prevalent confidence in science as the basis of all knowledge, Association members dedicated themselves to the discovery and dissemination of "the science of society." By promoting public discussion and lobbying politicians and bureaucrats behind the scenes, the Association contributed instrumentally to reforms in the law, education, and public health. The efforts of its members secured the appointment of the Royal Commission on Sanitary Law in 1869 and the passage of the Married Women's Property Act in 1870.[5] In turning to the Social Science Association, suffragists were going right to the body whose knowledge seemed to be legitimating reform. They were, in effect, entering the ground of male discourse, which, "in claiming science, politics, philosophy and all the higher regions of thought for [itself] and warning off intrusion by placarding them with the word *unfeminine*," had garnered the power that knowledge made possible in men's hands exclusively.[6]

Shortly after the formation of the Manchester Women's Suffrage Committee, suffrage societies in London, Edinburgh, and Bristol were organized. The four societies existed independently of one another, but participants soon recognized the need for a central body to coordinate activities and policy. The London National Society for Women's Suffrage served this purpose. Its executive body included Frances Power Cobbe and Millicent Garrett Fawcett. Fawcett's sister, Louisa Garrett Smith, acted as Honorary Secretary.[7]

The suffrage pioneers hailed from a variety of feminist organizations seeking to raise the status of women. Boucherette, Bodichon, and Bessie Raynor Parkes (later Belloc) formed the nucleus of the Langham Place group, which, beginning in 1855, had focused on securing earnings and property for married women and providing educational opportunities, occupations, and technical training for women. Emily Davies and Elizabeth Garrett became involved with the group, and in 1865, they founded the Kensington Society to promote higher education for women. Davies, with Barbara Bodichon, later founded Girton College at Cambridge. Garrett, after a long and arduous struggle to become registered as a physician, was instrumental in opening medicine as a profession for women. Louisa Garrett Smith, Helen Taylor, and Elizabeth Wolstenholme also belonged to the Kensington Society. Lydia Becker—author of *Botany for Novices*, published in 1864, and a book on elementary astronomy, which did not get into print—had founded the Manchester Ladies' Literary Society. Though short-lived, the Society aimed to disseminate scientific knowledge among women. At the first meeting, Becker read a paper by Darwin, sent to her with his best wishes for the ladies' success. These organizations, while aiming to eliminate separate and specific disabilities experienced by women, shared the common goal of achieving for women freedom and equality. All of them were "keenly alive to the importance of the suffrage,"[8] as a perhaps apocryphal conversation among Davies, Elizabeth Garrett, and Millicent Garrett indicates. Summing up their discussion of the women's cause, Davies said, "Well, Elizabeth, it's quite clear what has to be done. I must devote myself to securing higher education, while you open the medical profession. After these things are done we must see about getting the vote." Turning to Millicent, she added, "You are younger than we are, Millie, so you must attend to that."[9]

Mill's election to the House of Commons made votes for women a distinct possibility. When, in 1867, Disraeli's government introduced a bill to enfranchise a large proportion of the working classes, Mill seized upon the opportunity to enfranchise women as well. He introduced an amendment to the bill, proposing to replace the word "man" with "person," and thereby admit women to the franchise on the same basis as men.[10] The motion was defeated handily. Surprisingly, however, another amendment to replace the word "man" with "male" also went down to defeat, leading suffragists to hope that, on the basis of Lord Romilly's act of 1850, the word "man" applied to women as well. Lord Romilly's act had mandated that unless explicitly stated otherwise, the term "man" in Parliamentary statutes was to be used generically, including women as well as men under the jurisdiction of the law. After some debate in Parliament as to the relevance of Lord Romilly's act for the Reform Act of 1867, Disraeli ruled that it was a matter for the courts to decide. In the midst of the debate, Becker noted, one M.P. argued to the "effect that if a woman could be brought in under Lord Romilly's Act, so might a cow!!" She deduced from this that he "appeared to hold the belief that man and woman were distinct species of animals as much as man and horses." Becker was, of course, entirely correct and discovered that this particular M.P.'s views were widely held. The courts ruled that Lord Romilly's act did not apply to the Reform Act of 1867, one of the magistrates indicating that it could also be used to enfranchise a dog or a horse.[11]

Mill's role in the suffrage campaign went beyond that of parliamentary champion of the women's cause. His writings, and those of his wife, Harriet Taylor Mill, provided a theoretical foundation for the arguments suffragists advanced throughout their fifty-year campaign. Harriet Taylor Mill's "Enfranchisement of Women," published in the *Westminster Review* in 1851, "was widely circulated by the Women's Suffrage Society in 1868."[12] To her, J. S. Mill attributed most of the ideas he presented in *The Subjection of Women*, published in 1869 but written eight years earlier. His analysis of women's position, the power and scope of which amazed feminists when the book was reissued in the 1960s, was seized upon by suffragists. Millicent Garrett's future husband, Henry Fawcett, and Mill were close friends and political allies; Millicent herself regarded Mill as one of "the three best men I have known" and often consulted with him on matters of suffragist policy and strategy.[13] It is to the Mills, then, that we must first turn for an understanding of the motives and aims of the suffrage campaign.

The writings of John Stuart Mill and Harriet Taylor Mill constitute an analysis of what Kate Millett has termed "sexual politics."[14] Millett has claimed that society's view of sex as a caste structure validated by "nature" served as "the very prototype of institutionalized inequality," superseding all other forms of "inegalitarianism"—racial, political, and economic. The sexual politic, she has argued, lies at the base of all other power relations.[15] As Alice Rossi has put it, unless "we go to the very center of the sexual politic and root out the power and violence there, all our efforts at liberation will only land us again in the same primordial stews."[16]

In "Enfranchisement of Women," Harriet Mill spoke directly to the notion of sexual politics that Millett analyzed over a century later. Mill referred to men as belonging to "the aristocracy of sex," to whom is given exclusively political liberty and personal freedom of action as "the prerogative of [their] caste." She pointed to the primacy of the sexual politic in determining other power relations. "[T]he division of mankind into two castes," she argued, "one born to rule over the other, is . . . a source of perversion and demoralization . . . forming a bar, almost insuperable while it lasts, to any really vital improvement, either in the character or in the social condition of the human race." John Stuart Mill echoed her sentiments in *The Subjection of Women*. "All the selfish propensities, the self-worship, the unjust self-preference, which exist among mankind, have their source and root in, and derive their principal nourishment from, the present constitution of the relation between men and women," he asserted. Unless the sexual politic could be eliminated, reforms in politics, economy, and society would be to no avail. "All that education and civilization are doing to efface the influences on character of the law of force, and replace them by those of justice, remains merely on the surface, as long as the citadel of the enemy is not attacked."[17]

The Mills pointed out that the distinctions between the sexes imposed by society were purported to be those delineated by nature, that the private sphere belonged to woman, and the public sphere to men, because of biological and physiological differences between the two. Separate sphere ideology, encompassing the notion of natural differences between the sexes, justified the exclusion of women from power and reinforced and perpetuated the stereotype of women as "the Sex," making them vulnerable to abuse by men. The campaign for the vote as much as the admission of women to the medical profession was designed to eliminate the notions of separate spheres and natural differences between the sexes insisted upon by patriarchy. As Harriet Mill noted, "many persons think they have sufficiently justified the restrictions of women's field of action, when they have said that the pursuits from which women are excluded are *unfeminine*, and that the *proper sphere* of women is not politics or publicity, but private and domestic life." She insisted that cultural constructions of masculinity and femininity bore no relation to the reality of male and female character, stating, "we deny the right of any portion of the species to decide for another portion, or any individual for another individual, what is and what is not their 'proper sphere.' The proper sphere for all human beings is the largest and highest which they are able to attain to."[18]

Harriet Mill made no attempt to deny that male and female natures, as evident in her society, certainly differed markedly. She was not, however, prepared to concede that these differences were necessarily natural or inherent to the two sexes. In the case of sexuality, for instance, she noted that "whether nature made a difference in the nature of men and women or not, it seems now that all men, with the exception of a few lofty minds, are sensualists more or less—women on the contrary are quite exempt from this trait, however it may appear otherwise in the cases of some." She thought that the most likely explanation was socialization, "that the habits of freedom and low indulgence on which boys grow up and the contrary notion of what is called purity in girls may have produced the appearance of different natures in the two sexes."[19]

Harriet Mill suggested that separate sphere ideology camouflaged and made palatable a system of power relationships. The designation of "self-will and self-assertion" as "manly virtues," and those of "abnegation of self, patience, resignation, and submission to power" as "the duties and graces required of women," she maintained, meant, in reality, "that power makes itself the centre of moral obligation, and that a man likes to have his own will, but does not like that his domestic companion should have a will different from his." The so-called influence of woman within the private sphere, stemming from her special purity and morality, concealed only a distinct lack of power to determine her life. "What is wanted for women," Harriet Mill declared, "is equal rights, equal admission to all social privileges; not a position apart, a sort of sentimental priesthood."[20]

Membership in this sentimental priesthood entailed dependence upon men for subsistence, "a position," John Stuart Mill pointed out, "which in nine cases out of ten, makes her either the plaything or the slave of the man who feeds her." He believed that the "first and indispensable step" toward the enfranchisement of women was the reconstruction of cultural stereotypes of masculinity and femininity. The woman must be "so educated, as not to be dependent either on her father or her husband," he insisted. His confidence in the power of education, or socialization, rested upon his conviction that "what women are is what we have required them to be." "What is now called the nature of women is an eminently artificial thing," he argued, "the result of forced repression in some directions, unnatural stimulation in others."[21]

J. S. Mill emphasized the link between power in the public sphere and that in the private sphere. He believed that patriarchal society insisted upon the continued exclusion of women from public power because men feared the corresponding power that they would obtain in the private sphere. "I believe that their disabilities elsewhere," he stated, "are only clung to in order to maintain their subordination in domestic life." Male "antipathy to the equal freedom of women" concealed a real fear "lest they should insist that marriage should be on equal conditions."[22]

Two developments, according to J. S. Mill, might "abate the exaggerated self-abnegation which is the artificial ideal of feminine character" that rendered her powerless to men. One was "equality of rights." The other was a comprehension of "the laws of the influence of circumstances on character"—or a determination of the real differences between male and female natures, those not induced by education or external circumstances. Here Mill hinted at the close relation between the campaign for medical women—their entry into the domain of scientific investigation—and that for the vote.[23]

Mill argued that because no one had undertaken a study to determine just which gender differences could not be explained as the result of education or external circumstances, no one possessed sufficient knowledge to make pronouncements upon the natural differences between the sexes, upon which the exclusion of women from the public sphere was based. "Medical practitioners and physiologists have ascertained, to some extent, the differences in bodily constitution," he conceded. Respecting, however, "the mental characteristics of women; their observations are of no more worth than those of common men. It is a subject on which nothing final can be known, so long as those who alone can really know it, women themselves, have given but little testimony, and that little, mostly suborned."[24]

Following the Mills, feminists repeatedly articulated their belief in the primacy of the sexual politic. In an address to the third annual meeting of the Edinburgh branch of the National Society for Women's Suffrage in 1872, Helen Taylor, Harriet Taylor Mill's daughter, argued that the position of women in society had nothing to do with what were supposed to be natural differences between the sexes. Physical power had determined male supremacy. "In the beginning," she asserted, "man and woman were created equals, made in the same divine image. God blessed them unitedly, and gave them conjoint dominion over the world." The superior size and strength of men naturally conferred upon them the role of protector of women. Gradually, she maintained, what had been a matter of expediency developed

> into a sovereignty that increased with exercise, until mere physical power established a supremacy that has existed in greater or lesser degree until now. Under this arbitrary rule

woman has been more or less degraded to the position of a slave; been treated in many respects as a mere chattel, and she has rarely, if ever, been in a position fully to develop and freely to use the powers which God has gifted her.

Men had determined what women were and were not, what women were and were not to do, Taylor stated; woman was now demanding for herself "the right to perfect liberty in fulfilling her duties to the world in accordance with nature's teachings and her own convictions."[25]

Five years later, in a speech delivered to the London National Society for Women's Suffrage, Arabella Shore again drew the link between so-called scientific justifications and the political arguments against women's suffrage. As women possessed in many cases the requisite criteria for voting, politicians were compelled to come up with other justifications for their exclusion. The "great Nature argument," as Shore termed it, effectively dehumanized women, making them politically ineligible. "[W]e are told of the peculiarities of our nature, our conditions, our duties, and our character; that is, in other words, our physical and mental inferiority, our home sphere," she noted. Challenging the "great Nature argument," she insisted on knowing "what is meant by Nature. Is it ancient usage or established convention, the law or custom of our country, training, social position, the speaker's own particular fancy or prejudice, or what?" She refused to accept the separate sphere argument, the idea that private and public issues had nothing to do with one another. "We cannot separate domestic politics from social conditions of life. If then we are told that we have nothing to do with politics, we can but answer that politics have a great deal to do with us." Finally, Shore realized that public powerlessness meant for women powerlessness in the private sphere as well. "With respect to the home as woman's natural sphere," she maintained, "[it] is by no means her domain, for as wife and mother she has no legal power, hardly any legal rights. . . . So that this distinction seems to result in man's keeping the supremacy in every sphere to himself."[26]

THE PIONEER suffragists and their supporters expected an early victory.[27] The defeat of Mill's amendment to the Reform Act of 1867 compelled suffragists to rely on private bills introduced by their parliamentary allies, bills that—lacking government backing—had little chance of passing. In each year from 1870 to 1883, with the exception of 1880, suffrage measures were introduced, and in each year they were defeated. In 1884, Gladstone's government put forth a bill to enfranchise the agricultural workers, generating great optimism among suffragists, who had secured the support of a majority of M.P.s. They quickly moved to amend the bill to include women on the same lines as men. Gladstone, however, remained adamant in his opposition to women's enfranchisement and imposed party discipline upon Liberals to defeat the amendment.

Because historians have viewed the campaign for votes for women as simply that—a campaign for votes—they have been able to state with confidence that for the thirty-five years following 1870 there was virtually no progress, "no forward movement," for suffragists. Fulford, for instance, dismissed as "minor measures affecting women" the passage of the Married Women's Property Act and the repeal of the Contagious Diseases Acts.[28] He and others have failed to see that, for the women, action in all arenas that demanded their right to some degree of equality with men constituted the same fundamental challenge to patriarchy as did the vote. Suffragists, cognizant now of just how great was the opposition to their cause, realized this and after 1870 "were drawn off to the special provinces of women's progress with which they had been originally identified."[29] This fragmentation of the movement may have been a conscious policy decision, designed to dilute opposition strength. As Strachey noted, "it was obvious, of course, to all the suffragists that the education movement and the political movement and the medical women's movement were all part of the same thing. But each of these reforms was separate, and all were battling against prejudice and obstruction; and it seemed rather dangerous to let the general public see what a close connection there was between them all."[30] The danger lay in the profoundly radical aims of the feminist movement to transform the sexual culture of England, although opponents were soon to realize the feminists' goals.

Efforts to secure property rights and higher education, and to open the medical profession to women, were successful during the last quarter of the nineteenth century. These gains, and especially the repeal of the Contagious Diseases Acts, which Strachey described as "of immense importance to the ultimate Women's Suffrage victory," contributed significantly to the gradual invalidation of the notions of separate spheres and of women as "the Sex."[31] Millicent Garrett Fawcett certainly understood that ultimate victory depended upon these incremental challenges to the cultural constructions of femininity. "Women's suffrage," she believed, "will not come, when it does come, as an isolated phenomenon, it will come as a necessary corollary of the other changes which have been gradually and steadily modifying during this century the social history of our country. It will be a political change . . . based upon social, educational, and economic changes which have already taken place."[32]

Fawcett was "deeply involved" in many of the individual feminist campaigns that were successful during the period of "doldrums" that characterized the suffrage movement from 1870 to 1905. She brought her considerable political experience to the Married Women's Property Act lobbying effort and used her husband's connections at Cambridge to help gain admission of Newnham College students to the Cambridge Honours exams. Though wholly supportive of Josephine Butler's repeal campaign, she decided, after consulting with Mill, to stay out of the CD Acts agitation. She could not, however, remain aloof from the controversy raised by Stead's exposé of white slavery in the *Pall Mall Gazette*; she spent a considerable amount of time writing and speaking about the need for an effective Criminal Law Amendment Act. Stead's articles revealing the traffic in young girls for the purpose of prostitution roused Fawcett "as she had never been roused before, and [she] burnt and flamed with rage against the evils he described." The evils he described represented in the extreme for Fawcett the exploited position of women in English society. She believed that "a knowledge of the facts [raised by Stead] will make a great many people understand for the first time one of the reasons why women ought to have votes."[33] The fact that Parliament acted quickly in the wake of the scandal did not placate her, for she believed that M.P.s had responded not to their consciences or to the desire to protect the interests of women but to political pressure. "If women had been able to protect themselves by the legitimate use of the parliamentary franchise," she insisted, "the Criminal Law Amendment Bill would have been passed in the ordinary course of things without the necessity of shaking the whole of England by the recent agitation."[34]

The white-slavery incident imposed upon Fawcett a single-minded determination to achieve votes for women. The "rottenness of public opinion on morals," which made possible and encouraged the degradation of women, she claimed, stemmed directly from "the low position of women generally." Piecemeal reforms such as the repeal of the Contagious Diseases Acts and the Criminal Law Amendment Act were important but failed to penetrate the heart of the problem. Fawcett regarded the suffrage as the best way to strike at the core, to raise the position of women to a status that would make the sexual abuse of them impossible.[35] After 1885, and certainly by 1905, with the advent of militancy, the whole of the feminist movement centered around suffrage as the means by which women could free themselves from servile bondage to men. As a symbol of civic and political personality, the vote would be an effective agent in eliminating the notion of women as "the Sex." As an instrument of power, it would enable women to recreate, they believed—as did their opponents—a sexual culture in Britain that would reflect the needs, desires, and interests of women.

WITH THE ARRIVAL of the Women's Social and Political Union, under the leadership of Emmeline and Christabel Pankhurst, the suffrage campaign took on new life and meaning. The militant tactics of the WSPU electrified the country and galvanized the whole of the suffrage movement. From 1897, when all suffrage societies were federated in the National Union of Women's Suffrage Societies (NUWSS), to 1903, when the WSPU was formed, the NUWSS encompassed only sixteen societies. By 1909, fifty-four additional societies had come into being and joined the NUWSS. In 1911, 305 societies made up the constitutional group; that number swelled to 400 by 1913.[36] As a result of militant tactics, Strachey explained, "to hundreds and thousands . . . the thing came as a new gospel; even those who had believed in the Cause before now began to see it in a new light, and an almost religious fervour entered into their support."[37]

In marked contrast to the strategies pursued by the NUWSS, the WSPU followed a policy of "sensational public protest." "Deeds not Words" was its motto. The first of the WSPU's big public demonstrations took place in 1907, when 3,000 women participated in the "Mud March" from Hyde Park to Exeter Hall, carrying banners and marching to the cacophony of numerous brass bands. Until the summer of 1909, militant action was nonviolent; suffragettes heckled Cabinet ministers and obstructed political meetings, and they marched on Parliament to meet with men who refused to see them. When the police learned to anticipate and try to cut short militant deputations to Parliament, the suffragettes responded with surprises and clever disguises to circumvent them. The Pankhurst followers "arrived in all sorts of guises, and appeared in all sorts of places," Strachey related.

Now one would appear as a messenger boy, now another as a waitress. Once they chained themselves to the railings in Downing Street, and so gained time to make some long-ish speeches before being haled [sic] off to Bow Street; another was found chained to a statue in the lobby of the House of Commons, a thoroughly strategic position. They sprang out of organ lofts, they peered through roof win-dows, and leapt out of innocent-looking furniture vans; they materialised on station platforms, they harangued the terrace of the House from the river, and wherever they were least expected there they were.[38]

Suffragettes regularly conducted "raids" on Parliament, processions that were actually quite orderly and peaceful. Often, however, the women met with violence at the hands of police— "sometimes as many as a thousand strong, on foot and on horse-back," according to Strachey—and civilian bystanders. "[T]he women were usually knocked about, sometimes pretty severely," and then arrested.[39] In the summer of 1909, the militants took up stone-throwing. In a symbolic protest against the politicians who refused to meet their demands, they broke countless gov-ernment windows. Stone-throwing had a more pragmatic effect as well—it cut short sometimes brutal struggles with the police and therefore diminished "considerable physical suffering before arrest."[40]

In the summer of 1909, militant suffragists began a hunger strike in prison. They demanded that their sentences be reduced to reflect more accurately the severity of their crimes—heckling, demonstrating, and stone-throwing—and that the courts regard them as political prisoners rather than common criminals. In-stead, the authorities responded with forced feeding, an intru-sive procedure symbolizing for suffragists "horrible outrage" and "violated bodies" as great as that of "instrumental rape" under the CD Acts.[41]

"[T]he Wardresses forced me on to the bed," wrote Mary Leigh, describing her ordeal, and the two doctors came in with them, and while I was held down a nasal tube was inserted. It is two yards long with a funnel at the end—there is a glass junction in the middle to see if the liquid is passing. The end is put up the nostril, one one day, and the other nostril, the other. Great pain is experienced during the process . . . the drums of the ear seem to be bursting, a horrible pain in the throat and the breast. The tube is pushed down 20 inches. I have to lie on the bed, pinned down by War-dresses, one doctor stands up on a chair holding the funnel at arms length, so as to have the funnel end above the level, and then the other doctor, who is behind, forces the other end up the nostrils.

The one holding the funnel end pours the liquid down.
. . . The after effects are a feeling of faintness, a sense of great pain in the diaphragm or breast bone, in the nose and the ears.[42]

The violence of forced feeding led to a great outcry against the government's actions from sympathizers and opponents of women's suffrage alike. Its analogy to rape undoubtedly aided the suffrage societies in their recruitment efforts.[43]

Despite the success of the WSPU in focusing enormous public-ity on the suffrage issue, the parliamentary response remained "deeply discouraging." Suffragists enjoyed a great deal of sup-port in Parliament, but Asquith, the Prime Minister, refused to back a women's suffrage measure. After the election of 1910, however, it appeared that a women's suffrage bill had a good chance of passing. A Conciliation Committee, composed of members from all parties, was formed to draft a bill that would enjoy the support of all shades of political opinion. In order to give the Conciliation Bill a chance, the WSPU called a truce in militancy. For six months, the suffrage societies carried on "an unparalleled intensity of propaganda."[44] The Conciliation Bill passed its second reading in July 1910, but before it could go any further, Asquith, with the complicity of Lloyd George, torpedoed the bill.[45]

The militants immediately abandoned their truce. On 18 November, suffragettes led by Emmeline Pankhurst and Elizabeth Garrett Anderson marched from Caxton Hall to Parliament, where they were attacked and sexually molested by police and male bystanders (see Chapter VI). This incident—the notorious "Black Friday"—has been presented by some male historians as evidence that the women wanted to be sexually abused. As David Mitchell has imagined it, the men who fell upon the women were only responding to the wishes of the women for sexual contact: "Wasn't this, they argued, what these women REALLY wanted? . . . Perhaps in some cases, and in a deeply unconscious way it was."[46] Mitchell has failed to see that these displays of male violence against women brought into public view the "sex war" that the suffrage was designed to eliminate and increased significantly the numbers of women determined to achieve success. As Emmeline Pethick Lawrence had announced four years earlier, "the struggle has begun. It is a life and death struggle . . . the harder the fight the better. What we are going to get is a great revolt of the women against their subjection of body and mind to men."[47]

The sexual abuse of suffragettes, like the sexual threats against Josephine Butler forty years earlier, stemmed logically from the ideology of separate spheres. The ideology equated women in public with prostitutes—public women whose appearance indicated their possession of sexual knowledge and their quest for sex. The presence of suffragists in public indicated their possession of (sexual) knowledge and their attempts to exploit their knowledge for a price. Respectable women were deemed to be naturally and contentedly confined to the private sphere by virtue of their sexual and reproductive functions. Those who stepped out of their God-given realm to venture into the public sphere were obviously "unsexed," suffering from some sexual malaise or incompleteness. The fact that a large proportion of suffragists were single or widowed corroborated this view. Providing what "these women REALLY wanted"—sex—amounted to providing what prostitutes really wanted. By identifying these women with prostitutes, women whose degradation allegedly justified all sorts of sexual abuse, the men of "Black Friday" were able to give vent to their anger and aggression toward suffragists.

The Conciliation Bill was revived in 1911, and again militants called a truce in their activities. When the government appeared to throw over the bill for a second time by introducing a measure for manhood suffrage, the WSPU erupted in acts of deliberate law-breaking.[48] On Friday, 1 March 1912, Emmeline Pankhurst and two other women broke the windows at 10 Downing Street, while over 200 other women, in a simultaneous attack, shattered windows all over London. In a few minutes there was damage worth thousands of pounds, Sylvia Pankhurst reported. "In Piccadilly, Regent Street, Oxford Street, Bond Street, Coventry Street and their neighbourhood, in Whitehall, Parliament Street, Trafalgar Square, Cockspur Street and the Strand . . . well-dressed women suddenly produced strong hammers from innocent-looking bags and parcels, and fell to smashing the shop windows." Police arrested 217 women. Mrs. Pankhurst and the Pethick Lawrences were charged with inciting to riot. Court officials also issued a warrant for Christabel Pankhurst's arrest, but she evaded their grasp by fleeing to Paris. The following Monday, 4 March, suffragettes struck again in Knightsbridge. "That day," Sylvia Pankhurst stated, "the British Museum and all the picture galleries in the centre of London were already closed. . . . Nine thousand police were stationed in . . . [Trafalgar] Square."[49]

Mrs. Pankhurst and the Pethick Lawrences received sentences of nine months in the Second Division and immediately embarked on a hunger strike. They became so ill that officials released them from prison shortly thereafter. Mrs. Pankhurst intended to continue the violent activities of the WSPU, and in fact to expand them to include arson. The Pethick Lawrences objected to such tactics and left the WSPU, taking their newspaper, *Votes for Women*, with them. Christabel Pankhurst, from Paris, started publishing the *Suffragette* in its stead.[50]

In January 1913, Asquith's government introduced its manhood suffrage bill, having earlier promised suffragists that it would be open to amendment. When it reached the floor of the House, the government announced that it would not permit an amendment for women's suffrage. Crying betrayal, the WSPU embarked upon another campaign of destruction. Christabel Pankhurst designed a strategy that included the "pouring of acids into pillar boxes, the cutting of telegraph wires, and the slashing of pictures in public galleries. . . . [Suffragettes] set fire to empty houses, they destroyed golf-courses, they threw bombs at churches." In February 1913, someone attempted to burn down Lloyd George's country house. Mrs. Pankhurst was arrested, charged with inciting to commit a felony, and given three years penal servitude. Anticipating that she would go on a hunger strike and thereby obtain early release, the government passed what became known as the "Cat and Mouse Act." Aimed specifically at the suffragettes, the law enabled the government to release a hunger-striking prisoner and reincarcerate her after she recovered from her ordeal.[51] Mrs. Pankhurst entered Holloway on 3 April 1913. She refused all food, became ill, and was released on 12 April. Having recovered by the end of May, she was sent to prison once again, refused to eat, and was out five days later.

The next day, 31 May 1913, was Derby Day. In the midst of the race, Emily Wilding Davison threw herself in front of the King's horse and was trampled to death. The militant suffragettes had gained their first true martyr to the Cause. Mrs. Pankhurst tried to march in Davison's funeral procession but was stopped by police and returned to Holloway. Indomitable, she continued to refuse food. By April of 1914, she had conducted twelve hunger strikes and had served, under the Cat and Mouse

Act, only thirty days toward her sentence.[52] It is impossible to imagine how far the militants might have gone in their efforts to achieve votes for women had not World War I intervened to bring their activity to a sudden and decisive halt.

Such militant behavior on the part of respectable women shocked society and provoked numerous attempts at explanation. "Physiological conditions" consequent upon "the severe sexual restrictions" faced by surplus women in England, asserted Sir Almroth Wright, M.D., were at the root of the militant suffrage campaign. In a letter published in the *Times* in 1912, he stated that "the mind of a woman is always threatened with danger from the reverberations of her physiological emergencies." The "mental disorder" displayed by those "mixed up with the woman's movement" was a product of "the physiological emergencies" experienced by "the million of our excess female population," those women who, denied husbands, were "sexually embittered" and "incomplete." In 1913, Wright elaborated upon his views in a book titled *The Unexpurgated Case against Woman Suffrage*. "[T]he question of suffrage," he submitted, "and with it the larger question as to the proper sphere of woman, finally turns upon the question as to what imprint woman's sexual system leaves upon her physical frame, character, and intellect." As a physiologist, he knew "that the sexual products influence every tissue of the body"; in women the sexual products devolved upon them "intellectual immoralities and limitations" as "secondary sexual characteristics." Women's character defects, "as irremediable as 'racial characters,'" delineated her proper sphere and settled once and for all any nonsense as to women's suffrage.[53]

As Christabel Pankhurst noted in 1913, the ideology of separate spheres and its justification for the subjection of women only camouflaged the "doctrine that woman is sex and beyond that nothing." In a series of articles published first in the *Suffragette* and later compiled in a book titled *The Great Scourge*, she offered a scathing attack on the interdependent cultural constructions of masculinity and femininity and of male and female sexuality. "Sometimes this doctrine [of woman as sex]," she argued, "is dressed up in the saying that women are mothers and beyond that nothing. What a man who says that really means is that women are created primarily for the sex gratification of men, and secondarily, for the bearing of children if he happens to want them, but of no more children than he wants."[54] The man who opposed women's suffrage did so because he held women to be "a sub-human species useful in so far as female, but not otherwise." He valued women "only because of their sex functions, which functions he also believes are to be used at the orders and in the service of men."[55]

In accordance with this value system, Pankhurst continued, men had divided women into two classes. "Those belonging to the first class are expected to give birth to legitimate children. They are not recognized by the law as 'persons,' and they are not recognized as legal parents of their own children. They are called 'wives.' " Those belonging to the second class "are called 'prostitutes.' They are used for the physical satisfaction of men." There was also a third class of women—neither wives nor prostitutes—called "superfluous." Because they neither bore legitimate children nor served as an outlet for "that exaggerated development of the sex instinct which is supposed to be natural where men are concerned," man had no use for them. "In fact, he has a peculiar fear and horror of them."[56] Pankhurst may have had Wright in mind when she made this last point. Of the superfluous woman who so notoriously flocked to the suffrage banner, he wrote, "the State would be well rid of her if she were crushed under the soldiers' shields like the traitor woman at the Tarpeian rock."[57] Single women defied sexual classification, threatened the sexual organization of society, and undermined the concept of separate spheres that guaranteed patriarchal hegemony. Pankhurst's clarion call to women to remain single contained, at least implicitly, this message. Her importuning constituted a radical but utterly consistent extension of suffrage

aims—the elimination of separate sphere ideology that justified
the sexual classification of women. The suffrage movement was,
she insisted, "a revolt against the evil system under which
women are regarded as sub-human and as the sex slaves of
men."[58]

OLIVE BANKS has argued that feminism in Britain contained at
least two strands of thought, distinct intellectual traditions that
did not prevent feminists from allying with one another but that
produced a degree of conflict in their approaches. The first,
embracing the notion of the natural purity or innate moral superiority of women, derived from evangelical Christianity and
encouraged feminist involvement in moral and social reform.
The second emphasized the similarities rather than the differences between the sexes. Arising from the Enlightenment belief
in reason, this "face" of feminism saw the differences between
men and women as products of the environment, not as natural
or biologically determined sexual characteristics. Banks has
claimed that the superiority school tended increasingly to dominate feminist thought, until by the turn of the century, conser-
vatism characterized the women's movement. "During the years
between 1870 and 1914," she has maintained,

> most of the radicalism that the pioneering feminists had
> inherited from the Enlightenment disappeared. As femi-
> nism grew in influence and became, in the great suffrage
> campaign of the early twentieth century, something of a
> mass movement, it shed not only its more radical goals but
> its more radical conception of womanhood. Most signifi-
> cantly of all, it passed from a concern with the social con-
> struction of the female based ultimately upon Enlighten-
> ment views on the effect of the environment upon human
> nature, to an acceptance of the essential uniqueness of the
> female. By the end of the nineteenth century, the feminist
> movement was based, not so much on the doctrine of male

and female equality as on a notion of female superiority that was accepted not only by women but by many of their male supporters.[59]

There are two basic problems with Banks's interpretation. First, she has drawn the line between the strands of feminism far too starkly. As Jane Lewis has observed, the two were in no way distinct, and both in fact challenged the idea of a natural separation of spheres.[60] Feminists holding the equality position dismissed the idea of any inherent sexual difference. Those, like Swiney, who believed that women were the natural guardians of morality sought to extend the qualities associated with the feminine, domestic role to the public sphere so as to create a more moral world. Frequently, moreover, feminists espoused the tenets of both strands as they demanded simultaneously equal rights and moral reform. Elizabeth Wolstenholme Elmy, a great friend and admirer of Swiney and active in the Contagious Diseases Acts repeal effort, nonetheless could write, "I do not admit the superiority of women over men. Women have been repressed in every way whilst men's appetites have been equally encouraged."[61] Banks, in fact, later concedes that "in Britain, the doctrine of female superiority is less in evidence within feminism than it is in the United States, and it is possible that it was less significant, especially in the campaign for the suffrage."[62]

Olive Schreiner rejected outright any suggestion of an innate female moral superiority, and although she believed that women had a "deep and over-mastering . . . hunger for motherhood," she did not preclude men from sharing that same desire for parenthood.[63] In 1912, she exclaimed to Havelock Ellis that to be a mother, emotionally and intellectually, was the highest function in life, "except to be a real father."[64] Schreiner refused to accept the ideology of separate spheres based on biological differences. In a letter to Ellis in 1884, she complained, "I object to anything that divides the two sexes. My main point is this: human development has now reached a point at which sexual difference has become a thing of altogether minor importance. We make too much of it; we are men and women in the second place, human beings in the first."[65] In *Woman and Labour*, she insisted that "any attempt to divide the occupations in which male and female intellects and wills should be employed, must be to attempt a purely artificial and arbitrary division." "*We take all labour to be our province!*" she cried.[66]

Second, although it is quite true that feminists began increasingly to focus on the vote almost exclusively after the turn of the century, it does not follow that their goals were thus less radical. If anything, the vote was perhaps one of the most radical demands they could have made, as Ellen DuBois has suggested for the American case.[67]

The radical nature of the vote lay in its challenge to the ideology of separate spheres. Suffragists and suffragettes demanded votes for women on the same terms as it was or should be granted to men. Historians have tended to regard this as a conservative demand, as the franchise was based on the ownership or occupation of property. Prior to the passage of the Married Women's Property Acts in the 1870s and 1880s, coverture would have limited even further the number of women qualified to vote. But as Constance Rover has observed, though without extending her argument to its ultimate conclusions, "the prime object of the suffragists was to break down the sex barrier to the parliamentary franchise, not to see the vote extended to all."[68] Suffragists realized the power of political constructions such as those symbolized by enfranchisement and disenfranchisement. The vote, Christabel Pankhurst asserted,

> is the symbol of freedom and equality. Any class which is denied the vote is branded as an inferior class. Women's disenfranchisement is to them a perpetual lesson in servility, and to men it teaches arrogance and injustice where their dealings with women are concerned. The inferiority of women is a hideous lie which has been enforced by law

and woven into the British Constitution, and it is quite
hopeless to expect reform between [sic] the relationship of
the sexes until women are politically enfranchised.[69]

Sex equality as symbolized by the vote constituted "an important
ideological battle," an undermining of the "rationale for the
maintenance of male power," as Elizabeth Sarah has noted. The
principle of sex equality challenged "the power of men at its
very basis"—in the ideology of separate spheres and in the categories of "masculine" and "feminine" by which those spheres
were justified.[70]

Christabel Pankhurst and other suffragists pointed out that
the male monopoly on power was not limited to their control of
the political and economic processes or to the organization of
society. It extended well into the realm of the personal. Men
controlled the scientific and cultural institutions that defined
sexuality; they had constructed a paradigm of female sexuality
that reflected and served their sexual and psychological definitions of masculinity. Foucault suggested that in this period sexual identity came to form the core of individual identity—that
personal, political, social identity finally came down to the category of sexuality. This phenomenon helps to explain why suffragists focused so much of their attention on sexual issues and
consciously associated them with their demand for the vote: they
were convinced of the intimate connection between their exclusion from political power and their sexual powerlessness and
vulnerability. Separate sphere ideology neatly encompassed and
justified both aspects of their powerlessness; it imposed a male-
defined sexual organization upon women and barred their way
from positions of power that might challenge that organization.

For suffragists, the double standard of morality arose and received its legitimacy from ideological prescriptions of natural
differences between the sexes. It reflected the prevalent acceptance of an innate male sexual drive and concomitantly justified
the institutionalization of prostitution, with its consequences of

widespread venereal disease. The double standard was perhaps the single greatest issue in the suffrage campaign, serving as the symbol that best exemplified women's subject status and the dangers consequent to it. It was the one issue around which virtually all suffragists could unite. Many women ascribed to it the motive and rationale for their activism.[71]

But much more than an insistence on purity was involved in the critique of the double standard. Feminists underscored the political implications inherent in a creed that condoned men's sexual transgressions and punished those of women; they emphasized the dynamics of power at work within it. Without the theoretical language available to feminists of the 1970s, suffragists nonetheless held the belief that "the personal is political." The sexual subjugation of women had everything to do with their political subjugation; their political enfranchisement was intricately bound up with their sexual status. Feminists argued that the two issues could not be treated as discrete entities, and they incorporated demands for change in both areas explicitly. "Votes for Women, Chastity for Men" is only the most notorious summation of their theoretical analysis. Maria Grey, in 1881, had insisted that "no political, no educational, no professional equality will avail [woman] till she obtains moral equality with man in the primal relation between man and woman."[72]

"*The demand for women's political enfranchisement*," testified Lady Chance, "*is rooted in and springs from one main fact . . .* the deep-seated and firm conviction that *so long as women are men's inferiors in the State—that is, are not full citizens—so long must the evil continue of the double standard of morality* for men and women." She believed that sexual and political identity were intertwined, and that the transformation of one required the transformation of the other. "[O]ur desire to win direct political power," she wrote, "is founded upon our belief that in that way only shall we become possessed of the power and the weapons necessary to fight this terrible evil. The Women's Movement is in fact a great Moral Movement. It means the lifting up of

women to be the equals of men in the eyes of the whole nation."
A sexual identity that rendered women sexual objects could be
altered only by a political identity that gave them citizenship and
power. Suffragists regarded the vote as the means by which
power could be attained. As both symbol and pragmatic instrument, "all women—or rather—women as a sex, *need* it . . . for
protection," insisted Chance.[73] For, as Christabel Pankhurst protested, "so long as the subjection of women endures, and is
confirmed by law and custom, so long will . . . women be victimised."[74]

Political or civic equality, feminists believed, was the requisite
precondition to the elimination of notions of the natural differences between masculine and feminine sexuality that legitimated
male aggression against the female. Access to Parliament, Ethel
Snowdon held, provided "the instrument by which the equality
of women before the law could be secured—a necessary reform
if the value of women in the eyes of men is to be raised."[75]
Cultural constructions of femininity, Emmeline Pethick Lawrence maintained, had devalued women to so low a point that
"the deep respect for women on the part of men" had been
utterly lost, replaced by "that sense of sex superiority, that attitude of indulgent (or sometimes not indulgent) contempt which
is the very reverse of that sentiment in which the practice of
chivalry was rooted." Raising themselves to the level of political
peerage with men, reestablishing their "birthright and due in-
heritance" as human beings, was the only way that women were
"going to get any counterpart of chivalry, anything that tallies
with it" from men.[76]

Contempt for women and the sexual abuse it encouraged,
feminists argued, had resulted from prescriptions that had
stripped them of humanity. By raising woman to the level of an
angel, Victorian ideology conferred upon her superhuman status. By reducing her to sexual, animal characteristics, it presented her as subhuman. Dehumanization, the "mixture of sentimentality and contempt which has been the attitude of the

majority of men toward" women, as Hale put it, had justified women's exclusion from positions of power and legitimated their continued subjugation to men in all aspects of life.[77] Conferring upon woman a civic personality would "assure due respect for her mind and body by the ordinary man," argued the Elmys in 1898, "as being no longer a nullity, but his own equal."[78] "Every step in their economic and political position gained by women," urged Hale, "means a step away" from the stereotypes of femininity that dehumanized them and made them sexual objects. Every step constituted an "assertion that a woman has a human individuality apart from her sex functions."[79] The granting of women's suffrage, Louise Creighton argued, "by the recognition of their full citizenship . . . would inevitably . . . do away with the idea that women exist for the pleasure and the use of men" and was the key to the elimination of prostitution and venereal disease.[80] The "only cure" for "this canker of venereal disease," Christabel Pankhurst had stated in her "Great Scourge" articles, was "Votes for Women, which is to say the recognition of the freedom and human equality of women." Women's enfranchisement would teach men "that women are their human equals," she claimed, "and not the sub-human species men now think them, not slaves to be bought and soiled [sic] and degraded and then cast away."[81] Fawcett perceived the suffrage campaign as "a great human movement which was gradually . . . raising the position of women from absolute subjection to free citizenship." She recognized that the absolute subjection of women to men contained the notion that women's sexual functions were valued only insofar as they served the pleasure of men. After the vote was won in 1918, she noted with satisfaction that "the lives of women in childbirth were taken account of by Parliament in quite a different spirit directly women acquired the status of citizens."[82]

The vote also symbolized for women self-determination and choice. "It is, after all," wrote Hale, "a fragment of sovereignty."[83] Enfranchisement represented the right of women to determine for themselves their identity, their roles, their interests, and their actions. As Cicely Hamilton observed in 1912, the suffrage movement reflected women's "efforts to overthrow the barriers that have so far hemmed them in, to discover their own needs, strengths, weakness and purpose in life—to ascertain, in short, the essentials of their own identity."[84] The prime object of militancy, Teresa Billington-Greig agreed, consisted of "the assertion of the woman's right to be herself, the undermining of the customs, habits, and conventions, which . . . bar the way to the real emancipation of women."[85] In demanding the vote, women demanded that men "love women for what they are, not what it amuses men to think they are."[86] Civic personality constituted the first step in the individual woman's formation of personal identity, for the vote "is the symbol and medium of human will and human power shaping the circumstances and conditions of the outside human world," Emmeline Pethick Lawrence maintained.[87] "Through the vote," Christabel Pankhurst proclaimed, "women will gain a new confidence in themselves and a real power to help themselves."[88] It would enable them to develop a sense of dignity based on personal worth rather than on their relationship to men. "The outcome of enfranchisement will be to make women hate more than anything else in the world the very thought of selling themselves into slavery as under the conditions of the present day so many of them do sell themselves," she asserted.[89]

As a badge of civic personality, a symbol of women's humanity and equality with men, the vote had a powerful appeal. But suffragists also expected to use it pragmatically, to effect through their electoral power reforms that would raise the status of women, increase their welfare, and protect them from the destructive manifestations of male sexuality. Their ultimate goal was to bring about a profound transformation in the sexual culture of Britain, to create a society based upon reconstructions of masculinity and femininity and of male and female sexuality.

Feminists refused to accept the idea that male lust was an

inherent trait. "English women," asserted Meakin, "are at last refusing to believe that man was fashioned lower than the brute, that instincts have been given him by his Creator which he has not the power to control, which must therefore entail the ruin of a fellow-creature before they can be pacified. English women have a higher opinion of their Creator than this, and a higher opinion of His handiwork."[90] Drawing upon the works of female physicians such as Blackwell, Garrett Anderson, and Ker, they hoped to change societal stereotypes of male sexuality through the scientific education of the young. The Elmys published a sex education book, *The Human Flower*, in 1895. Maintaining that "at whatever age a reader is sufficiently interested to follow and try to understand what is here written, that age is a sufficient one for the contained information to be at his or her disposal," they presented in straightforward terms the facts of human sexual anatomy and reproduction. Their hope was that "from fuller knowledge will arise a truer purity; with general teaching and recognition of the natural facts relating to our own physiology shall come the worthier man, the happier woman." For women, knowledge would enable them to understand and assert control over their bodies; they would no longer be the "helpless dupes" of unscrupulous men or inconsiderate husbands. Proper sex education for men would help to ensure that "the voice of lower passion will be overcome by the higher pleadings of justice, while the youth will be no more deluded by false counsel and evil example into the ways of heartless or thoughtless wrong-doing."[91]

Perhaps the most far-reaching and profound goal of feminism was the creation of a positive paradigm of female sexuality. Victorian society offered only two extreme models of female sexuality, that of Mary or that of Eve. "They are not simply contradictory," Elizabeth Janeway has observed, "they have existed in a balanced polarity of good and bad, sacred and profane. In one the female symbolizes chastity; in the other she embodies insatiate, nymphomaniac greed." Janeway has also noted that these models are external to women's emotional reality, the construction of male minds in a male-dominated society, serving male needs. Therefore, "coming out of alien understanding as they do, they are never really satisfactory even when they seem to be accepted and absorbed quite thoroughly." Neither pure nor purely sexual, British feminists sought a paradigm of female sexuality that reflected "the interior emotional reality of the female self."[92] Its creation would both enhance and be enhanced by a larger female identity that did not rely on sex as its fundamental criteria. As Hamilton argued, "no natural ethical code emanating from within could have summed up woman's virtue in *a* virtue—physical purity. That confusion of one virtue with virtue in general was certainly of masculine origin arising from the masculine habit of thinking of woman only in connection with her relations to himself."[93]

Billington-Greig maintained that the Eve/Mary models dehumanized women and encouraged men and women alike in

acting as though [they] were merely sex. They called women "the sex" as though the race could be divided into feminine sex and masculine humanity. . . . To the man of one type she possessed all the virtues because she was a woman; to the man of the other she could possess no virtue but sex virtue and that was imposed upon her by inexorable pressures. But the point to mark is that from both sides her sex was emphasised and that both forces have been acting upon her for many generations.

As a result, she asserted, society produced two extremes of women as sex, neither of which fit the realities of the majority of women. "At the one extreme we have the narrow sexless and conventional prude, priding herself upon a purity that is merely sex anaemia; at the other we have the over-sexed woman in whom the imperative demands of sex are as insistent as in the man of the same type; in between we have that normal majority of women in whom despite theories of inferiority and bitter relations both sex and humanity are healthily balanced." If the relations of men and women were to be placed on better footing, the realities of this majority of women had to be acknowledged. Society must face up to the fact that "woman belonged to the same genus as man, that she was fully human, and human only, not an inferior animal or a superior angel but just a common human female."[94]

The first step, then, in constructing a positive female sexuality was a critique of the passionless, pure Mary. Marshalling their experience as a counter to ideology, some feminists asserted in the early twentieth century that sexual feeling and emotion were natural and beneficial, and that repression was harmful socially, emotionally, and physiologically. Restraint in sex matters, Billington-Greig warned women, if carried too far, "may sometimes cease to be a virtue and become a disease."[95] Maude Royden, a suffragist affiliated with the NUWSS and the Church League for Women's Suffrage, observed in 1917 that "the horrifying superstition . . . that 'physical' means degraded, or base or impure; that a woman, at least, should love without physical desire, and that a really refined and civilized woman should not only be indifferent to, but perhaps actually repelled by, the physical side of marriage . . . [has] had [its] disastrous consequences." It often imposed "an almost insurmountable barrier" between husband and wife and made sexual intercourse for women "something rather horrible." As for the woman who did have sexual feelings, "she has been burdened with a sense of guilt from which her nature forbade her escape . . . perpetually pretending, even to herself, a sexlessness she could not feel, and afraid to show herself a generous lover even to her husband . . . what a perpetual repression and deceit this meant for her!"[96] Women must be taught, Maud Braby declared in 1908, that sex is "the pivot on which the world turns . . . the instincts and emotions of sex are common to humanity, and in themselves not base or degrading, nor is there any cause for shame in possessing them." She called for educating young girls "to regard sex as a *natural* and *ordinary* fact. . . . Let us bring them up to think that loving wifehood, passionate motherhood are the proper expression of a woman's nature."[97]

Within even the youngest generation of feminists, however, differences of opinion about sexual issues often divided the women. "[T]here lingered even among the youngest suffragists some of the earlier prudery," wrote Meikle. "Even among them there were some who saw in sex nothing but degradation for women, who thought love disgusting and the most thoroughly married motherhood a fall from virtue."[98] She might have been describing Christabel Pankhurst, who, according to her mother, "would never be deflected from her purpose in life by her affections, as most women were apt to be."[99] Sheila Rowbotham and Jeffrey Weeks have maintained that Pankhurst "had no sympathy for a growing current in the feminist movement which was asserting active female sexuality and discussing demands which related to the biological situation of women as women."[100]

"Hotly opposed to these extremists of the right wing" represented by Christabel Pankhurst and her followers, Meikle found "the wild spirits of the extreme left. One met them in every suffragist league and union and society. . . . They flaunted their insurgency."[101] Surely the contributors to *The Freewoman* met this criteria, but so did more moderate women such as Billington-Greig, who, Sylvia Pankhurst related, "declaimed on the virtue of flouting Mrs. Grundy, and expiated with youthful excitement on the joys of her love affair with the worthy Scotsman, Greig, whom she presently married."[102] Billington-Greig belonged more properly to the third group of women discussed by Meikle, that majority of suffragists who made up the "Centre," "the women whose attitude toward sex was creating a new feminism. . . . They differed momentously from the older suffragists, inasmuch as while enormously interested in aspects of sex—biological, social and pathological—which had been hid [sic] from the sentimental Victorians, the adventurous young were neither greatly startled by those aspects nor greatly shocked."[103] While recognizing the beneficial service done by the "wild spirits" in decrying Victorian sexual mores and demanding sexual pleasure and sexual freedom for women, the moderates sought to temper their "extremism."

The Freewoman made its debut in November of 1911 but lasted only until the following May, when financial difficulties forced its demise. It reappeared in 1913 as *The New Freewoman* but could not sustain itself for long. Established by Dora Marsden and Mary Gawthorpe, both very active in the WSPU, the paper enjoyed only a rather small readership. Les Garner has discovered a subscription list of over 300 subscribers, though "the total number of readers clearly exceeded this."[104] Correspondence from and articles by Rebecca West, H. G. Wells, Edward Carpenter, Havelock Ellis, Billington-Greig, Stella Browne, and many others openly challenged contemporary morality as it pertained to marriage, sexuality, and reproduction. Contraception, sexual pleasure, lesbianism, and menstruation were freely discussed in its columns, provoking much displeasure among the leaders of the suffrage campaign. Millicent Garrett Fawcett found the paper "objectional [sic] and mischievous and tore it up into small pieces." Maude Royden called it "nauseous."[105] Even Olive Schreiner, whom we might expect to have been more sympathetic than her more conventional colleagues, found *The Freewoman* appalling, suggesting that it be renamed *The Licentious Male*. Writing to Ellis in 1912, she exclaimed, "Almost all the articles are by men and not by women. It's got the tone of the most licentious females or prostitutes. It's unclean, and sex is so beautiful."[106]

For in rejecting the model of Mary for female sexuality, most feminists were not advocating sexual freedom or sexual promiscuity as symbolized by Eve. Eve, Janeway has pointed out, "does not serve women, but patriarchy." The cultural depictions of Eve in the twentieth century present her not as a sexual being but as a sexual object. Media images of Eve "are intended to teach us how to behave in a 'sexy' new way not because that will be liberating or rewarding, or even just fun, but because with Mary gone, men are now free to forget about chastity."[107] Feminists of the 1970s and 1980s have slowly come to see that sexual liberation following a male model can involve a great deal of sexual exploitation; the first wave of feminists recognized this danger early.[108] Sexual liberation for women that did not also bring them economic, legal, and political autonomy was no liberation at all; coupled with the still general unavailability of effective contraceptives, it meant greater subjection. As Billington-Greig noted, those theorists of the "sexual liberty school" of her generation were blind to "the fact that very few women can yet achieve economic independence and therefore sexual liberty, and . . . the fact that in order to be as free sexually as man woman will have to avoid motherhood and therefore fight nature as well as society."[109]

Feminists such as Schreiner, Billington-Greig, Royden, and Elmy sought a middle ground for female sexuality, a paradigm that acknowledged sexuality in women but did not involve the obsession with women as sex. Male models of sexuality, Billington-Greig maintained, had imbued society with a "disproportionate exaggeration of sex in human affairs"; this sex-obsession would have to be eliminated before women could assert a sexual identity that served their interests and needs. She called for a "new movement to reduce sex to its natural proportions," a new creed for humanity, in which "sex is but a part," to replace that by which "all our other human qualities and powers have been too long sacrificed to sex."[110] Tolerance, rationality, sincerity, frank discussion, and "recognition of both sex and human needs"—specifically the absolute right of the woman to control intercourse and reproduction—formed the cornerstone of the new creed. With it, "the liberty of woman must come; and it will come without destroying love or the best form of the family or the permanent mating of lovers."[111]

The new sexual culture envisaged by feminists coupled the physical with the spiritual. It rejected the inexorability of male sex drives and men's "desire for mastery" in the sexual relationship, as Royden put it. It excoriated the "old idea that childbearing was 'what women were for' " and the notion of conjugal rights. It would educate men to an understanding "that love can never *take* what must always be *given*—or destroyed . . . [that] there must be equality in passion, or one is shamed." In the new sexual culture, Royden insisted, "the body is equally honoured with the spirit, and nothing but a love which embraces all is truly marriage."[112]

As all feminists held, it was the responsibility of women to raise the relationship between the sexes from one of subjection and mastery to one of equality. The new relationship was not based on the old idea of separate spheres, with its constructions of "masculine" and "feminine," but on a single sphere for men and women, in which the positive attributes of each sex were seen to pertain to both. "Feminism does not seek the extinction of strength and courage in men, nor of beauty and softness and tenderness in women, but the recognition that these . . . qualities are the heritage of men and women alike," wrote Ethel Snowdon.[113] Through the "emancipation and autonomy of woman," claimed the Elmys, the new sexual culture of "psychic" and "physical" love would replace forever that in which male values had ensured that women were "steeped in . . . grossness." In 1897, they published *Phases of Love*, in which they offered a description of their first sexual union as an example of what was to be with a reordering of society along egalitarian lines. Upon completion of their coupling,

> so knew we that it was now our deepest courtship—of soul by soul—[that had] had full initiation, and was entering upon higher existence and fruition. . . . And the first thought to cheer us was that though only after long and patient endeavour had we, or the few, few others, so far attained, yet would the path be increasingly easier, the bliss continually greater and more certain to a newer, truer generation; born and bred to the realisation of justice, equality, and sympathy between the sexes.[114]

EPILOGUE

You will wonder at passionate struggles that accomplished so little. . . . You will marvel at the labour
that ended in so little.

OLIVE SCHREINER, 1911

In the end, what matters is an attitude of mind.

WINIFRED HOLTBY, 1934

With the outbreak of World War I, the NUWSS, WFL, and
WSPU ceased all suffrage activity as their leaders devoted their
energies to the war effort. For all intents and purposes, "votes
for women" was dead for the duration of the war. In 1917, however, the government became concerned about the need to call
a new election, and on the basis of the old franchise the men of
the armed forces and those serving in related industries would
no longer be eligible to vote. (After 1884, men were qualified to
vote if they occupied a residence for twelve months prior to July
15 of an election year.) Various suggestions for the amelioration
of this injustice were advanced, but Parliament finally agreed on
the need for a new franchise. At this point, Millicent Garrett
Fawcett and the NUWSS stepped in, demanding that women also
be included. The timing was propitious. Steadfast opponents of
women's suffrage could not ignore the contribution made by
British women to the war effort and were inclined to reward
them for their service. Asquith himself announced his conversion to votes for women on just this basis. "It is true," he said,
"[that women] cannot fight in the sense of going out with rifles
and so forth, but . . . they have aided in the most effective way
in the prosecution of the war."[1]

Over a period of months, Fawcett negotiated with Cabinet

officials and M.P.s, and an agreement was reached. The 1918 Representation of the People Bill gave men the vote on the basis of residence of premises, a grant of universal manhood suffrage. It restricted the vote to those women who were householders or the wives of householders, and had attained the age of thirty, enfranchising some six million out of eleven million adult women. The age requirement served to ensure that women would not enjoy a majority over men; the acceptance of it by the NUWSS constituted an abandonment of the long-held principle of sex equality—votes for women on the same lines as it was or should be granted to men. Fawcett and other NUWSS leaders explained to their discontented Labour followers, most of whom would not be admitted to the franchise because they were under age, that they did not want to "risk their prospects for partial success by standing out for more."[2]

The NUWSS, known after 1919 as the National Union of Societies for Equal Citizenship (NUSEC), continued to pursue its earlier goal—"to obtain the parliamentary franchise for women on the same terms as it is or may be granted to men"—and enlarged its scope to include "all other such reforms, economic, legislative, and social, as are necessary to secure a real equality of liberties, status, and opportunities between men and women."[3] Many of its efforts paid off. The Eligibility of Women Act of 1918, which permitted women to stand for Parliament, passed unopposed. The same year, the Bastardy Laws of 1872 were amended, thus increasing from five to ten shillings a week the amount a father could be made to pay to support an illegitimate child. In 1919, the passage of the Sex Disqualification Removal Act gave women access to all branches of the legal profession. By 1925, despite the ferocious opposition of entrenched bureaucrats, the Civil Service admitted women to its competitive examinations, though it refused to pay female civil servants the salaries given to men holding the same position. The Matrimonial Causes Act of 1923, a direct outcome of intense feminist lobbying, eliminated the double standard of divorce. Officially adopting birth control as a fundamental right for women in 1925, NUSEC explicitly rejected the older notion of sex for procreation only. The organization called for the dissemination of contraceptive information at the maternity clinics, joining a host of other feminist and socialist (as well as eugenicist) associations. The Ministry of Health, in 1930, began to make such advice available. In 1928, after sixty-one years, women finally obtained the franchise on the same terms as it was granted to men.

Although organized feminism continued to lobby for and indeed obtain important changes in the legal, political, economic, and social position of women during the interwar period, it never achieved its prewar size or status as a mass movement. According to Ray Strachey and Winifred Holtby, writing in the 1930s, feminists found themselves on the defensive after 1918. "Modern young women know amazingly little of what life was like before the war," Strachey lamented, "and show a strong hostility to the word 'feminism' and all which they imagine it to connote."[4] "Why," asked Holtby in despair, "in 1934, are women themselves often the first to repudiate the movements of the past hundred and fifty years, which have gained for them at least the foundations of political, economic, educational and moral equality?"[5]

The answer is a complex one, and space permits only the barest outline. At least three factors contributed to the demise of feminism as a mass movement, with its ability to attract and hold the public's attention: the postwar economic situation and the threat of fascism, the rise of anti-feminism throughout Europe generally and in Britain in particular, and ideological and institutional division within the organized women's movement. Each was intricately bound up with the others.

The shortage of labor occasioned by the war enabled women to find employment in well-paying, traditionally male occupations in all sectors of the economy. With the armistice, however, women's new-found prosperity ended. As the soldiers were mustered out of the army, the women were dismissed from their jobs. "Everyone assumed, of course, that they would go back to their homes," Strachey explained, "and that everything could be as it had been before."[6] But the economic changes and demographic carnage wrought by world war made it imperative that women work if they were to survive, no matter their feelings on the subject. Society failed to grasp these facts, however, and turned on the women it supposed were maliciously denying to returning soldiers any means of livelihood. "The tone of the Press swung, all in a moment, from extravagant praise to the opposite extreme, and the very same people who had been heroines and the saviours of their country a few months before were now parasites, blacklegs, and limpets," wrote Strachey.[7] We saw in Chapter VI how the anti-feminist Kenealy threatened women with extinction if they did not give up their jobs; Brian Harrison has described how "unemployed Bristol ex-servicemen . . . smashed the windows of tramcars and attacked conductresses in 1920 to protest against women's employment on public services there."[8]

The pressure on women to return to their domestic sphere was intense, and if propaganda and government policy did not always succeed in their aims, they contributed to an ideological backlash against the victories women had secured before and during the war. "Every woman in industry," argued Lord Birkenhead in *Good Housekeeping* in 1928, "who, by underselling her labour, deprives a man of his post, is making more difficult the setting up of a home by that man. This prevents some other woman from becoming mistress of his home and from exercising the rights and privileges inseparable from that position."[9] This kind of persuasion was all too effective, reported Strachey, for women "made little protest, and let their gains slip from them, allowing the old rigid exclusions to be reimposed because they thought it was their duty."[10] The depression only exacerbated the immediate postwar employment problem for women while international political developments diverted time and energies away from the amelioration of women's grievances. In the face of some three million unemployed and the looming threat of fascism, even the most committed activist could hardly be expected to give priority to feminist goals. As Rowbotham has put it, "In the context of the hunger marches, Spain, and anti-fascism young women who inclined toward radicalism had more pressing political choices."[11]

The attempts to remove women from their wartime positions constituted only one aspect of "a wave of anti-feminism" that inundated Europe after 1918, from which Britain was by no means immune. Some form of "Kinder, Küche, Kirche" ideology found favor in almost every European country and was legitimated by psychoanalytic theory.[12] With the popularization of Freudian theories in the 1920s, separate sphere ideology based on constructions of masculinity and femininity received additional "scientific" justification. While undermining the belief in the sexlessness of the female, Freud and his followers reinforced the notion that anatomy is destiny, that biological factors determined the differences between masculinity and femininity and male and female sexuality. Freud argued that the personality development of the female centered upon her discovery in early childhood that she lacked a penis; penis envy created in the female child a lifelong dissatisfaction with her identity as a woman.[13] This dissatisfaction could only be overcome, Freud asserted, through the substitution of the penis with a child. Happiness and health for women, in other words, depended upon motherhood. As Erik Erikson stated in 1964, fulfillment for the mature woman rests on the "fact" that her "somatic design harbors an 'inner space' destined to bear the offspring of chosen men, and with it, a biological, psychological, and ethical commitment to take care of human infancy."[14] Twentieth-century politicians, no less than their nineteenth-century forebears, seized on these scientific "truths" as evidence that women politicians were "aberrant." Leo Abse, for example, suggested that "since anatomy is destiny . . . [aren't] many of our women politicians the little girls who refused to recognise the unwelcome fact that they lacked a penis and, defiantly rebellious, exaggerated their masculinity?"[15]

As much as psychoanalysis, perhaps, the fashion and cosmetic industries contributed mightily to an atmosphere that was antithetical to feminism in the twentieth century. As Holtby noted, "the psychology of clothes is not unimportant." She protested against "this powerful movement to reclothe the female form in swathing trails and frills and flounces, to emphasise the difference between men and women—to recall Woman, in short, to Her True Duty—of . . . the bearing of sons and recreation of the tired warrior."[16] Sylvia Pankhurst, too, lamented the widespread "reaction from the ideal of an intellectual and emancipated womanhood, for which the pioneers toiled and suffered, to be seen in painted lips and nails, and the return of trailing skirts and other absurdities of dress which betoken the slavewoman's sex appeal rather than the free-woman's intelligent companionship."[17]

The response of organized feminism to these attempts to reestablish separate spheres was ambiguous and reflected division within its ranks. While NUSEC campaigned against legislation that barred married women from many—chiefly professional—occupations, it embarked, under the leadership of Eleanor Rathbone, on a "new" feminist course. "New feminism" stressed the needs of mothers and sought reforms that would improve the position of women in the home and protect them in the workplace. As Rathbone explained it, the new direction meant that "at last we can stop looking at all our problems through men's eyes and discussing them in men's phraseology. We can demand what we want for women, not because it is what men have got but because it is what women need to fulfil the potentialities of their own natures and to adjust themselves to circumstances of their own lives."[18] Family allowances paid directly to women, protective legislation, and easy access to birth control appeared to Rathbone and her followers to be the most efficacious means of providing economic and sexual autonomy to women; to legitimate these demands, NUSEC emphasized the role of women at home. To women like Fawcett and the members of the Six Point Group and the Equal Rights Council, who espoused a strictly egalitarian line, such views were anathema, reminiscent of antifeminist arguments promulgated in the nineteenth and early twentieth centuries in order to deny women their equal rights. Fawcett and her supporters left NUSEC in 1926, and the women's movement split over the "new" feminist ideology, which indeed, as Vicinus has explained, "left women peculiarly vulnerable to the reassertion of traditional male-dominated political and economic structures."[19]

Moreover, as support for such reforms as birth control and family allowances became more widespread, the issues became much less distinctly feminist. The advocates of birth control had always relied on Malthusian arguments, and eugenicists soon superseded feminists in the movement for control over reproduction. Labour supported family allowances, as did conservatives, who viewed them as a way to build a strong race and turn back the German threat. During the interwar period, Banks has noted, feminists joined forces with many unlikely allies, and in the process their ideology "was swallowed up."[20] As Vicinus has observed,

> Rathbone's efforts highlight the classic dilemma of feminism: how to unite the need for equality of opportunity and equality before the law with the demand for legislation to overcome the socially determined inequalities of women. If women are the bearers of children and chiefly responsible for bringing them up, then—argued Rathbone to NUSEC—feminists must struggle to help change the laws to meet women's specific needs. For the egalitarians, this change seemed to imply the legal enshrinement of women in the home rather than doing everything to help them choose whether to stay there or to leave.[21]

Because, as Jane Lewis has argued, interwar feminists employed "the same analytic frameworks as anti-feminists," the goals and visions of prewar feminism—a wholly new system of relations between men and women—were undermined and then lost.[22]

BECAUSE feminists accepted the terms of liberal political discourse—that power lay in the vote—they directed the brunt of their attack on the centralized power of the state. Feminists gained access to state institutions, but they failed to gain control of the sexual discourse—particularly that sexual discourse articulated by the psychoanalytic profession—and thereby reconstruct the models of "masculinity" and "femininity." Feminists sought to achieve a sexual revolution, but as Millett has noted, "the arena of sexual revolution is within human consciousness even more pre-eminently than it is within human institutions." The suffrage campaign challenged both human consciousness and human institutions but succeeded only in the latter. Suffragists were unable to "penetrate deeply enough into the substructure of patriarchal ideology and socialization."[23]

The articulate leaders of the first wave of feminism insisted that their subordinate and inferior status, and their vulnerability to sexual abuse, rested upon constructions of masculinity and femininity and of male and female sexuality. While the movement comprised diverse, and sometimes discrete, campaigns for various concrete reforms, the common denominator of sexuality—the need to redefine sexual constructions—informed each effort. At bottom, the fundamental issue was that of the relations between the sexes.

So it remains today. Feminists of the second wave—operating from various ideological assumptions, disciplines, and organizations such as Marxism, psychoanalysis, or the National Organization for Women—seek profound and fundamental change in the relations between the sexes. The feminist movement of the late twentieth century is nothing if not diverse, factionalized, and often acrimonious. Some groups seek changes in law, some in socialization practices; others posit the need for a complete reordering of capitalist society. All, however, recognize, at least tacitly, that the oppression of women rests upon the sexual constructions of masculinity and femininity. The rallying cry of the 1970s, "the personal is political," derives from a feminist claim that sexuality, or the sexual politic, forms the core of their secondary status. The great majority of feminist reforming efforts center on sexual issues: rape, pornography, sexual harrassment, sexual preference, and birth control and abortion. The key to women's autonomy, liberation, and power lies in the redefinition and reconstruction of sexuality, upon which notions of masculinity and femininity are based. Success may depend, therefore, on the degree to which feminists gain access to the normalizing, controlling agents that exercise power through the sexual discourse.

For this reason, psychoanalytic theory has received intense scrutiny and challenge by feminists of late. Again, diversity among women in the psychological and psychoanalytic professions is the rule, but the common denominator of sexuality informs their work.

Juliet Mitchell, for instance, has suggested that patriarchal ideology and socialization, or the cultural identifications of masculinity and femininity and of male and female sexuality, are located in unconscious psychic experience, specifically in the resolution by boys and girls of the Oedipal conflict. Her analysis rests upon her assertion that although the situation of women may vary by culture, the oppression of women in patriarchal society is universal and independent of specific political institutions or even social arrangements. Neither trivial nor historically transitory, she has argued, the oppression of women has been so effectively maintained because "it courses through the mental and emotional bloodstream."[24]

According to Freud, the human male or female, in the pre-Oedipal stage, possesses a "bisexual" or androgynous psychological disposition. With the resolution of the Oedipal conflict, the

human becomes, Mitchell has noted, "the sexed social creature—the man or the woman." She has argued that Freud perceived the Oedipus complex to be the psychoanalytic analog to
the origins of human (patriarchal) culture—the establishment of
kinship structures based on totemism and exogamy, or the role
of the father and the exchange of women. Mitchell has asserted
that "understanding the laws of the unconscious thus amounts
to a start in understanding how ideology functions, how we ac-
quire and live the ideas and laws within which we must exist."[25]

With the resolution of the Oedipal conflict, the boy, having
accepted symbolic castration from his father, identifies with the
father and internalizes the law of the father, or patriarchy. The
girl resolves her Oedipal conflict when she is "seduced/raped
by, and/or seduces the father" and "learns her feminine destiny
with this symbolic seduction." Unable to internalize the law of
the father, she must identify with the mother. As Mitchell has
analyzed the process,

> instead of taking on qualities of aggression and control [the
> girl] acquires the art of love and conciliation. Not being
> heir to the law of culture, her task is to see that mankind
> reproduces itself within the circularity of the supposedly
> natural family. The family is, of course, no more "natural"
> than the woman, but its place within the law is to take on
> "natural" functions. For sexuality, which supposedly unites
> the couple, disrupts the kingdom if uncontrolled; it, too,
> must be contained and organized. Woman becomes, in her
> nineteenth-century designation, "the sex." Hers is the
> sphere of reproduction.[26]

Mitchell, and the French feminists of "*politique et psychana-
lyse*" by whom she has been so influenced, see in the unconscious a fertile ground for the resocialization of men and
women, the reconstructions of masculinity and femininity. The
analysis of the Oedipal complex in Mitchell's *Psychoanalysis and
Feminism*, however, implies that, because the individual learns

society's laws and ideas by recapitulating during the Oedipal stage the primal creation of human society, there is no possibility of learning new laws and ideas. What different original event in human history could be relived through Oedipal resolution? More directly, the challenges to patriarchy made by the feminists presented in this study offer historical evidence that undermines Mitchell's contentions and point up the dangers of a transhistorical analysis of individual identity formation.

Other feminist theorists—utilizing the tools, though not necessarily the theories, of analysis made available by Freud—have contributed a great deal to the challenge to patriarchy's ideological underpinnings. Emphasizing external factors over those of inner, mental processes in the development of sexuality, Nancy Chodorow and Dorothy Dinnerstein, for instance, have argued that adult personalities are warped by the intense involvement between mother and child in the early years of childhood development and have called for the involvement of both mother and father in the raising of children.[27] Carol Gilligan's most recent work has asserted that the exclusion of women's experiences from models of human development has resulted in "a limitation in the conception of human condition, an omission of certain truths about life."[28] These women challenge the dominant discourse by affirming the positive aspects of feminine values, but they nonetheless tend to accept sex-role stereotyping, if not an essentialist notion of femininity.

The experience of the feminists of the first wave holds a valuable lesson for people today who seek to eliminate the subjection and oppression of women. The suffragists' attack on power located in one place—in patriarchal institutions and laws—helped to reorder and recast society along more egalitarian lines. But effective, fundamental societal change depends upon alterations of human attitudes, beliefs, and consciousness. The reconstruction of notions of masculinity and femininity requires a strategy of multifaceted attacks on multiple sources of power. The broader the attack, the more likely an effective challenge to patriarchy and the greater the chance of reconstructing masculine and feminine stereotypes. The fragmentation of the second wave of feminism, then, should not be perceived as a negative development but as a positive one. Diversity and a willingness to challenge sexual stereotypes in a wide variety of areas offer the best chance of achieving autonomy and freedom for women.

NOTES

INTRODUCTION

1. Patricia Stubbs, *Women and Fiction: Feminism and the Novel, 1880-1920* (London, 1981), p. 126.
2. See Olive Banks, *Faces of Feminism: A Study of Feminism as a Social Movement* (New York, 1981); Les Garner, *Stepping Stones to Women's Liberty. Feminist Ideas in the Women's Suffrage Movement, 1900-1918* (Rutherford, NJ, 1984); and Brian Harrison, *Separate Spheres: The Opposition to Women's Suffrage in Britain* (London, 1978), although Harrison refers, in his conclusion, to suffragists as "purely political activists" (p. 238).
3. Richard Evans, *The Feminists: Women's Emancipation Movements in Europe, America and Australasia, 1840-1920* (London, 1977), p. 39 n. 1, pp. 66-67.
4. Ibid., p. 23.
5. Ibid., pp. 29-30.
6. Roger Fulford, *Votes for Women, The Story of a Struggle* (London, 1957), p. 289.
7. Andrew Rosen, *Rise Up, Women! The Militant Campaign of the Women's Social and Political Union, 1903-1914* (London, 1974), p. 203.
8. Ibid. "[T]he markedly dominant/submissive character of [Pankhurst's] relationships with Mrs. Tuke and Annie Kenney certainly seems to resemble the psychology of many Lesbian relationships" (p. 209). Leaving aside Rosen's fatuous notion of lesbian relationships, it is disturbing to find historians raising the specter of lesbianism for early feminists as a way to dismiss or disguise the radical nature of feminism. Veterans of the second wave will not be surprised to discover that charges of lesbianism plagued the early feminist movement,

usually leveled at women who were described as "unsexed" or "viragoes."

9. Ibid., pp. 210-211.

10. Ibid., p. 205.

11. O. R. McGregor, *Divorce in England* (London, 1957), p. 92.

12. Rosen, in fact, insisted that Pankhurst gave no source for her statistics, failing to mention that in articles subsequent to the one he quoted, she cited the medical men from whom she had gathered her data. Rosen, *Rise Up, Women*, p. 205.

13. I am indebted to Joan Scott for this and countless other valuable insights in the course of our communication.

14. David Mitchell, *Queen Christabel: A Biography of Christabel Pankhurst* (London, 1977), p. 160. See also Elizabeth Sarah, "Christabel Pankhurst: Reclaiming Her Power," in *Feminist Theorists, Three Centuries of Key Women Thinkers*, ed. Dale Spender (New York, 1983), p. 259.

15. George Dangerfield, *The Strange Death of Liberal England, 1910-1914* (New York, 1961), p. 149.

16. William O'Neill, *The Woman Movement* (London, 1969), p. 38.

17. Judith Walkowitz, *Prostitution and Victorian Society, Women, Class, and the State* (Cambridge, 1980).

18. Ibid., p. 255.

19. Ibid. for this and the previous quotation.

20. Ibid., pp. 5-6.

21. Emilie Venturi to Henry Wilson, 10 December 1872. Josephine Butler Collection, Fawcett Library, London.

22. Walkowitz, *Prostitution*, p. 133.

23. Millicent Garrett Fawcett, *Josephine Butler* (London, 1927), p. 29.

24. Josephine Butler, *Personal Reminiscences of a Great Crusade* (London, 1898), p. 44. "[T]he fact that this new legislation *directly* and shamefully attacked the dignities and liberties of women . . . consolidated the women of our country, and gradually of the world, by the infliction on them of a double

wrong, an outrage on free citizenship, and an outrage on the sacred rights of womanhood" (p. 42).

25. Quoted in Glen Petrie, *A Singular Iniquity: The Campaigns of Josephine Butler* (London, 1971), pp. 19-20.

26. Ibid.

27. Josephine Butler, *An Autobiographical Memoir*, ed. G. W. Johnson and Lucy A. Johnson (London, 1928), pp. 93-94.

28. See Constance Rover, *Love, Morals and the Feminists* (London, 1970), p. 55.

29. Josephine Butler to Maria Grey, 9 June 1871. Butler Collection.

30. Ray Strachey, *Millicent Garrett Fawcett* (London, 1931), p. 52.

31. Fawcett, *Butler*, p. 105.

32. Frances Swiney, *The Awakening of Women*, 3d ed. (London, 1908), p. 92.

33. Ethel Colquhoun, "Modern Feminism and Sex-Antagonism," *Quarterly Review* 219 (1913): 156-157.

34. H. M. Swanwick, *I Have Been Young* (London, 1935), pp. 83-84.

35. Ibid., p. 82.

36. Cicely Hamilton, *Life Errant* (London, 1935), p. 282.

37. Teresa Billington-Greig, manuscript notes for an autobiography. Teresa Billington-Greig Collection, Fawcett Library, London.

38. Ibid.

39. Beatrice Forbes-Robinson Hale, *What Women Want* (New York, 1914), p. 19.

40. Ethel Snowdon, *The Feminist Movement* (London, n.d.), p. 15.

41. Ibid., pp. 16-17. Zoë Fairfield insisted that the "Women's Movement derives its passion and gathers its momentum from the fact that it . . . touches the fundamental things of life, the forces which carry on the race." Zoë Fairfield, *The Woman's Movement* (London, 1914), p. 12. An April 1910 editorial in

Common Cause spoke plainly to the issue of women's fundamental demand for personhood outside of sexual considerations. "Her sex," asserted the writer, perhaps Swanwick, "is
the ground of her disability . . . all the questions of women's
economic, legal and political subjection, the future of the
race, the hope of humanity, are involved in the question
whether the rival trades of prostitution and of marriage are
those alone which shall be open to women. According to this
view, men can do anything they *can* do; women are to exist
merely for the propagation of the race and for the enjoyment
of man. . . . So long as women are in the degrading stultifying
servitude of sex, you cannot work for their liberation if you
never name their sex and all it implies." *Common Cause*, 14
April 1910, p. 3.

42. Butler, *Autobiographical Memoir*, pp. 75-76.
43. Josephine Butler to Miss Priestman, 1873. Butler Collection.
44. Josephine Butler, *An Address Delivered at Croyden, July 3,
1871* (Manchester, 1871), p. 12.
45. Fawcett, *Butler*, p. 6.
46. Millicent Garrett Fawcett, *The Women's Victory—and After:
Personal Reminiscences, 1911-1918* (London, 1920), p. 72.
47. See Strachey, *Fawcett*, p. 121.
48. *Common Cause*, quoting Butler, highlighted the importance
of women's sense of sexual abuse to the suffrage campaign.
"[A]t the bottom of that desire [for the vote]," it proclaimed,
"underneath many other good motives, there lies a bitterness
of woe which is the most powerful stimulus towards the desire for representation in the legislature." *Common Cause*, 19
May 1910, p. 82.
49. Elizabeth Wolstenholme Elmy to Harriet McIlquham, 21
May 1897. Elizabeth Wolstenholme Elmy Collection, British
Library, London.
50. Michel Foucault, *The History of Sexuality*, Volume 1: *An Introduction* (New York, 1980), pp. 22, 30, 33, 18.
51. Ibid., pp. 41, 47.

52. Ibid., pp. 68, 103, 104. My use of the (non)word "hysteri-zation" is taken from the translation of Foucault's book.

53. Ibid., p. 123.

54. Ibid., p. 103.

55. See Jill Liddington and Jill Norris, *One Hand Tied Behind Us: The Rise of the Women's Suffrage Movement* (London, 1978), passim.

56. E. Sylvia Pankhurst, *The Suffragette Movement* (London, 1977), p. 26. "As to the child, he grew up puny and frail and lacking in initiative. His want of vigour is not surprising. Al-ways poor, always working for a living, and always giving to the Causes she had at heart a wealth of unpaid service, unable to employ household aid, or aid in attending to her child, could it be otherwise? Undoubtedly he was stunted from his birth, by solitude and by lack of material things, knowing only the care of that work-driven mother, who was here, there and everywhere upon her mission, and whose tiny hand daily cov-ered a multitude of closely-written sheets on the all-important questions of women's emancipation. She was an instrument in the grasp of Progress; he was a victim of her time and work."

57. Wilma Meikle, *Towards a Sane Feminism* (London, 1916), pp. 82, 83.

58. See Anne Crawford, Tony Hayter, Ann Hughes et al., *The Europa Biographical Dictionary of British Women* (Detroit, 1983), p. 175.

59. Swanwick, *I Have Been Young*, p. 228.

60. See Joan Lock, *The British Policewoman: Her Story* (London, 1979).

61. A. Maude Royden, *A Threefold Cord* (London, 1948).

62. Meikle, *Sane Feminism*, pp. 86-87.

CHAPTER I: "THE SEX"

1. See J. A. Banks and Olive Banks, *Feminism and Family Plan-ning in Victorian England* (Liverpool, 1964), passim.

2. Mary Lyndon Shanley, "Marriage Contract and Social Contract in Seventeenth-Century English Political Thought," *Western Political Quarterly* 32 (1979): 79.

3. Randolph Trumbach, *The Rise of the Egalitarian Family: Aristocratic Kinship and Domestic Relations in Eighteenth-Century England* (New York, 1978), p. 3. See also Lawrence Stone, *The Family, Sex and Marriage in England, 1500-1800* (New York, 1977), passim.

4. Stone, *Family, Sex and Marriage*, Chapter 8.

5. Quoted in Trumbach, *Egalitarian Family*, p. 153.

6. See ibid., pp. 154-155.

7. Quoted in Ray Strachey, *The Cause: A Short History of the Women's Movement in Britain* (Rpt., London, 1978), p. 15.

8. See ibid., p. 15. See also Patricia Branca, *Women in Europe since 1750* (New York, 1978), pp. 160-164.

9. See O'Neill, *Woman Movement*, p. 40.

10. Quoted in Jane Lewis, *Women in England, 1870-1950: Sexual Divisions and Social Change* (Bloomington, 1984), p. 120.

11. See McGregor, *Divorce*, pp. 17-18.

12. Keith Thomas, "The Double Standard," *Journal of the History of Ideas* 20 (1959): 210.

13. See Branca, *Women in Europe*, p. 170.

14. Trumbach, *Egalitarian Family*, p. 4.

15. This chapter is informed by the definition of gender proposed by Joan W. Scott in her unpublished paper read before the meetings of the American Historical Association, December 27, 1985, titled "Is Gender a Useful Category of Historical Analysis?" "Gender is a process of constituting social relationships based on perceived differences between the sexes. Gender is a primary way of conceptualizing relationships of power" (pp. 24-25).

16. L. J. Jordanova, "Natural Facts: A Historical Perspective on Science and Sexuality," in *Nature, Culture and Gender*, ed. Carol MacCormack and Marilyn Strathern (Cambridge, 1980), p. 43.

17. Quoted in Banks and Banks, *Feminism and Family Planning*, p. 59.

18. Ibid.

19. Ibid., p. 58.

20. Ibid., p. 22. Another moralist, Mrs. S. A. Sewell, argued that "it is the man's place to rule, and a woman's to yield. He must be held up as the head of the house, and it is her duty to bend so unmurmuringly to his wishes, that the rest of the household will follow her example, and treat him with the due respect his sex demands." Ibid., p. 60.

21. See Jill Conway, "Stereotypes of Femininity in a Theory of Sexual Evolution," in *Suffer and Be Still: Women in the Victorian Age*, ed. Martha Vicinus (Bloomington, 1972), pp. 140, 141.

22. Quoted in ibid., p. 146.

23. Ibid., p. 147.

24. Nancy Cott, "Passionlessness: An Interpretation of Victorian Sexual Ideology, 1790-1850," *Signs* 4 (1979): 220, 221.

25. Ibid., pp. 222-223.

26. Ibid., pp. 223, 224.

27. Ibid., pp. 227-228.

28. Ibid., p. 233.

29. Quoted in John Haller and Robin Haller, *The Physician and Sexuality in Victorian America* (New York, 1977), pp. 98, 97.

30. Foucault, *History of Sexuality*, p. 139.

31. Quoted in Jean L'Esperance, "Doctors and Women in Nineteenth-Century Society: Sexuality and Role," in *Health Care and Popular Medicine in Nineteenth-Century England*, ed. John Woodward and David Richards (New York, 1977), pp. 111, 112.

32. Ibid., p. 114.

33. Quoted in Jeffrey Weeks, *Sex, Politics and Society: The Regulation of Sexuality Since 1800* (London, 1981), p. 147.

34. Mary Douglas, *Purity and Danger, An Analysis of Concepts of Pollution and Taboo* (New York, 1966), p. 2.

35. Carroll Smith-Rosenberg, "Sex as Symbol in Victorian Prudery," in *Turning Points: Historical and Sociological Essays on the Family*, ed. John Demos and Sarane Spence Boocock. A Supplement of the *American Journal of Sociology* 84 (1978): 230.
36. Ibid., p. 229.
37. Douglas, *Purity and Danger*, p. 4.
38. See Olivia Harris, "The Power of Signs: Gender, Culture and the Wild in the Bolivian Andes," in *Nature, Culture and Gender*, ed. MacCormack and Strathern, p. 77.
39. Douglas, *Purity and Danger*, p. 36.
40. Ibid., p. 158.
41. Cott, "Passionlessness," p. 235.
42. See Floyd Bryan Strong, *Sex, Character, and Reform in America, 1830-1920* (Ann Arbor, 1972), p. 18.
43. Quoted in Lewis, *Women in England*, p. 84.
44. Quoted in G. J. Barker-Benfield, "The Spermatic Economy: A Nineteenth-Century View of Sexuality," in *The American Family in Social-Historical Perspective*, ed. Michael Gordon, 2d ed. (New York, 1978), p. 383. As Barker-Benfield has noted, "the paradox of confining a woman's identity to the distinction of her sexual organs while at the same time claiming she was sexless should be apparent. Sexless woman was a sexual definition. Men's fantastic and unappeasable demands that women not be what they were rested on what they could not avoid perceiving women to be" (ibid.).
45. See W. O. Priestly and Horatio R. Storer, eds., *The Obstetric Memoirs and Contributions of James Y. Simpson, M. D., F.R.S.E.* (Philadelphia, 1855). I owe this insight to Barker-Benfield in a personal communication.
46. Quoted in Elaine Showalter, "Victorian Women and Insanity," in *Madhouses, Mad-Doctors, and Madmen, The Social History of Psychiatry in the Victorian Era*, ed. Andrew Scull (Philadelphia, 1981), p. 323.
47. Quoted in Barker-Benfield, "Spermatic Economy," p. 383.

48. Quoted in Showalter, "Victorian Women," p. 327.

49. Quoted in Barker-Benfield, "Spermatic Economy," p. 383.

50. Henry Maudsley, "Sex in Mind and Education," *Fortnightly Review* 15 (1874): 466.

51. Ibid., pp. 467, 468, 477.

52. Ibid., p. 473.

53. See Lorna Duffin, "The Conspicuous Consumptive: Woman as Invalid," in *The Nineteenth-Century Woman: Her Cultural and Physical World*, ed. Sara Delamont and Lorna Duffin (London, 1978), p. 35.

54. Quoted in Showalter, "Victorian Women," p. 323.

55. Quoted in Weeks, *Sex, Politics and Society*, pp. 147, 146.

56. Sherry Ortner, "Is Female to Male as Nature is to Culture?" in *Woman, Culture, and Society*, ed. Michelle Rosaldo and Louise Lamphere (Stanford, 1978), pp. 72, 73.

57. Ibid., pp. 73-74, 87.

58. Jordanova, "Natural Facts," pp. 44, 67, 44-45, 49, 59.

59. Barker-Benfield, "Spermatic Economy," p. 385.

60. Isaac Baker Brown, *On the Curability of Certain Forms of Insanity, Epilepsy, and Hysteria in Females* (1866), quoted in Janet Murray, *Strong-Minded Women and Other Lost Voices from Nineteenth-Century England* (New York, 1982), pp. 130-131.

61. See Duffin, "The Conspicuous Consumptive," p. 42.

62. See Weeks, *Sex, Politics and Society*, p. 54 n. 27. Clitoridectomies were discontinued not because they were deemed to be ineffective but because the publicity surrounding the Baker Brown case cast so negative a light on the medical profession. See Chapter IV.

63. See Duffin, "The Conspicuous Consumptive," p. 42.

64. See Barker-Benfield, "Spermatic Economy," pp. 387, 389, 389-390, for the preceding quotations.

65. Quoted in Showalter, "Victorian Women," p. 327.

66. Simone de Beauvoir, *The Second Sex* (New York, 1953), p. 239.

67. See Gillian Gillison, "Images of Nature in Gini Thought," in *Nature, Culture and Gender*, ed. MacCormack and Strathern, p. 143.
68. Ortner, "Female to Male," p. 73.
69. Smith-Rosenberg, "Sex as Symbol," p. 230.
70. Jordanova, "Natural Facts," pp. 45, 66.
71. See Lewis, *Women in England*, pp. 76, 77.
72. Ibid., pp. 78, 125-126, 79, 78-79.
73. See Weeks, *Sex, Politics and Society*, pp. 42, 91, 92, 141.
74. Quoted in ibid., p. 147.
75. Lillian Faderman, *Surpassing the Love of Men: Romantic Friendships and Love Between Women from the Renaissance to the Present* (New York, 1981), p. 16.
76. Ibid., p. 154.
77. Eliza Lynn Linton, *The Rebel of the Family*, 3 vols. (London, 1880), vol. 1, p. 74; vol. 2, pp. 48, 50-51.
78. Vineta Colby, *The Singular Anomaly, Women Novelists of the Nineteenth Century* (New York, 1970), p. 20.
79. Faderman, *Surpassing the Love of Men*, pp. 176-177.
80. See ibid., pp. 241, 238, 242, for the quotations of Westphal, Krafft-Ebing, and Ellis.
81. Quoted in Constance Rover, *Women's Suffrage and Party Politics in Britain, 1866-1914* (London, 1967), p. 43.
82. Ibid., p. 39.
83. Jordanova, "Natural Facts," pp. 66, 66-67.
84. See Rover, *Women's Suffrage*, pp. 43, 51-52, 120, for the preceding quotations.
85. Ibid., p. 38.
86. *Common Cause*, 14 April 1910, p. 3.
87. Frederic Harrison, *Votes for Women* (London, 1909), p. 1.
88. Quoted in Rover, *Women's Suffrage*, p. 52.
89. Quoted in ibid.
90. Quoted in Walkowitz, *Prostitution*, p. 88.
91. Frederic Harrison, *Votes for Women*, p. 7.
92. Olive Banks, *Faces of Feminism*, p. 86.

93. Lewis, *Women in England*, pp. 88-89.
94. Quoted in Garner, *Stepping Stones*, p. 27.
95. Olive Banks, *Faces of Feminism*, p. 90.

Chapter II: Prostitution

1. I do not mean to imply that women's behavior conformed in every case to prescribed norms, or that a monolithic sexual culture existed in Britain. Carl Degler has argued that for middle-class American women at the turn of the century, what ought to be was not always what was. Carl Degler, "What Ought to Be and What Was: Women's Sexuality in the Nineteenth Century," *American Historical Review* 79 (1974): 1467-1490. Walkowitz has found that the actual behavior and patterns of working-class women and prostitutes in England bore no resemblance to the scenarios conjured up by respectable members of society. Walkowitz, *Prostitution*, passim. It is difficult to distinguish between prescribed norms and actual behavior in any culture, but we might fairly say that prescribed norms often constitute the boundaries within which women, in particular, are free to operate without incurring the wrath or disdain of society.

2. William Acton, *Functions and Disorders of the Reproductive Organs* (1857), quoted in Erna Hellerstein, Leslie Parker Hume, and Karen Offen, eds., *Victorian Women* (Stanford, 1981), p. 178.

3. Ibid., p. 179.

4. See Walkowitz, *Prostitution*, pp. 43, 42, 45.

5. See Vern Bullough and Bonnie Bullough, *Sin, Sickness, and Sanity, A History of Sexual Attitudes* (New York, 1977), pp. 136-137.

6. Quoted in Strong, *Sex, Character, and Reform*, p. 89.

7. McGregor, *Divorce*, p. 73. Governmental attempts to suppress the dissemination of birth-control literature in the 1870s, Walkowitz has noted, when juxtaposed against the passage of the

Contagious Diseases Acts, demonstrates that "it was more respectable to uphold the necessity of prostitution than to advocate" family planning. Walkowitz, *Prostitution*, p. 43.

8. Quoted in Edward Bristow, *Vice and Vigilance* (Dublin, 1977), p. 98.

9. Catherine Gasquoine Hartley, *The Truth About Woman* (London, 1913), p. 341.

10. Banks and Banks, *Feminism and Family Planning*, p. 108.

11. Butler, *Autobiographical Memoir*, p. 23.

12. Snowdon, *Feminist Movement*, p. 253.

13. See Bristow, *Vice and Vigilance*, p. 78.

14. Walkowitz, *Prostitution*, p. 70.

15. Gordon Rattray Taylor, *Sex in History* (New York, 1954), p. 219.

16. See Strong, *Sex, Character and Reform*, p. 54.

17. See Walkowitz, *Prostitution*, p. 3.

18. Quoted in ibid., p. 81.

19. Butler, *Personal Reminiscences*, p. 42.

20. Olive Schreiner, *Woman and Labour* (London, 1978), pp. 191, 194-195.

21. Barbara Taylor, *Eve and the New Jerusalem, Socialism and Feminism in the Nineteenth Century* (New York, 1983), p. 31.

22. Quoted in Walkowitz, *Prostitution*, pp. 6, 141.

23. *Shield*, 13 July 1872, p. 1003.

24. "Report from the Royal Commission on the Administration and Operation of the Contagious Diseases Acts 1866-9 (1871)," *Parliamentary Papers*, 1871 (C.408-I), XIX, p. 447.

25. Mary Taylor, *The First Duty of Women* (London, 1870), passim.

26. Lady K. Amberley, "The Claims of Women," *Fortnightly Review* 9 (January 1871): 99.

27. Mary Hume-Rothery, *A Letter Addressed to the Right Hon. W. E. Gladstone, M.P.* (Manchester, 1870), p. 8.

28. Josephine Butler, *Sursum Corda* (Liverpool, 1871), p. 33.

29. Josephine Butler, *Speech Delivered by Mrs. Josephine Butler*

at the Fourth Annual Meeting of the Vigilance Association for the Defense of Personal Rights, October 15, 1871 (London, n.d.), p. 8.

30. Swiney, *Awakening*, p. 170.

31. O'Neill, *Woman Movement*, p. 40.

32. Walkowitz, *Prostitution*, p. 128.

33. See O'Neill, *Woman Movement*, p. 40.

34. Hume-Rothery, *Letter*, p. 18.

35. Josephine Butler, *A Letter on the Subject of Mr. Bruce's Bill Addressed to the Repealers of the Contagious Diseases Acts* (Liverpool, 1872), p. 16.

36. Butler, *Sursum Corda*, p. 33.

37. Elizabeth Blackwell, *Opening the Medical Profession to Women* (New York, 1977), p. 242. Elizabeth Blackwell, *Essays in Medical Sociology*, 2 vols. (London, 1902), vol. 1, pp. 171-172.

38. Blackwell, *Essays*, vol. 1, p. 167.

39. See Josephine Butler to the *Shield*, n.d. Butler Collection.

40. Josephine Butler, *The Demand for Moral Members of Parliament* (London, n.d.), p. 2.

41. Josephine Butler to Harriet Meuricoffre, n.d., probably 1872. Butler Collection.

42. Quoted in "Report from the Royal Commission," pp. 440, 439, 443.

43. Butler, *Sursum Corda*, p. 36.

44. Josephine Butler to Henry Wilson, 23 December 1872. Butler Collection. Butler later remarked, "It seems strange that I should have been engaged in taking up the cudgel against men when my father, brother, husband and sons have all been so good." Quoted in Walkowitz, *Prostitution*, p. 121.

45. Quoted in Petrie, *Iniquity*, p. 134.

46. Ibid., p. 139.

47. See Chapters III and IV.

48. Josephine Butler, *Speech to Leister Hall, Dublin, 1878* (Liverpool, 1878), p. 4.

49. Butler, *Croyden*, pp. 10-11.

50. Josephine Butler, "Letter to an M.P.," February 1883. Butler Collection.

51. Annette Meakin, *Woman in Transition* (London, 1907), p. 70.

52. Hale, *What Women Want*, p. 89.

53. Fairfield, *Woman's Movement*, pp. 14-15.

54. Josephine Butler, "Letter to an M.P.," February 1883. Butler Collection.

55. Butler, *Autobiographical Memoir*, p. 105.

56. Ibid., p. 215.

57. Ladies' National Association for the Repeal of the Contagious Diseases Acts, *Twelfth Annual Report, 1881*, p. 1.

58. Butler, *Leister Hall*, p. 2.

59. Josephine Butler, *The New Era* (Liverpool, 1872), pp. 51-52.

60. Quoted in Bristow, *Vice and Vigilance*, p. 83.

61. Butler, *New Era*, pp. 53, 52-53.

62. Ibid., p. 54.

63. Josephine Butler, *A Few Words Addressed to True-Hearted Women* (Liverpool, 1872), p. 4.

64. Swiney, *Awakening*, pp. 175-176.

65. Walkowitz, *Prostitution*, p. 128.

66. See Ladies' National Association, *Eighth Annual Report 1877*, pp. 26, 27-28, for the following quotations.

67. *Shield*, 21 March 1870, p. 18.

68. Mrs. Ormiston Chant, *Speech of Mrs. Ormiston Chant, at the Annual Meeting of the Ladies' National Association* (1886), p. 1.

69. An English Lady, *Letter to My Countrywomen* (Manchester, 1871), p. 1.

70. Butler, *Vigilance Association*, p. 6.

71. Josephine Butler, *An Appeal to the People of England on the Recognition and Superintendance* [sic] *of Prostitution by Government*, 2d ed. (1870), p. 18.

72. Ibid., p. 4.

73. Quoted in Petrie, *Iniquity*, pp. 140-141.

Chapter III: Marriage

1. W. L. Burn, *The Age of Equipoise, A Study of the Mid-Victorian Generation* (New York, 1965), p. 37.
2. Mary Scharlieb, *What It Means to Marry* (London, 1914), p. 34.
3. Ibid., p. 33.
4. Daniel Defoe, *Complete English Tradesman* (1726), quoted in Barbara Taylor, *Eve*, p. 34.
5. Burn, *Equipoise*, p. 37.
6. See Harry Quilter, ed., *Is Marriage a Failure?* (London, 1888), passim.
7. Burn, *Equipoise*, p. 37.
8. See Banks and Banks, *Feminism and Family Planning*, p. 38; even Lewis, *Women in England*.
9. Elizabeth Garrett to Millicent Garrett, 25 December 1870. Elizabeth Garrett Collection, Fawcett Library, London.
10. See Dale Spender, *Women of Ideas and What Men Have Done to Them* (London, 1982), pp. 438, 431.
11. Sylvia Pankhurst, *Suffragette Movement*, p. 31.
12. Quoted in Banks and Banks, *Feminism and Family Planning*, pp. 103-104.
13. Quoted in ibid., pp. 111-112.
14. A. R. Cunningham, "The 'New Woman Fiction' of the 1890's," *Victorian Studies* 17 (December 1973): 178.
15. Ibid.
16. Ibid., p. 180.
17. Sarah Grand, *Ideala, A Study From Life* (London, 1888).
18. See Cunningham, "New Woman Fiction," pp. 181, 180.
19. Mona Caird, *The Morality of Marriage and Other Essays on the Status and Destiny of Woman* (London, 1897), pp. 67, 54.
20. Teresa Billington-Greig, manuscript notes. Billington-Greig Collection.
21. See Chapter VII.
22. See Jean Elshtain, "Feminist Discourse and Its Discontents:

Language, Power, and Meaning," in *Feminist Theory, A Critique of Ideology*, ed. Nannerl Keohane, Michelle Rosaldo, and Barbara Gelpi, (Chicago, 1982), pp. 130, 134.

23. Cicely Hamilton, *Marriage as a Trade* (New York, 1909), pp. 17, 18.

24. Gasquoine Hartley, *Truth*, p. 253.

25. Hamilton, *Marriage*, pp. 18-19.

26. Ibid., pp. 36, 36-37.

27. Ibid., pp. 37-38.

28. See Hellerstein, Hume, and Offen, *Victorian Women*, p. 164.

29. Caird, *Marriage*, pp. 217-218, 57.

30. *The Freewoman*, 20 June 1912, p. 81.

31. Mona Caird, *Daughters of Danaus* (London, 1894), p. 129.

32. See Lewis, *Women in England*, p. 130.

33. Caird, *Marriage*, pp. 57-58.

34. Ibid., pp. 54-55.

35. See Banks and Banks, *Feminism and Family Planning*, p. 60.

36. Ibid., passim. See also J. A. Banks, *Prosperity and Parenthood, A Study of Family Planning Among the Victorian Middle Classes* (London, 1954), passim.

37. Banks and Banks, *Feminism and Family Planning*, pp. 62, 72, 75.

38. "[T]he changes of the prosperous decades of the nineteenth century," Banks and Banks have argued, "increased the middle-class woman's subservience by relegating her to the position of status object." Women may have found "release from the burden of domesticity," but they were reduced to the trivial and humiliating role of ornament and symbol of conspicuous consumption. Ibid., pp. 12, 67.

39. See Frances Swiney, *The Bar of Isis* (London, 1912).

40. "Motherhood," *Common Cause*, 8 September 1910, p. 351.

41. Elizabeth Wolstenholme Elmy, *The Emancipation of Women* (London, 1888), p. 3.

42. Marion Leslie, letter to the *Women's Penny Paper*, 13 December 1912.

43. Elizabeth Wolstenholme Elmy, *The Criminal Code in its Relation to Women* (Manchester, 1880), pp. 8, 9, 10.

44. Quoted in Vera Brittain, *Lady Into Woman* (London, 1953), pp. 24, 25.

45. Elizabeth Wolstenholme Elmy to Harriet McIlquham, 29 May 1897. Elmy Collection.

46. Elizabeth Wolstenholme Elmy to Harriet McIlquham, 13 December 1896. Elmy Collection.

47. Kathlyn Oliver, letter to *The Freewoman*, 11 July 1912, p. 156.

48. F. W. Stella Browne, "The Sexual Variety and Variability among Women and their Bearing upon Social Reconstruction," in *A New World for Women*, ed. Sheila Rowbotham (London, 1977), p. 112.

49. Frances Power Cobbe, "The Final Cause of Woman," in *Woman's Work and Woman's Culture*, ed. Josephine Butler (London, 1869), p. 8.

50. Caird, *Marriage*, p. 85.

51. Hamilton, *Marriage*, pp. 59, 6.

52. Blackwell, *Medical Profession*, p. 30.

53. Hamilton, *Marriage*, p. 193.

54. Caird, *Marriage*, pp. 134, 173.

55. Caird, *Daughters*, p. 251.

56. Quoted in Eric Trudgill, *Madonnas and Magdalens: The Origins and Development of Victorian Sexual Attitudes* (New York, 1976), p. 61.

57. Quoted in Quilter, *Failure?*, p. 177.

58. Ellis Ethelmer [Elizabeth Wolsteholme Elmy and Ben Elmy], *Life to Woman* (1896), pp. 31-32.

59. Ibid., pp. 29-30.

60. Frances Swiney, *Man's Necessity* (n.d.), p. 1.

61. Frances Swiney, *Women Among the Nations* (London, 1913), p. 31.

62. Swiney, *Isis*, p. 38.

63. Billington-Greig, manuscript notes. Billington-Greig Collection.

64. Hamilton, *Marriage*, pp. 33-34.

65. Caird, *Daughters*, pp. 188, 187.

66. Caird, *Marriage*, p. 173.

67. Hamilton, *Marriage*, pp. 193-194.

68. Caird, *Daughters*, pp. 254-255.

69. I. D. Pearce, Letters to *The Freewoman*, 30 November 1911, p. 32, and 14 December 1911, p. 71.

70. Caird, *Marriage*, pp. 13, 87.

71. Ibid., pp. 5, 1, 83, 81-82, 98-99, 100.

72. Grand, *Ideala*, pp. 145, 13.

73. These quotations taken from Quilter, *Failure?*, pp. 22, 22-23.

74. Olive Schreiner, *The Story of an African Farm* (New York, 1883), p. 154.

75. Caird, *Daughters*, pp. 427, 306, 343.

76. Scharlieb, *What It Means*, p. 35.

77. Quoted in Quilter, *Failure?*, p. 188.

78. Lady Emily Acland, *Marriage as the Foundation of the Home* (London, 1902), pp. 28-29.

79. Ethel Harrison, "A Woman's View of Divorce," *Nineteenth Century and After* 69 (1911): 333-334.

80. Caird, *Marriage*, p. 219.

81. Sarah Grand et al., "Does Marriage Hinder a Woman's Self-Development?" *Lady's Realm*, March 1899, p. 576.

82. Quoted in Quilter, *Failure?*, pp. 35-36.

83. Ibid., p. 26.

84. Quoted in Banks and Banks, *Feminism and Family Planning*, pp. 92, 93.

85. See Lewis, *Women in England*, pp. 129-130.

86. Ethelmer, *Life*, pp. 60-61.

87. Swiney, *Isis*, pp. 41-42, 43, 31-32.

88. Butler, *Appeal*, p. 14.

89. Quoted in Walkowitz, *Prostitution*, p. 130.

90. Hamilton, *Marriage*, pp. 73, 74, 253.

91. Lily Waring, "Codes of Honour," *Common Cause*, 14 April 1910, p. 4.

92. Fawcett, *Women's Victory*, p. 24.

93. Christabel Pankhurst, "A Woman's Question," *Suffragette*, 8 August 1913, p. 737.

94. Christabel Pankhurst, "The End of a Conspiracy," *Suffragette*, 1 August 1913, p. 717.

95. Christabel Pankhurst, "Woman's Question," p. 737.

96. See Walkowitz, *Prostitution*, pp. 50, 270.

97. Quoted in ibid., pp. 55, 55-56.

98. Elizabeth Blackwell, *Medical Responsibility in Relation to the Contagious Diseases Acts*, 3d ed. (London, 1897), p. 4.

99. Scharlieb, *What It Means*, pp. 114, 113.

100. See Harris, "Power of Signs," p. 77.

101. Douglas, *Purity*, pp. 3-4, 142.

102. Ibid., p. 113.

103. Ethelmer, *Life*, pp. 8, 9-10, 64.

104. Ibid., p. 24. It would be wrong—and anachronistic—to dismiss the Elmys' views as absurd and unscientific. Here again, the language and meaning of their statements, not the accuracy of their observations, are the important factors. At the time of their writing, and well into the twentieth century, doctors did not understand the function or process of menstruation, confusing it with ovulation. Early twentieth-century physicians and scientists believed that intercourse without fear of pregnancy would best take place two weeks after the onset of menstruation. The Elmys believed that doctors had covered up the "facts" of menstruation in order to permit the sexual subjugation of women, and that the "science" of female physicians would set things straight.

105. Ibid., pp. 31-32.

106. Caird, *Daughters*, p. 256.

107. Quoted in Banks and Banks, *Feminism and Family Planning*, p. 102.

108. *Woman's Herald*, 24 January 1891, p. 211.
109. Ellis Ethelmer [Elizabeth Wolstenholme Elmy and Ben Elmy], *The Human Flower* (1895), p. 43.
110. Snowdon, *Feminist Movement*, pp. 248-249, 24-25.
111. Blackwell, *Essays*, p. 78.
112. Alice Ker, *Motherhood: A Book for Every Woman* (Manchester, 1891), pp. 27, 29.
113. Ibid., p. 30.

Chapter IV: The Doctors

1. Foucault, *History of Sexuality*, pp. 54, 56, 104.
2. "Obstetrical Society of London," *Lancet*, 6 April 1867, p. 430.
3. "The Removal of a Fellow from the Obstetrical Society," *Lancet*, 6 April 1867, p. 420.
4. "Obstetrical Society of London," p. 431.
5. "Removal of a Fellow," p. 420.
6. "Obstetrical Society of London," p. 439.
7. Ibid., pp. 434, 437, 435.
8. Ibid., p. 438.
9. Ibid., p. 439.
10. Ibid., p. 432.
11. Walkowitz, *Prostitution*, pp. 130, 129.
12. Petrie, *Iniquity*, p. 111.
13. *The Geneva Conference on Public Morality* (London, 1877), p. 23.
14. Ladies' National Association, *Eighteenth Annual Report, 1887*, pp. 57-58.
15. J. J. Garth Wilkinson, *The Forcible Introspection of Women for the Army and Navy by the Oligarchy* (London, 1870), pp. 14-15.
16. "Report from the Royal Commission," p. 445.
17. Josephine Butler to Mr. Edmondson, 28 March 1872. Butler Collection.

18. Mary Hume-Rothery, *Women and Doctors: or Medical Despotism in England* (London, 1871), p. 5.
19. Ibid., pp. 5, 6.
20. Josephine Butler, "A Few Words Addressed to True-Hearted Women," 18 March 1872 (draft). Butler Collection.
21. "The Female Medical Movement," *Shield*, 18 April 1870, p. 56.
22. Duffin, "Conspicuous Consumptive," p. 46.
23. Quoted in Sophia Jex-Blake, *Medical Women*, 2d ed. (Edinburgh, 1886), p. 52.
24. Frances Power Cobbe, "The Little Health of Ladies," *Contemporary Review* 31 (January 1878): 295.
25. Butler, *Appeal*, p. 5.
26. Quoted in Rover, *Love, Morals and the Feminists*, p. 82.
27. Quoted in Wilkinson, *Introspection*, p. 25.
28. Quoted in Jex-Blake, *Medical Women*, pp. 54, 52.
29. Ladies' National Association, *Twelfth Annual Report, 1881*, p. 1.
30. Quoted in G. J. Barker-Benfield, *The Horrors of the Half-Known Life: Male Attitudes Toward Women and Sexuality in Nineteenth-Century America* (New York, 1976), p. 61.
31. Blackwell, *Medical Profession*, pp. 214-215.
32. Wilkinson, *Introspection*, p. 26.
33. Elizabeth Blackwell, *Medicine and Morality* (London, 1881), p. 13.
34. Cobbe, "Little Health," pp. 294-295.
35. Blackwell, *Medical Profession*, p. 72.
36. Quoted in Edythe Lutzker, "Medical Education for Women in Great Britain" (Master's thesis, Columbia University, 1959), pp. 26-27.
37. "Standards of Feminine Propriety," *Englishwoman's Review* 14 (April 1873): 118.
38. Blackwell, *Medicine and Morality*, pp. 5-6.
39. Blackwell, *Essays*, pp. 67-68.
40. Blackwell, *Medicine and Morality*, p. 4.

41. Jex-Blake, *Medical Women*, pp. 7-8.
42. Ibid., pp. 7-8, 49, 50.
43. Quoted in ibid., p. 50.
44. Cobbe, "Little Health," p. 294.
45. Snowdon, *Feminist Movement*, p. 98.
46. Quoted in Jex-Blake, *Medical Women*, pp. 42, 48.
47. Cobbe, "Little Health," p. 294.
48. Quoted in Duffin, "Conspicuous Consumptive," p. 35.
49. Quoted in Jex-Blake, *Medical Women*, pp. 49-50.
50. See Ellen S. Gaskell, letter to *The Freewoman*, 18 April 1912, p. 438.
51. See Walkowitz, *Prostitution*, p. 55.
52. Blackwell, *Medical Profession*, p. 93.
53. Jex-Blake, *Medical Women*, p. 60.
54. Blackwell, *Medical Profession*, pp. 253-254.
55. Elizabeth Garrett to J.G.S. Anderson, 20 August 1870. Garrett Collection.
56. Brian Harrison, "Women's Health and the Women's Movement in Britain: 1840-1940," in *Biology, Medicine and Society, 1840-1940*, ed. Charles Webster (Cambridge, 1981), passim.
57. Jex-Blake, *Medical Women*, p. 49.
58. Cobbe, "Little Health," p. 296.
59. Waring, "Codes of Honour," p. 4.
60. Hale, *What Women Want*, p. 88.
61. Snowdon, *Feminist Movement*, p. 254.
62. Blackwell, *Medical Profession*, pp. 200-201.
63. Blackwell, *Medical Responsibility*, p. 13.
64. Louisa Martindale, *Under the Surface* (Brighton, n.d.), p. 70.
65. Blackwell, *Medical Profession*, pp. 116-117, 119.
66. Ibid., pp. 4-5, 28-29, 30.
67. Ibid., pp. 24, 25.
68. Blackwell, *Medical Responsibility*, p. 13; *Medical Profession*, p. 251.
69. Blackwell, *Medical Profession*, p. 251.
70. Elizabeth Garrett Anderson, "Sex in Mind and Education:

A Reply," *Fortnightly Review* 15 (1874): 583, 585, 586-587, 588.
71. See Helena Normanton, letter to *The Woman's Leader*, 19 September 1924, p. 275.
72. Hale, *What Women Want*, p. 244.
73. Blackwell, *Medical Profession*, p. 85.
74. Blackwell, *Essays*, pp. 48, 51, 32, 16.
75. Ibid., pp. 51, 16, 52, 53.
76. Blackwell, *Medical Profession*, p. 85.

CHAPTER V: THE LAW

1. C. Nina Boyle, "A Grave Abuse," *Vote*, 17 October 1913, p. 406.
2. Butler, *Demand For Moral Members*, p. 1.
3. National Union of Women's Suffrage Societies, *Parliament & Moral Reform* (London, 1913).
4. *Common Cause*, 27 October 1910, p. 460.
5. Quoted in McGregor, *Divorce*, p. 21.
6. See Josephine Butler, letter to the Ladies' National Association, 4 December 1882. Butler Collection.
7. "Report from the Royal Commission," p. 439.
8. Millicent Garrett Fawcett, "Speech or Silence," *Contemporary Review* 48 (September 1885): 330.
9. Mrs. Henry Fawcett, *Paper Read at the Bristol Meeting of the Central Conference of Women Workers Among Women and Children* (London, 1892), pp. 7, 8.
10. Frances Swiney, *The Sons of Belial* (London, n.d.), p. 26.
11. National Union, *Parliament & Moral Reform*.
12. Lady Chance, *Women's Suffrage and Morality* (London, 1912), p. 11.
13. Women's Freedom League, *Some Social Problems and Votes for Women* (London, n.d.).
14. National Union, *Parliament & Moral Reform*.
15. Swiney, *Awakening*, p. 219.
16. Walkowitz, *Prostitution*, p. 256. See also Ellen DuBois and

Linda Gordon, "Seeking Ecstasy on the Battlefield: Danger and Pleasure in Nineteenth-Century Feminist Sexual Thought," *Feminist Studies* 9 (Spring 1983), passim.

17. Martha Vicinus, "Sexuality and Power: A Review of the Current Work in the History of Sexuality," *Feminist Studies* 8 (Spring 1982): 144.

18. Swanwick, *I Have Been Young*, pp. 83-84.

19. See S. C. Cronwright-Schreiner, ed., *The Letters of Olive Schreiner, 1876-1920* (London, 1924), pp. 44, 79, passim. See also Lewis, *Women in England*, p. 129.

20. See Ruth First and Ann Scott, *Olive Schreiner* (London, 1980), pp. 18-19, 291.

21. Phyllis Grosskurth, *Havelock Ellis* (London, 1980), p. 80.

22. First and Scott, *Olive Schreiner*, pp. 291, 18-19.

23. Ibid., pp. 158, 160, 151-152, 162, 179.

24. Schreiner, *Woman and Labour*, p. 25.

25. Quoted in First and Scott, *Olive Schreiner*, pp. 276, 293.

26. Schreiner, *Woman and Labour*, p. 25.

27. Boyle, "Abuse," p. 406.

28. Ibid.

29. See Strachey, *Fawcett*, p. 121.

30. Boyle, "Abuse," p. 406.

31. "Gladstone's Speech on the Reform Bill of 1866," quoted in Brian Tierney, Donald Kagan, and L. Pearce Williams, eds., *Great Issues in Western Civilization*, 3d ed., vol. 2 (New York, 1976), pp. 396, 397.

32. Emmeline Pethick Lawrence, *The Meaning of the Woman's Movement* (London, n.d.), pp. 4-5.

33. Chance, *Women's Suffrage*, p. 5.

34. Frances Power Cobbe, "Wife-Torture in England," *Contemporary Review* 32 (April 1878): 62, 80.

35. Swiney, *Sons of Belial*, p. 29.

36. Martindale, *Under the Surface*, p. 7.

37. Swiney, *Sons of Belial*, pp. 23, 11.

38. [Constance Smedley], *Woman: A Few Shrieks* (Letchworth, n.d.), p. 66.

39. Chance, *Women's Suffrage*, pp. 10-11.
40. "Wife Beating Made Easy," *Woman's Herald*, 3 January 1891, p. 168.
41. Eunice Murray, *The Illogical Sex?* (Edinburgh, n.d.), p. 3.
42. "Brutal Assaults," *Englishwoman's Review* 26 (June 1875): 382-383.
43. Quoted in Swiney, *Awakening*, p. 213.
44. *Common Cause*, 27 October 1910, pp. 460-461.
45. *Common Cause*, 26 May 1910, p. 106.
46. See Vicinus, "Sexuality and Power," p. 144.
47. Quoted in Petrie, *Iniquity*, pp. 123, 116.
48. Walkowitz, *Prostitution*, p. 109.
49. Butler, *Demand for Moral Members*, p. 1.
50. Quoted in Strachey, *Fawcett*, pp. 121, 120.
51. "Correspondence between Mrs. Fawcett and the Right Honorable A. J. Balfour, M. P. Respecting Mr. Cust's Candidature for North Manchester, 1894," p. 2. Millicent Garrett Fawcett Collection. Fawcett Library, London.
52. Ibid., pp. 2-3, 5, 15, 16, 17.
53. See Strachey, *Fawcett*, p. 120.
54. "Correspondence between Mrs. Fawcett and the Right Honorable A. J. Balfour," Fawcett Collection, p. 22.
55. See Sylvia Pankhurst, *Suffragette Movement*, p. 521.
56. Christabel Pankhurst, "The Truth About the Piccadilly Flat," *Suffragette*, 25 July 1913, p. 693.
57. Swiney, *Awakening*, p. 228.
58. Christabel Pankhurst, "Piccadilly Flat," p. 693.
59. Quoted in Sylvia Pankhurst, *Suffragette Movement*, p. 181.
60. See Boyle, "Abuse," p. 406.
61. Chance, *Women's Suffrage*, p. 14.

CHAPTER VI: SEX WAR

1. Pethick Lawrence, *Woman's Movement*, p. 8.
2. Meikle, *Sane Feminism*, p. 83.
3. Ibid., pp. 83, 83-84, 84-85, 86, 92.

4. Ibid., p. 98.
5. Fawcett, *Women's Victory*, p. 71.
6. Quoted in Andro Linklater, *An Unhusbanded Life, Charlotte Despard: Suffragette, Socialist and Sinn Feiner* (London, 1980), pp. 121-122.
7. Teresa Billington-Greig, "Modern Women and Divorce" (unpublished manuscript), p. 1. Billington-Greig Collection.
8. Gasquoine Hartley, *Truth*, p. 332.
9. Quoted in Rosen, *Rise Up*, p. 208.
10. Sylvia Pankhurst, *Suffragette Movement*, p. 181.
11. Hale, *What Women Want*, pp. 88-89.
12. *Common Cause*, 26 May 1910, p. 106.
13. Frances Swiney, *Woman and Natural Law*, 2d ed. (London, 1912), pp. 10, 15.
14. Ibid., p. 21.
15. Frances Swiney, *The Ancient Road* (London, 1918), pp. 33-34.
16. Swiney, *Natural Law*, pp. 42-43.
17. Frances Swiney, "The Woman Movement," *The Race Builder* 2 (November 1904-October 1905): 94.
18. Schreiner, *Woman and Labour*, p. 12.
19. Swiney, "Woman Movement," p. 95.
20. Caird, *Marriage*, p. 97.
21. Gasquoine Hartley, *Truth*, pp. 10-11.
22. See Lucy Re-Bartlett, *Towards Liberty* (London, 1913), pp. 45, 69.
23. Gasquoine Hartley, *Truth*, p. 247.
24. Swiney, *Awakening*, p. 116.
25. Annie Swan, *Courtship and Marriage* (London, 1893), pp. 31-32.
26. Caird, *Marriage*, pp. 196-197.
27. Grand, *Ideala*, p. 157.
28. Swiney, *Natural Law*, p. 46.
29. Quoted in Brittain, *Lady Into Woman*, p. 18.
30. Fawcett, *Butler*, p. 74.

31. Quoted in Rover, *Women's Suffrage*, p. 169.
32. Priscilla Barker, *The Secret Book, Containing Private Information and Instruction for Women and Young Girls* (Brighton, 1888), p. 19.
33. Grand, *Ideala*, pp. 22-23.
34. [Smedley], *Woman*, pp. 18, 21-22.
35. Ibid., pp. 36, 40, 188-199.
36. See Cicely Hamilton, "Man," *English Review* 11 (April 1912): 120.
37. Ellis Ethelmer [Elizabeth Wolstenholme Elmy and Ben Elmy], "Feminism," *Westminster Review* 149 (1898): 61.
38. "Speculations on Sex War," *The Freewoman*, 14 December 1911, p. 65.
39. Maud Braby, *Modern Marriage and How to Bear It* (London, 1908), pp. 10, 12-13.
40. M.O.W.O., "The Grievances of Women," *Fraser's Magazine* 21 (May 1880): 698.
41. Gasquoine Hartley, *Truth*, pp. 265, 266.
42. Cronwright-Schreiner, *Letters of Olive Schreiner*, pp. 35-36.
43. Hamilton, "Man," p. 121.
44. Laura Morgan-Brown, "The Whitechapel Murder," *Woman's Herald*, 14 March 1891, p. 324.
45. Snowdon, *Feminist Movement*, pp. 173-174.
46. Swiney, *Awakening*, pp. 170, 171-172.
47. "Speculations," *The Freewoman*, p. 65.
48. Louise Creighton, *The Social Disease and How to Fight It* (London, 1914), pp. 61-62, 12, 19.
49. Vera Laughton Matthews, *The Woman's Movement and Birth Control* (London, n.d.), p. 3.
50. Hale, *What Women Want*, pp. 150, 150-151, 54.
51. Caird, *Daughters*, pp. 441, 473.
52. See Rover, *Love, Morals and the Feminists*, pp. 141-142.
53. Eliza Lynn Linton, "The Wild Women: As Politicians," *Nineteenth Century* 30 (July 1891): 88.
54. Brian Harrison, *Separate Spheres*, p. 77.

55. Swanwick, *I Have Been Young*, p. 183.
56. Quoted in Sylvia Pankhurst, *Suffragette Movement*, p. 297.
57. Ibid., pp. 343, 344.
58. Mitchell, *Queen Christabel*, p. 160.
59. Sylvia Pankhurst, *Suffragette Movement*, p. 392.
60. Hale, *What Women Want*, pp. 206, 207.
61. Re-Bartlett, *Towards Liberty*, pp. 45, 49.
62. See Brian Harrison, *Separate Spheres*, p. 55.
63. See George Layard, *Mrs. Lynn Linton, Her Life, Letters, and Opinions* (London, 1901).
64. See Brian Harrison, *Separate Spheres*, p. 55.
65. See Brittain, *Lady Into Woman*, p. 32.
66. Snowdon, *Feminist Movement*, p. 164.
67. Lynn Linton, "Wild Women: As Politicians," p. 88.
68. Brian Harrison, *Separate Spheres*, p. 81.
69. Eliza Lynn Linton, *Ourselves: A Series of Essays on Women* (London, 1869), p. 12. Eliza Lynn Linton, "The Partisans of the Wild Women," *Nineteenth Century* 31 (1890): 460.
70. Lynn Linton, "Partisans," p. 460.
71. Arabella Kenealy, *Feminism and Sex-Extinction* (London, 1920), p. 186.
72. Kenealy, *Feminism*, pp. 10, 179-180.
73. Ibid., pp. 179-180.
74. *Anti-Suffrage Review*, September 1910, p. 5.
75. Olive Katharine Parr, *Woman's "Emancipation"* (Devon, n.d.), pp. 9-10.
76. Kenealy, *Feminism*, pp. 178, 186.
77. Quoted in Layard, *Lynn Linton*, p. 140.
78. Eliza Lynn Linton, *The One Too Many*, 3 vols. (London, 1894).
79. Eliza Lynn Linton, "The Wild Women as Social Insurgents," *Nineteenth Century* 30 (October 1891): 602.
80. Parr, *Woman's "Emancipation"*, pp. 9-10.
81. *Anti-Suffrage Review*, September 1910, p. 6.
82. Kenealy, *Feminism*, p. 108.

83. Marie Corelli, *Woman, or—Suffragette?* (London, 1907), p. 3.

84. See Brian Harrison, *Separate Spheres*, p. 18.

85. *Anti-Suffrage Review*, December 1908, p. 7.

86. Women's National Anti-Suffrage League, *Why the Women's Enfranchisement Bill, 1908, Would Be Unfair to Women If It Became Law* (London, 1908).

87. Ethel Harrison, *The Freedom of Women* (London, 1908), pp. 26-27.

88. Women's National Anti-Suffrage League, *Women's Suffrage and the National Welfare*, 3d ed. (London, 1909), pp. 1-2.

89. *Anti-Suffrage Review*, August 1909, p. 1.

90. Heber Hart, *Nature's Reason Against Woman Suffrage* (London, 1908), pp. 2, 3, 4.

91. Frederic Harrison, *Votes for Women*, pp. 5-6.

92. *Common Cause*, 15 September 1910, p. 367.

93. Ibid.

94. Hale, *What Women Want*, p. 214.

95. Colquhoun, "Modern Feminism," pp. 163, 166.

CHAPTER VII: SUFFRAGE

1. See Rover, *Women's Suffrage*, p. 28.

2. Strachey, *The Cause*, pp. 304, 305.

3. See Fulford, *Votes for Women*, pp. 54, 56.

4. See Strachey, *The Cause*, p. 87.

5. See Donald Read, *England: 1868-1914* (London, 1979), pp. 128, 129.

6. See Helen Blackburn, *Women's Suffrage: A Record of the Women's Suffrage Movement in the British Isles* (Rpt., New York, 1970), p. 78.

7. Ibid., pp. 63, 52.

8. Ibid., pp. 46-47, 51, 52, 38-39.

9. See Strachey, *The Cause*, p. 101.

10. See Patricia Hollis, ed., *Women in Public, 1850-1900: Docu-*

ments of the Victorian Women's Movement (London, 1979), p. 304.

11. See Blackburn, *Women's Suffrage*, pp. 78, 85.
12. Ibid., p. 20.
13. See Strachey, *Fawcett*, pp. 88, 53.
14. Kate Millett, *Sexual Politics* (New York, 1971).
15. Ibid., p. 39.
16. John Stuart Mill and Harriet Taylor Mill, *Essays on Sex Equality*, ed. Alice S. Rossi (Chicago, 1970), p. 52.
17. Ibid., pp. 96, 97, 97-98, 218, 220.
18. Ibid., p. 100.
19. Ibid., p. 84.
20. Ibid., pp. 108, 120.
21. Ibid., pp. 74, 60, 148.
22. Ibid., pp. 181, 156.
23. Ibid., pp. 172, 150.
24. Ibid., p. 150.
25. Quoted in Hollis, *Women in Public*, pp. 294-295.
26. Ibid., p. 309.
27. See Blackburn, *Women's Suffrage*, pp. 67, 68.
28. Fulford, *Votes for Women*, pp. 75-76.
29. Blackburn, *Women's Suffrage*, p. 102.
30. Strachey, *Fawcett*, pp. 44-45.
31. Ibid., p. 52.
32. Quoted in Rover, *Women's Suffrage*, p. 2.
33. Strachey, *Fawcett*, pp. 75, 83, 52, 53, 108, 110.
34. Fawcett, "Speech or Silence," p. 330.
35. See Strachey, *Fawcett*, p. 121.
36. See Rover, *Women's Suffrage*, p. 66.
37. Strachey, *The Cause*, pp. 303-304.
38. Ibid., pp. 310, 309, 306, 311-312.
39. Ibid., p. 312.
40. See Rover, *Women's Suffrage*, pp. 80-82.
41. See Rosen, *Rise Up*, p. 124; Walkowitz, *Prostitution*, p. 256.
42. Quoted in Rosen, *Rise Up*, p. 124.

43. See Sylvia Pankhurst, *Suffragette Movement*, pp. 317, 318. Rosen, *Rise Up*, pp. 124, 125.

44. See Strachey, *The Cause*, pp. 315, 315-316.

45. See Rover, *Women's Suffrage*, pp. 81-82.

46. Mitchell, *Queen Christabel*, p. 160.

47. Quoted in Fulford, *Votes for Women*, p. 143.

48. See Rover, *Women's Suffrage*, p. 82.

49. Sylvia Pankhurst, *Suffragette Movement*, pp. 373, 374.

50. See Strachey, *The Cause*, p. 326.

51. Ibid., pp. 329-330.

52. Ibid., p. 333.

53. Almroth E. Wright, *The Unexpurgated Case Against Woman Suffrage* (New York, 1913), pp. 136-137, 168, 168-169, 12-13, 81, 141.

54. Christabel Pankhurst, "A Woman's Question," p. 737.

55. Christabel Pankhurst, "Piccadilly Flat," p. 693.

56. Ibid.

57. Wright, *Unexpurgated Case*, p. 181.

58. Christabel Pankhurst, "Piccadilly Flat," p. 693.

59. Olive Banks, *Faces of Feminism*, p. 84.

60. Lewis, *Women in England*, pp. 89, 88.

61. Elizabeth Wolstenholme Elmy to unnamed person, n.d., probably early 1898. Wolstenholme Elmy Collection.

62. Olive Banks, *Faces of Feminism*, p. 95.

63. Olilve Schreiner, *Woman and Labour*, pp. 171, 67.

64. See First and Scott, *Olive Schreiner*, p. 281.

65. Cronwright-Schreiner, *Letters of Olive Schreiner*, p. 51.

66. Schreiner, *Woman and Labour*, pp. 160, 84.

67. Ellen Carol DuBois, *Feminism and Suffrage: The Emergence of an Independent Women's Movement in America, 1848-1869* (Ithaca, 1978).

68. Rover, *Women's Suffrage*, pp. 21, 24.

69. Quoted in Sarah, "Christabel Pankhurst," p. 269.

70. See ibid.

71. See Snowdon, *Feminist Movement*, pp. 22-23, 24.

72. Maria Grey, "Men and Women: A Sequel," *Fortnightly Review* 29 (1881): 786.

73. Chance, *Women's Suffrage*, pp. 6, 9.

74. Christabel Pankhurst, "A Woman's Question," p. 737.

75. Snowdon, *Feminist Movement*, p. 252.

76. Pethick Lawrence, *Woman's Movement*, pp. 11, 10.

77. Hale, *What Women Want*, p. 117.

78. Ethelmer, "Feminism," p. 53.

79. Hale, *What Women Want*, pp. 117, 99.

80. Creighton, *Social Disease*, p. 79.

81. Christabel Pankhurst, "A Woman's Question," p. 737.

82. Fawcett, *Women's Victory*, pp. 41, 159.

83. Hale, *What Women Want*, p. 184.

84. Hamilton, "Man," p. 116.

85. Billington-Greig, Manuscript notes. Billington-Greig Collection.

86. Hale, *What Women Want*, p. 55.

87. Pethick Lawrence, *Woman's Movement*, pp. 4-5.

88. Christabel Pankhurst, "To Cure White Slavery. A Medical Question," *Suffragette*, 25 April 1913, p. 475.

89. Christabel Pankhurst, "A Woman's Question," p. 737.

90. Meakin, *Woman in Transition*, p. 71.

91. Ethelmer, *Human Flower*, pp. 12, 37.

92. Elizabeth Janeway, "Who Is Sylvia? On the Loss of Sexual Paradigms," in *Women: Sex and Sexuality*, ed. Catharine Stimpson and Ethel Person Spector (Chicago, 1980), pp. 5, 6.

93. Hamilton, *Marriage*, pp. 78-79.

94. Teresa Billington-Greig, "Feminine Vice and Virtue," unpublished manuscript, pp. 3, 2. Billington-Greig Collection.

95. Ibid., p. 1.

96. A. Maude Royden, "Modern Love," in *The Making of Women*, ed. Victor Gollancz (London, 1917), pp. 38-39, 41-42.

97. Braby, *Modern Marriage*, pp. 102-103, 104.

98. Meikle, *Sane Feminism*, p. 88.
99. Quoted in Sylvia Pankhurst, *Suffragette Movement*, p. 192.
100. Sheila Rowbotham and Jeffrey Weeks, *Socialism and the New Life: The Personal and Sexual Politics of Edward Carpenter and Havelock Ellis* (London, 1977), pp. 17-18.
101. Meikle, *Sane Feminism*, p. 89.
102. Sylvia Pankhurst, *Suffragette Movement*, p. 208.
103. Meikle, *Sane Feminism*, p. 91.
104. Garner, *Stepping Stones*, p. 61.
105. Quoted in ibid., p. 64.
106. See First and Scott, *Olive Schreiner*, pp. 291-292.
107. Janeway, "Who Is Sylvia?" pp. 16-17.
108. See Sarah Evans, *Personal Politics: The Roots of Women's Liberation in the Civil Rights Movement and the New Left* (New York, 1980), passim.
109. Teresa Billington-Greig, "Sex and Morality," unpublished manuscript outline for article by that title, p. 2. Billington-Greig Collection.
110. Ibid., pp. 1, 2.
111. Billington-Greig, "Feminine Vice and Virtue," p. 4. Teresa Billington-Greig, "The Things That Matter," unpublished manuscript outline for suggested topics for publication, p. 6. Billington-Greig Collection.
112. Royden, "Modern Love," pp. 59, 51, 43, 44.
113. Snowdon, *Feminist Movement*, p. 13.
114. Ellis Ethelmer [Elizabeth Wolstenholme Elmy and Ben Elmy], *Phases of Love* (1897), pp. 20, 8-9.

Epilogue

1. Quoted in Strachey, *The Cause*, p. 354.
2. Fawcett, *Women's Victory*, p. 146.
3. Fawcett, *Women's Victory*, p. 160.
4. Ray Strachey, *Our Freedom and Its Results* (1936), quoted in

Sheila Rowbotham, *Hidden From History* (New York, 1976), p. 163.

5. Winifred Holtby, *Women and a Changing Civilization* (Rpt., Chicago, 1978), p. 96.

6. Strachey, *The Cause*, pp. 370-371.

7. Ibid., p. 371.

8. Brian Harrison, *Separate Spheres*, p. 230.

9. Quoted in ibid.

10. Strachey, *The Cause*, p. 371.

11. Rowbotham, *Hidden From History*, p. 163.

12. See Brian Harrison, *Separate Spheres*, pp. 229, 242.

13. See Lois Banner, *Women in Modern America: A Brief History* (San Diego, 1984), p. 151.

14. Erik Erikson, "Inner and Outer Space: Reflections on Womanhood" (1964), quoted in Naomi Weisstein, " 'Kinde, Küche, Kirche' as Scientific Law: Psychology Constructs the Female," in *Sisterhood is Powerful*, ed. Robin Morgan (New York, 1970), p. 229.

15. Quoted in Lewis, *Women in England*, pp. 101, 102.

16. Holtby, *Women*, pp. 118, 119.

17. Quoted in Brian Harrison, *Separate Spheres*, p. 243.

18. Quoted in Martha Vicinus, *Independent Women: Work and Community for Single Women, 1850-1920* (Chicago, 1985), p. 283.

19. Ibid., p. 281.

20. Olive Banks, *Faces of Feminism*, p. 150.

21. Vicinus, *Independent Women*, pp. 283-284.

22. Lewis, *Women in England*, pp. 104, 105.

23. Millet, *Sexual Politics*, pp. 63, 64.

24. Juliet Mitchell, *Psychoanalysis and Feminism* (New York, 1974), p. 362.

25. Ibid., pp. 402, 403.

26. Ibid., pp. 404, 405.

27. See Nancy Chodorow, *The Reproduction of Mothering* (Berke-

ley, 1978); Dorothy Dinnerstein, *The Mermaid and the Minotaur, Sexual Arrangements and Human Malaise* (New York, 1977).

28. Carol Gilligan, *In a Different Voice, Psychological Theory and Women's Development* (Cambridge, MA, 1982), p. 2.

BIBLIOGRAPHY

Archival Sources

London. British Library:
    Elizabeth Wolstenholme Elmy Collection.
    Maud Arncliffe Sennett Collection. Volume I.
London. Fawcett Library:
    Elizabeth Garrett Collection.
    Josephine Butler Collection.
    Millicent Garrett Fawcett Collection.
    Teresa Billington-Greig Collection.

Newspapers and Periodicals

Anti-Suffrage Review. London: 1908-1910.
Blackwood's Edinburgh Magazine. London: 1895, 1897.
Common Cause. London, 1910.
Contemporary Review. London: 1878, 1885, 1887.
Englishwoman's Review. London: 1870, 1873, 1875, 1889.
Fortnightly Review. London, 1871, 1874-1875, 1881, 1894, 1905-1906.
Fraser's Magazine. London: 1880.
The Freewoman. London, 1911-1913.
Lady's Realm. London, 1899.
Lancet. London, 1867.
Nineteenth Century. London: 1887, 1890, 1891, 1893, 1896.
Nineteenth Century and After. London: 1909, 1911.
Quarterly Review. London: 1913.
The Race Builder. London: 1904-1905.
Shield. London, 1870, 1872.
Suffragette. London: 1913.
Vote. London: 1912-1913.

Westminster Review. London: 1898.
Woman's Herald. London, 1891.
The Woman's Leader. London, 1924.
Women's Penny Paper. London, 1912.

PRIMARY SOURCES

Acland, Lady Emily. *Marriage as the Foundation of the Home*. London, 1902.
Amberley, Lady K. "The Claims of Women." *Fortnightly Review* 9 (January 1871): 95-110.
The Author of "John Halifax, Gentleman." "For Better For Worse." *Contemporary Review* 51 (1887): 570-576.
Balfour, Betty. *Letters of Constance Lytton*. London, 1925.
Barker, Priscilla. *The Secret Book, Containing Private Information and Instruction for Women and Young Girls*. Brighton, 1888.
Bewicke, Alicia. *Address by Miss Alicia Bewicke*. Bristol, n.d.
Billington-Greig, Teresa. "The Truth About White Slavery." *English Review* 14 (1913): 428-446.
Blackburn, Helen. *Women's Suffrage: A Record of the Women's Suffrage Movement in the British Isles*. Rpt., New York, 1970.
Blackwell, Elizabeth. *Essays in Medical Sociology*. 2 vols. London, 1902.
———. *Medical Responsibility in Relation to the Contagious Diseases Acts*. 3d ed. London, 1897.
———. *Medicine and Morality*. London, 1881.
———. *Opening the Medical Profession to Women*. Rpt., New York, 1977.
Boyle, C. Nina. "A Grave Abuse." *Vote*, 17 October 1913, p. 406.
Braby, Maud. *Downward: A "Slice of Life."* London, 1910.
———. *Modern Marriage and How to Bear It*. London, 1908.
Brittain, Vera. *Lady Into Woman*. London. 1953.
"Brutal Assaults." *Englishwoman's Review* 26 (June 1875): 382-383.

Butler, Josephine. *An Address Delivered at Croyden, July 3, 1871*. Manchester, 1871.

———. *Address Delivered in Craigie Hall, Edinburgh, February 24, 1871*. Manchester, 1871.

———. *An Appeal to the People of England on the Recognition and Superintendance of Prostitution by Government*. 2d ed. 1870.

———. *An Autobiographical Memoir*. Edited by G. W. Johnson and Lucy A. Johnson. London, 1928.

———. *The Constitution Violated*. Edinburgh, 1871.

———. *The Demand for Moral Members of Parliament*. London, n.d.

———. *A Few Words Addressed to True-Hearted Women*. Liverpool, 1872.

———. *A Letter on the Subject of Mr. Bruce's Bill Addressed to the Repealers of the Contagious Diseases Acts*. Liverpool, 1872.

———. *A Letter to the Members of the Ladies' National Association*. Liverpool, 1879.

———. *The New Era*. Liverpool, 1872.

———. *Paper on the Moral Reclaimability of Prostitutes*. 1870.

———. *Personal Reminiscences of a Great Crusade*. London, 1898.

———. *The Principles of the Abolitionists*. London, 1885.

———. *Speech Delivered by Josephine Butler*. London, 1874.

———. *Speech Delivered by Mrs. Josephine Butler at the Fourth Annual Meeting of the Vigilance Association for the Defense of Personal Rights, October 15, 1871*. London, n.d.

———. *Speech to Leister Hall, Dublin, 1878*. Liverpool, 1878.

———. *Sursum Corda*. Liverpool 1871.

———. *Truth Before Everything*. London, 1897.

Caird, Mona. *Daughters of Danaus*. London, 1894.

———. *The Morality of Marriage and Other Essays on the Status and Destiny of Woman*. London, 1897.

Chance, Lady. *Women's Suffrage and Morality*. London, 1912.

Chance, Lady. *Words to Working Women*. London, 1912.

Chant, Mrs. Ormiston. *Speech of Mrs. Ormiston Chant, at the Annual Meeting of the Ladies' National Association*. 1886.

Chesser, Elizabeth. *From Girlhood to Womanhood*. London, 1914.

Cobbe, Frances Power. "The Final Cause of Woman." In *Woman's Work and Woman's Culture*, edited by Josephine Butler. London, 1869.

―――. "The Little Health of Ladies." *Contemporary Review* 31 (January 1878): 276-296.

―――. "Wife-Torture in England." *Contemporary Review* 32 (April 1878): 55-87.

Colquhoun, Ethel. "Modern Feminism and Sex-Antagonism." *Quarterly Review* 219 (1913): 143-166.

―――. *The Vocation of Woman*. London, 1913.

Corelli, Marie. *Woman, or—Suffragette?* London, 1907.

Creighton, Louise. *The Social Disease and How to Fight It*. London, 1914.

Cronwright-Schreiner, S. C., ed. *The Letters of Olive Schreiner, 1876-1920*, London, 1924.

Davies, Emily. *Medicine as a Profession for Women*. 2d ed. London, 1863.

Elmy, Elizabeth Wolstenholme. *The Criminal Code in its Relation to Women*. Manchester, 1880.

―――. *The Emancipation of Women*. London, 1888.

An English Lady. *Letter to My Countrywomen*. Manchester, 1871.

Ethelmer, Ellis [Elizabeth Wolstenholme Elmy and Ben Elmy], "Feminism." *Westminster Review* 149 (1898): 50-62.

―――. *The Human Flower*. 1895.

―――. *Life to Woman*. 1896.

―――. *Phases of Love*. 1897.

―――. *Woman Free*. 1893.

Fairfield, Zoë. *The Woman's Movement*. London, 1914.

Faithfull, Emily. *Three Visits to America*. Edinburgh, 1884.

Fawcett, Millicent Garrett. *Josephine Butler*. London, 1927.

————. "Speech or Silence," *Contemporary Review* 48 (September 1885): 326-331.

————. *The Women's Victory—and After: Personal Reminiscences, 1911-1918*. London, 1920.

Fawcett, Mrs. Henry. *Paper Read at the Bristol Meeting of the Central Conference of Women Workers Among Women and Children*. London, 1892.

"The Female Medical Movement." *Shield*, 18 April 1870, p. 56.

Garrett, Elizabeth. *An Enquiry into the Character of the Contagious Diseases Acts of 1866-69*. London, 1870.

Garrett Anderson, Elizabeth. "Sex in Mind and Education: A Reply," *Fortnightly Review* 15 (1874): 582-594.

The Geneva Conference on Public Morality. London, 1877.

Goslett, Clare. *Things We Must Tell Our Girls*. London, 1911.

Grand, Sarah [F. E. MacFall]. *A Domestic Experiment*, London, 1891.

————. *Ideala, A Study From Life*, London, 1888.

————. *The Modern Man and Maid*. London, 1898.

———— et al. "Does Marriage Hinder a Woman's Self-Development?" *Lady's Realm*, March 1899, pp. 576-586.

Grey, Maria. "Men and Women: A Sequel." *Fortnightly Review* 29 (1881): 776-793.

Grove, Agnes. "The Present Disabilities of the Women of England." *Fortnightly Review* 80 (1906): 135-143.

Hale, Beatrice Forbes-Robinson. *What Women Want*. New York, 1914.

Hamilton, Cicely. *Life Errant*. London, 1935.

————. "Man." *English Review* 11 (April 1912): 115-125.

————. *Marriage as a Trade*. New York, 1909.

Hardy, Catherine. *Woman at the Crossroads*. Edinburgh, 1911.

Harrison, Ethel. *The Freedom of Women*. London, 1908.

————. "Then and Now." *Nineteenth Century and After* 66 (1909): 1051-1057.

————. "A Woman's View of Divorce." *Nineteenth Century and After* 69 (1911): 329-334.

Harrison, Frederic. *Votes for Women*. London, 1909.

Hart, Heber. *Nature's Reason Against Woman Suffrage*. London, 1908.

Hartley, Catherine Gasquoine. *Motherhood and the Relationships of the Sexes*. London, 1917.

———. *The Truth About Woman*. London, 1913.

Holmes, Marion. *The A.B.C. of Votes for Women*. London, n.d.

Holtby, Winifred. *Women and a Changing Civilization*. Rpt., Chicago, 1978.

Hume-Rothery, Mary. *A Letter Addressed to the Right Hon. W. E. Gladstone, M.P.* Manchester, 1870.

———. *The Prayer and Humble Petition, to Her Most Gracious Majesty, Queen Victoria*. 2d ed. London, 1870.

———. *Women and Doctors: or Medical Despotism in England*. London, 1871.

Huntley, Edith. *The Study and Practice of Medicine by Women*. Lewes, 1886.

Jeune, May. "The Revolt of the Daughters." *Fortnightly Review* 55 (1894): 267-276.

Jex-Blake, Sophia. *The Medical Education of Women*. London, 1874.

———. *Medical Women*. 2d ed. Edinburgh, 1886.

———. "Medical Women." *Nineteenth Century* 22 (1887): 692-707.

———. "Medical Women in Fiction." *Nineteenth Century* 33 (1893): 261-272.

———. "The Practice of Medicine by Women." *Fortnightly Review* 17 (1875): 392-407.

Kenealy, Arabella. *Feminism and Sex-Extinction*. London, 1920.

Ker, Alice. *Lectures to Women*. Manchester, 1884.

———. *Motherhood: A Book for Every Woman*. Manchester, 1891.

Ladies' National Association for the Abolition of State Regulation of Vice. *Letter to Fellow-women in Northern countries of Europe*. 1893.

Ladies' National Association for the Repeal of the Contagious Diseases Acts. *Annual Reports, 1870-1887.*

Layard, George. *Mrs. Lynn Linton, Her Life, Letters, and Opinions.* London, 1901.

London Society for Women's Suffrage. *Medical Women on Women's Suffrage.* London, 1908.

Lynn Linton, Eliza. *The One Too Many.* 3 vols. London, 1894.

———. *Ourselves: A Series of Essays on Women.* London, 1869.

———. "The Partisans of the Wild Women." *Nineteenth Century* 31 (1890): 455-464.

———. *The Rebel of the Family.* 3 vols. London, 1880.

———. "The Wild Women: As Politicians." *Nineteenth Century* 30 (July 1891): 79-88.

———. "The Wild Women as Social Insurgents." *Nineteenth Century* 30 (October 1891): 596-605.

M.A.B. "Normal or Abnormal." *Englishwoman's Review* (1889): 533-538.

Markham, Violet. *Woman's Sphere.* London, 1912.

Martindale, Louisa. *Under the Surface.* Brighton, n.d.

Matthews, Vera Laughton. *The Woman's Movement and Birth Control.* London, n.d.

Maudsley, Henry. "Sex in Mind and Education." *Fortnightly Review* 15 (1874): 466-483.

McIlquham, Harriet. " 'Of Women in Assemblies,' A Reply." *Nineteenth Century* 40 (1896): 777-781.

Meakin, Annette. *Woman in Transition.* London, 1907.

A Medical Woman. "The Falling Birthrate." *Suffragette*, 9 May 1913, p. 410.

Meikle, Wilma. *Towards a Sane Feminism.* London, 1916.

Mill, John Stuart, and Harriet Taylor Mill. *Essays on Sex Equality.* Edited by Alice S. Rossi. Chicago, 1970.

Morgan-Brown, Laura. "The Whitechapel Murder," *Woman's Herald*, 14 March 1891, p. 324.

"Motherhood." *Common Cause*, 8 September 1910, p. 351.

M.O.W.O. "The Grievances of Women." *Fraser's Magazine* 21 (May 1880): 698-710.

Murray, Eunice. *The Illogical Sex?* Edinburgh, n.d.

National Union of Women's Suffrage Societies. *Parliament & Moral Reform*. London, 1913.

———. *Service versus Subjection*. London, 1913.

———. *White Slave Traffic*. London, 1913.

"Obstetrical Society of London." *Lancet*, 6 April 1867, pp. 429-441.

"The Obstetrical Society's Charges and Mr. Baker Brown's Replies." *Lancet*, 6 April 1867, pp. 427-429.

Osler, Mrs. A. C. *Why Women Need the Vote*. Birmingham, n.d.

Pankhurst, Christabel. "Chastity and the Health of Men." *Suffragette*, 5 September 1913, p. 813.

———. "To Cure White Slavery. A Medical Question." *Suffragette*, 25 April 1913, p. 475.

———. "The Dangers of Marriage.—I." *Suffragette*, 12 September 1913, p. 829.

———. "The Dangers of Marriage.—II." *Suffragette*, 19 September 1913, p. 845.

———. "The End of a Conspiracy." *Suffragette*, 1 August 1913, p. 717.

———. "The Government and White Slavery." *Suffragette*, 18 April 1913, p. 451.

———. "How to Cure the Great Pestilence." *Suffragette*, 15 August 1913, p. 759.

———. "Plain Facts About a Great Evil." *Suffragette*, 29 August 1913, p. 797.

———. "The Truth About the Piccadilly Flat." *Suffragette*, 25 July 1913, p. 693.

———. "A Woman's Question." *Suffragette*, 8 August 1913, p. 737.

Pankhurst, E. Sylvia. *The Suffragette Movement*. London, 1977.

Parr, Olive Katharine. *Woman's "Emancipation."* Devon, n.d.

Pethick Lawrence, Emmeline. *The Meaning of the Woman's Movement*. London, n.d.

Priestly, W. O., and Horatio R. Storer, eds. *The Obstetric Memoirs and Contributions of James Y. Simpson, M.D., F.R.S.E.* Philadelphia, 1855.

Quilter, Harry, ed. *Is Marriage a Failure?* London, 1888.

Re-Bartlett, Lucy. *The Coming Order*. London, 1911.

―――. *Sex and Sanctity*. London, 1912.

―――. *Towards Liberty*. London, 1913.

"The Removal of a Fellow from the Obstetrical Society," *Lancet*, 6 April 1867, p. 420.

"Report from the Royal Commission on the Administration and Operation of the Contagious Diseases Acts 1866-9 (1871)." *Parliamentary Papers*, 1871 (C.408-I), XIX.

Royden, A. Maude. *Extracts from May Mission Speech*. London, 1910.

―――. *How Women Use the Vote*. London, 1912.

―――. "Modern Love." In *The Making of Women*, edited by Victor Gollancz. London, 1917.

―――. *The Moral Standards of the Rising Generation*. London, n.d.

―――. *Sex and Common Sense*. London, 1921.

―――. *A Threefold Cord*. London, 1948.

―――. "The Woman's Movement of the Future." In *The Making of Women*, edited by Victor Gollancz. London, 1917.

Scharlieb, Mary. *What It Means to Marry*. London, 1914.

Schreiner, Olive. *The Story of an African Farm*. New York, 1883.

―――. *Woman and Labour*. Rpt., London, 1978.

Sharp, Amy. *The Legal Protection of Young Girls*. London, 1884.

[Smedley, Constance]. *Woman: A Few Shrieks*. Letchworth, n.d.

Snowdon, Ethel. *The Feminist Movement*. London, n.d.

Some Social Problems and Votes for Women. London, n.d.

"Speculations on Sex War." *The Freewoman*, 14 December 1911, p. 65.

"Standards of Feminine Propriety." *Englishwoman's Review* 14 (April 1873): 118.

Strachey, Ray. *The Cause: A Short History of the Women's Movement in Britain*. Rpt., London, 1978.

——. *Millicent Garrett Fawcett*. London, 1931.

——, ed. *Our Freedom and Its Results*. London, 1936.

Stutfield, Hugh E. M. "The Psychology of Feminism." *Blackwood's Edinburgh Magazine* 161 (January 1897): 104-117.

——. "Tommyrotics." *Blackwood's Edinburgh Magazine* 157 (June 1895): 833-845.

Suffrage Annual and Women's Who's Who. London, 1913.

Swan, Annie. *Courtship and Marriage*. London, 1893.

Swanwick, H. M. *I Have Been Young*. London, 1935.

Swiney, Frances. *The Ancient Road*. London, 1918.

——. *The Awakening of Women*. 3d ed. London, 1908.

——. *The Bar of Isis*. London, 1912.

——. *Man's Necessity*. n.d.

——. *The Sons of Belial*. London, n.d.

——. *Woman and Natural Law*. 2d ed. London, 1912.

——. *Women Among the Nations*. London, 1913.

——. "The Woman Movement." *The Race Builder* 2 (November 1904-October 1905): 94.

Taylor, Mary. *The First Duty of Women*. London, 1870.

Ward, Mrs. Humphry [Mary]. *Speech by Mrs. Humphry Ward*. 3d ed. London, 1909.

Waring, Lily. "Codes of Honour." *Common Cause*, 14 April 1910, p. 4.

Wheeler, Maud. *Whom to Marry, or All About Love and Matrimony*. London, 1894.

"Wife Beating Made Easy." *Woman's Herald*, 3 January 1891, p. 168.

Wilkinson, J. J. Garth. *The Forcible Introspection of Women for the Army and Navy by the Oligarchy*. London, 1870.

Women's Freedom League. *Some Social Problems and Votes for Women*. London, n.d.

Women's National Anti-Suffrage League. *Is Parliamentary Suffrage the Best Way?* London, 1908.

———. *Queen Victoria and Women's Rights*. London, 1908.

———. *A Suffrage Talk*. 3d ed. London, 1909.

———. *Why the Women's Enfranchisement Bill, 1908, Would Be Unfair to Women If It Became Law*. London, 1908.

———. *Women's Suffrage and After*. 3d ed. London, 1909.

———. *Women's Suffrage and the National Welfare*. 3rd ed. London, 1909.

Wright, Almroth E. *The Unexpurgated Case Against Woman Suffrage*. New York, 1913.

Wright, Helena. *Marriage*. Kent, n.d.

SECONDARY SOURCES

Banks, J. A. *Prosperity and Parenthood, A Study of Family Planning Among the Victorian Middle Classes*. London, 1954.

Banks, J. A., and Olive Banks. *Feminism and Family Planning in Victorian England*. Liverpool, 1964.

Banks, Olive. *Faces of Feminism: A Study of Feminism as a Social Movement*. New York, 1981.

Banner, Lois. *Women in Modern America: A Brief History*. San Diego, 1984.

Barker-Benfield, G. J. *The Horrors of the Half-Known Life: Male Attitudes Toward Women and Sexuality in Nineteenth-Century America*. New York, 1976.

———. "The Spermatic Economy: A Nineteenth-Century View of Sexuality." In *The American Family in Social-Historical Perspective*, edited by Michael Gordon. 2d ed. New York, 1978.

Basch, Françoise. *Relative Creatures: Victorian Women in Society and the Novel*. New York, 1974.

Bell, E. Moberly. *Storming the Citadel*. London, 1953.

Branca, Patricia. *Women in Europe since 1750*. New York, 1978.

Bristow, Edward. *Vice and Vigilance*. Dublin, 1977.

Browne, F. W. Stella. "The Sexual Variety and Variability among Women and their Bearing upon Social Reconstruction." In *A New World for Women*, edited by Sheila Rowbotham. London, 1977.

Bullough, Vern. *Sexual Variance in Society*. New York, 1976.

Bullough, Vern, and Bonnie Bullough. *Sin, Sickness, and Sanity, A History of Sexual Attitudes*. New York, 1977.

Burn, W. L. *The Age of Equipoise, A Study of the Mid-Victorian Generation*. New York, 1965.

Burstyn, Joan. *Victorian Education and the Ideal of Womanhood*. New Brunswick, 1984.

Chodorow, Nancy. *The Reproduction of Mothering*. Berkeley, 1978.

Colby, Vineta. *The Singular Anomaly, Women Novelists of the Nineteenth Century*. New York, 1970.

Conway, Jill. "Stereotypes of Femininity in a Theory of Sexual Evolution." In *Suffer and Be Still: Women in the Victorian Age*, edited by Martha Vicinus. Bloomington, 1972.

Cott, Nancy. "Passionlessness: An Interpretation of Victorian Sexual Ideology, 1790-1850." *Signs* 4 (1979): 219-236.

Crawford, Anne, Tony Hayter, Ann Hughes et al. *The Europa Biographical Dictionary of British Women*. Detroit, 1983.

Crow, Duncan. *The Victorian Woman*. New York, 1972.

Cunningham, A. R. "The 'New Woman Fiction' of the 1890's." *Victorian Studies* 17 (December 1973): 177-186.

Dangerfield, George. *The Strange Death of Liberal England, 1910-1914*. New York, 1961.

De Beauvoir, Simone. *The Second Sex*. New York, 1953.

Degler, Carl. "What Ought to Be and What Was: Women's Sexuality in the Nineteenth Century." *American Historical Review* 79 (1974): 1467-1490.

Dinnerstein, Dorothy. *The Mermaid and the Minotaur, Sexual Arrangements and Human Malaise*. New York, 1977.

Donnison, Jean. *Midwives and Medical Men*. London, 1977.

Douglas, Mary. *Purity and Danger, An Analysis of Concepts of Pollution and Taboo*. New York, 1966.

DuBois, Ellen Carol. *Feminism and Suffrage: The Emergence of an Independent Women's Movement in America, 1848-1869*, Ithaca, 1978.

DuBois, Ellen Carol, and Linda Gordon. "Seeking Ecstasy on the Battlefield: Danger and Pleasure in Nineteenth-Century Feminist Sexual Thought." *Feminist Studies* 9 (Spring 1983): 7-25.

Duffin, Lorna. "The Conspicuous Consumptive: Woman as Invalid." In *The Nineteenth-Century Woman: Her Cultural and Physical World*, edited by Sara Delamont and Lorna Duffin. London, 1978.

Ehrenreich, Barbara, and Deirdre English. *For Her Own Good, 150 Years of Experts' Advice to Women*. New York, 1979.

Elshtain, Jean Bethke. "Feminist Discourse and Its Discontents: Language, Power, and Meaning." In *Feminist Theory, A Critique of Ideology*, edited by Nannerl Keohane, Michelle Rosaldo, and Barbara Gelpi. Chicago, 1982.

Evans, Richard. *The Feminists: Women's Emancipation Movements in Europe, America and Australasia, 1840-1920*. London, 1977.

Evans, Sarah. *Personal Politics: The Roots of Women's Liberation in the Civil Rights Movement and the New Left*. New York, 1980.

Faderman, Lillian. *Surpassing the Love of Men: Romantic Friendships and Love Between Women from the Renaissance to the Present*. New York, 1981.

Finnegan, Frances. *Poverty and Prostitution: A Study of Victorian Prostitutes in York*. Cambridge, 1979.

First, Ruth, and Ann Scott. *Olive Schreiner*. London, 1980.

Foucault, Michel. *The History of Sexuality*. Volume 1: *An Introduction*. New York, 1980.

Fulford, Roger. *Votes for Women, The Story of a Struggle*. London, 1957.

Garner, Les. *Stepping Stones to Women's Liberty. Feminist Ideas in the Women's Suffrage Movement, 1900-1918*. Rutherford, NJ, 1984.

Garrett Anderson, Louisa. *Elizabeth Garrett Anderson*. London, 1939.

Gilligan, Carol. *In a Different Voice, Psychological Theory and Women's Development*. Cambridge, MA, 1982.

Gillison, Gillian. "Images of Nature in Gini Thought." In *Nature, Culture and Gender*, edited by Carol MacCormack and Marilyn Strathern. Cambridge, 1980.

Goodale, Jane. "Gender, Sexuality and Marriage: A Kaulong Model of Nature and Culture." In *Nature, Culture and Gender*, edited by Carol MacCormack and Marilyn Strathern. Cambridge, 1980.

Gordon, Linda. *Woman's Body, Woman's Right, A Social History of Birth Control in America*. New York, 1977.

Gorham, Deborah. *The Victorian Girl and the Feminine Ideal*. Bloomington, 1982.

Grosskurth, Phyllis. *Havelock Ellis*. London, 1980.

Haller, John, and Robin Haller. *The Physician and Sexuality in Victorian America*. New York, 1977.

Harris, Olivia. "The Power of Signs: Gender, Culture and the Wild in the Bolivian Andes." In *Nature, Culture and Gender*, edited by Carol MacCormack and Marilyn Strathern. Cambridge, 1980.

Harrison, Brian. *Separate Spheres: The Opposition to Women's Suffrage in Britain*. London, 1978.

———. "Violence and the Suffragettes, 1904-1914." In his *Peaceable Kingdom, Stability and Change in Modern Britain*. Oxford, 1982.

———. "Women's Health and the Women's Movement in Britain: 1840-1940." In *Biology, Medicine and Society, 1840-1940*, edited by Charles Webster. Cambridge, 1981.

Hartman, Mary, and Lois Banner, eds. *Clio's Consciousness Raised*. New York, 1974.

Heath, Stephen. *The Sexual Fix*. New York, 1982.

Hellerstein, Erna, Leslie Parker Hume, and Karen Offen, eds. *Victorian Women*. Stanford, 1981.

Hollis, Patricia, ed. *Women in Public, 1850-1900: Documents of the Victorian Women's Movement*. London, 1979.

Houghton, Walter. *The Victorian Frame of Mind, 1830-1870*. New Haven, 1957.

Hume, Leslie Parker. *The National Union of Women's Suffrage Societies, 1897-1914*. New York, 1982.

Janeway, Elizabeth. "Who Is Sylvia? On the Loss of Sexual Paradigms." In *Women: Sex and Sexuality*, edited by Catharine Stimpson and Ethel Person Spector. Chicago, 1980.

Jordanova, L. J. "Natural Facts: A Historical Perspective on Science and Sexuality." In *Nature, Culture and Gender*, edited by Carol MacCormack and Marilyn Strathern. Cambridge, 1980.

Kunitz, Stanley S., and Howard Haycraft. *British Authors of the Nineteenth Century*. New York, 1936.

L'Esperance, Jean. "Doctors and Women in Nineteenth-Century Society: Sexuality and Role." In *Health Care and Popular Medicine in Nineteenth-Century England*, edited by John Woodward and David Richards. New York, 1977.

Lewis, Jane. *Women in England, 1870-1950: Sexual Divisions and Social Change*. Bloomington, 1984.

Liddington, Jill, and Jill Norris. *One Hand Tied Behind Us: The Rise of the Women's Suffrage Movement*. London, 1978.

Linklater, Andro. *An Unhusbanded Life, Charlotte Despard: Suffragette, Socialist and Sinn Feiner*. London, 1980.

Lock, Joan. *The British Policewoman: Her Story*. London, 1979.

Lutzker, Edythe. "Medical Education for Women in Great Britain." Master's thesis, Columbia University, 1959.

McGregor, O. R. *Divorce in England*. London, 1957.

Millett, Kate. *Sexual Politics*. New York, 1971.

Mitchell, David. *Queen Christabel: A Biography of Christabel Pankhurst*. London, 1977.

Mitchell, Juliet. *Psychoanalysis and Feminism*. New York, 1974.

Murray, Janet. *Strong-Minded Women and Other Lost Voices from Nineteenth-Century England*. New York, 1982.

O'Neill, William. *The Woman Movement*. London, 1969.

Ortner, Sherry. "Is Female to Male as Nature is to Culture?" In *Woman, Culture, and Society*, edited by Michelle Rosaldo and Louise Lamphere. Stanford, 1978.

Petrie, Glen. *A Singular Iniquity: The Campaigns of Josephine Butler*. London, 1971.

Read, Donald. *England: 1868-1914*. London, 1979.

Rosen, Andrew. *Rise Up, Women! The Militant Campaign of the Women's Social and Political Union, 1903-1914*. London, 1974.

Rover, Constance. *Love, Morals and the Feminists*. London, 1970.

———. *Women's Suffrage and Party Politics in Britain, 1866-1914*. London, 1967.

Rowbotham, Sheila. *Hidden From History*. New York, 1976.

Rowbotham, Sheila, and Jeffrey Weeks. *Socialism and the New Life: The Personal and Sexual Politics of Edward Carpenter and Havelock Ellis*. London, 1977.

Sarah, Elizabeth. "Christabel Pankhurst: Reclaiming Her Power." In *Feminist Theorists, Three Centuries of Key Women Thinkers*, edited by Dale Spender. New York, 1983.

Shanley, Mary Lyndon. "Marriage Contract and Social Contract in Seventeenth-Century English Political Thought." *Western Political Quarterly* 32 (1979): 79-91.

Showalter, Elaine. "Victorian Women and Insanity." In *Madhouses, Mad-Doctors, and Madmen, The Social History of Psychiatry in the Victorian Era*, ed. Andrew Scull, pp. 313-336. Philadelphia, 1981.

Smith-Rosenberg, Carroll. "Sex as Symbol in Victorian Prudery." In *Turning Points: Historical and Sociological Essays on the Family*, edited by John Demos and Sarane Spence

Boocock. A Supplement of the *American Journal of Sociology* 84 (1978): 212-247.

Spender, Dale. *Women of Ideas and What Men Have Done to Them*. London, 1982.

Stone, Lawrence. *The Family, Sex and Marriage in England, 1500-1800*. New York, 1977.

Strong, Floyd Bryan. *Sex, Character, and Reform in America, 1830-1920*. Ann Arbor, 1972.

Stubbs, Patricia. *Women and Fiction: Feminism and the Novel, 1880-1929*. London, 1981.

Taylor, Barbara. *Eve and the New Jerusalem, Socialism and Feminism in the Nineteenth Century*. New York, 1983.

Taylor, Gordon Rattray. *Sex in History*. New York, 1954.

Thomas, Keith. "The Double Standard." *Journal of the History of Ideas* 20 (1959): 195-216.

Tierney, Brian, Donald Kagan, and L. Pearce Williams, eds. *Great Issues in Western Civilization*. 3d ed., vol. 2. New York, 1976.

Trevelyan, Janet Penrose. *The Life of Mrs. Humphry Ward*. New York, 1923.

Trudgill, Eric. *Madonnas and Magdalens: The Origins and Development of Victorian Sexual Attitudes*. New York, 1976.

Trumbach, Randolph. *The Rise of the Egalitarian Family: Aristocratic Kinship and Domestic Relations in Eighteenth-Century England*. New York, 1978.

Vicinus, Martha. *Independent Women: Work and Community for Single Women, 1850-1920*. Chicago, 1985.

————. "Sexuality and Power: A Review of the Current Work in the History of Sexuality." *Feminist Studies* 8 (Spring 1982): 133-156.

Walkowitz, Judith R. "Jack the Ripper and the Myth of Male Violence." *Feminist Studies* 8 (Fall 1982): 543-574.

————. *Prostitution and Victorian Society, Women, Class, and the State*. Cambridge, 1980.

Weeks, Jeffrey. *Sex, Politics and Society: The Regulation of Sexuality Since 1800*. London, 1981.

Weisstein, Naomi. " 'Kinde, Küche, Kirche' as Scientific Law: Psychology Constructs the Female," in *Sisterhood is Powerful*, edited by Robin Morgan. New York, 1970.

Abortion Law Reform Association,
21
Abse, Leo, 224-225
Acland, Lady Emily, 103
Acton, William, 38, 39, 57, 60-61;
*Functions and Disorders of the
Reproductive Organs*, 38, 60-61
adultery, 84, 162
age of consent, 19, 20, 144. *See
also* Criminal Law Amendment
Act of 1885
Allbut, T. Clifford, 42, 48
Amberley, Lady K., 69, 158
Amos, Mrs, Sheldon, 140, 151
Anderson, Elizabeth Garrett, 10,
17, 18, 81, 114, 131, 132, 136, 137,
185-187, 200, 213
angel in the house, 33, 35, 55, 60,
65, 73, 76, 80, 99, 109, 163,
178. *See also* separate sphere ideology
anti-feminists, 52, 103, 104, 168,
169, 223, 224, 226, 227
Anti-Suffrage Review, 180, 181
anti-suffragists, 11, 54-57, 59, 103,
141, 149, 156, 160, 172, 175-183
Asquith, Herbert, 59, 199, 200,
202, 220

Balfour, A. J., 154
Banks, J. A., and Olive Banks, 90,
248n
Banks, Olive, 3, 58, 59, 63, 205,
206
Barker, Priscilla, 166
Barker-Benfield, G. J., 46, 48,
240n

Beale, Dorothea, 28
Beauvoir, Simone de, 48
Becker, Lydia, 82, 185-188
Bell, Gertrude, 176
Bell, W. Blair, 45
Belloc, Hilaire, 182
Besant, Annie, 105
Billington-Greig, 12, 20, 21, 84,
97, 160, 212, 214-218
birth control, 22, 104-105, 112, 113,
228. *See also* contraception
Black Friday, 173, 174, 200, 201
Blackstone, Sir William, 27
Blackwell, Elizabeth, 17, 18, 70-71,
105, 108, 109, 113, 125-127, 131-
138, 213
Blackwell, Emily, 125, 134
Bodichon, Barbara Leigh Smith,
28, 185, 186; *A Brief Summary
in Plain Language of the Most
Important Laws Concerning
Women*, 28
Boucherette, Jessie, 185, 186
Boyle, Nina, 20, 140, 141, 148
Braby, Maud, 167, 215
Bradlaugh, Charles, 105
Bright, Ursula (Mrs. Jacob), 82
Brittain, Vera, 147
Brown, Isaac Baker, 47, 116-118,
129
Browne, F. W. Stella, 21, 94, 217
Burn, W. L., 80, 81
Buss, Mary Frances, 28
Butler, George, 18, 72
Butler, Josephine, 8-11, 13, 14, 18,
60, 63, 64, 66-76, 78-79, 81,
82, 106, 110, 111, 114, 119-122,

Butler, Josephine (*cont.*)
124, 141, 142, 144, 152, 153, 155,
156, 159, 185, 195, 196, 200,
234n, 245n

Caird, Mona, 20, 81, 83-84, 88-
90, 95-102, 104, 112, 163, 165,
171; *Daughters of Danaus*, 84,
171
Carpenter, Edward, 51, 146, 217
Cat and Mouse Act, 202, 203
Cause, the, 18-20, 167, 184, 197.
See also women's suffrage cam-
paign
Chamberlain, Austen, 54
Chance, Lady, 149, 156, 209, 210
Chodorow, Nancy, 230
Church League for Women's Suf-
frage, 215
clitoridectomy, 47, 116-118, 241n.
See also gynecological surgery;
medical profession, abuse by
Clouston, T. S., 44; *Clinical Lec-
tures on Mental Diseases*, 44
Cobbe, Frances Power, 18, 82-83,
94, 123, 126, 129, 130, 132-133,
150, 165, 186; *The Duties of
Women*, 82
Colby, Vineta, 52
Colquhon, Ethel, 11, 183
Common Cause, 11, 20, 55, 106,
133, 141, 152, 160, 182, 184,
236n
Conciliation Bill, 54, 199, 201
conspiracy of silence, 64, 73, 107,
131, 159
Contagious Diseases Acts (CD
Acts), 3, 8, 9, 63-70, 72, 73, 75-
78, 106, 109, 119-122, 124, 131,
142, 143, 152, 153, 155, 195, 196,

198; repeal campaign, 7-11, 18-
20, 63, 64, 66, 67, 72, 119, 152,
153, 159, 194-196, 206
Contemporary Review, 143
contraception, 50, 105, 217, 222,
226. *See also* birth control
Conway, Jill, 35
Cott, Nancy, 35-37, 41
coverture, 27
Creighton, Louise, 170, 211
Criminal Code Bill of 1880, 92
Criminal Law Amendment Act of
1885, 18, 20, 140, 142, 143, 155,
196
Cunningham, A. R., 83
Cust, Henry, 153-155
Custody Act of 1839, 27
custody rights, 19, 27-28, 67, 89,
96, 142, 158, 176

Daily News, 178
Daily Telegraph, 81, 96-97, 101,
104
Dangerfield, George, 7
Davies, Emily, 10, 82, 185-187
Davison, Emily Wilding, 202
Defoe, Daniel, 80
Despard, Charlotte, 160
Dialectical Society, 92
Dinnerstein, Dorothy, 230
Disraeli, Benjamin, 187
divorce, 26, 29, 88, 103, 142, 221,
222; reform, 14, 89. *See also*
Matrimonial Causes Act of 1857,
1923
Divorce Law Reform Union, 21
Dixie, Lady Florence, 112
double standard: of law, 22, 27,
29, 141, 142, 147, 153, 221-222;
of morality, 7-9, 12, 19, 20, 22,

26, 62-63, 65, 67, 71, 76, 157, 208, 209. *See also* sexual ideology

Douglas, Mary, 39, 40, 48-49, 109, 110

Drysdale, George, 38, 39; *The Elements of Social Science*, 38-39

DuBois, Ellen, 207

Edmondson, Joseph, 120-121

Eligibility of Women Act of 1918, 221

Ellis, Havelock, 20, 39, 51, 53, 145, 146, 168, 206, 217

Ellis, Sarah Stickney, 33, 34

Elmy, Ben, 82. *See also* Elizabeth Wolstenholme Elmy

Elmy, Elizabeth Wolstenholme, 14, 18, 19, 82, 92-93, 97, 105, 110-112, 167, 185, 186, 206, 211, 213, 219, 237n; *The Criminal Code and its Relation to Women*, 92; and Ben Elmy, *Life to Woman*, 110, 251n; and Ben Elmy, *Phases of Love*, 219

Elshtain, Jean, 85

Englishwoman's Review, 83, 112, 127, 151, 158

Equal Rights Council, 226

Erikson, Erik, 224

Ethelmer, Ellis. *See* Elmy, Elizabeth Wolstenholme and Ben Elmy

Evans, Richard, 3, 4, 7

Examiner, 123

Faderman, Lillian, 51-53

Fairfield, Zoë, 74, 235n

Fawcett, Henry, 18, 188

Fawcett, Millicent Garrett, 9, 10,

14, 18, 59, 81, 106, 142, 143, 148, 153-155, 158, 160, 165, 186-188, 195, 196, 211, 217, 220, 221, 226

Female Medical Society, 130

femininity, 30-32, 115, 212, 224. *See also* sexuality, female

feminism, 19, 24, 81, 170, 195, 196, 209, 222, 225; education, 8-10, 14, 18, 19, 28, 52, 69, 83, 96, 141, 158-159, 176, 186, 195; employment, 18, 83, 142, 143, 158, 186; equality of the sexes, 3, 4, 25-29, 67, 89, 101, 141, 142, 149, 159, 208, 210, 211, 219, 221; property rights, 8, 9, 14, 19, 96, 142, 158, 176, 186, 195. *See also* women's suffrage campaign

feminists, 3, 22, 31, 33, 52, 58-60, 68, 76, 81, 85, 86, 88, 89, 92, 94, 109, 116, 119, 121, 123, 141, 147-149, 152, 158, 159, 161, 162, 164, 166-169, 171, 184, 209, 210, 212, 214-216, 226-228; identification with prostitutes, 72-76, 119, 147

First, Ruth, 146

Foucault, Michel, 14-16, 24, 38, 41, 114, 208; *The History of Sexuality*, 14

Fowler, Ellen Thorneycroft, 177-178, 180

Fraser's Magazine, 167

Freewoman, 21, 88, 167, 170, 216, 217

Freud, Sigmund, 65, 224, 228-230

Fulford, Roger, 5, 194

Gardner, A. K., 42

Garner, Les, 3, 217
Garrett, Elizabeth. *See* Elizabeth
  Garrett Anderson
Garrett, Millicent. *See* Millicent
  Garrett Fawcett
Gaskell, Elizabeth, 64
Gasquoine Hartley, Catherine, 63,
  80, 87, 160, 163-164, 168
Gawthorpe, Mary, 217
Geddes, Patrick, and J. Arthur
  Thomson, 35, 36, 39, 51, 161,
  164; *The Evolution of Sex*, 35
Gerald, Queenie, 155
Gilliam, David, 48
Gilligan, Carol, 230
Girton College, 20, 28, 186
Gladstone, William, 55, 69, 70,
  148-149, 166, 194
Good Housekeeping, 223
Grand, Sarah, 20, 83-84, 101, 104,
  157, 165, 166
Greg, W. R., 61, 96
Greig, Frederick, 21, 216
Grey, Sir Edward, 172
Grey, Maria, 10, 209
Guardianship of Infants Act of
  1886, 28
Gull, Sir William, 129
gynecological surgery, 46-49, 117.
  See also clitoridectomy; medical
  profession, abuse by; ovarioto-
  mies

Haden, Seymour, 115
Haig, Cecilia, 174
Hale, Beatrice Forbes-Robinson,
  13, 74, 137, 160, 170, 174, 183,
  211
Hamilton, Cicely, 12, 20, 21, 86-
  88, 95-98, 106, 168-169, 212,
  214; "Man," 168-169

Harrison, Brian, 3, 132, 172, 176,
  223
Harrison, Ethel, 103, 181
Harrison, Frederic, 56, 57, 182
Hart, Heber, 182
Holtby, Winifred, 220, 222, 225
homosexuality, 51. *See also* lesbian-
  ism
Hopkins, Ellice, 63
Hume-Rothery, Mary, 69, 70, 121,
  122, 185; *Women and Doctors: or
  Medical Despotism in England*,
  121
hunger strike, 198, 199, 201, 202

incest, 22, 143, 160
Inverness *Courier*, 130

Janeway, Elizabeth, 213-214, 217
Jex-Blake, Sophia, 17, 18, 127-129,
  131, 132; *Medical Women*, 127,
  128
Jordanova, L. J., 31, 46, 49, 54

Kenealy, Arabella, 177, 178, 180,
  223; *Feminism and Sex-Extinc-
  tion*, 177
Kensington Society, 186
Ker, Alice, 113, 213
Kingsley, Charles, 185
Krafft-Ebing, Richard von, 53

Labour Party, 21
Ladies' National Association (LNA)
  for the Repeal of the Contagious
  Diseases Acts, 8-10, 64, 66, 68,
  74, 75, 77, 78, 119, 124
Lady Margaret Hall, 21
Lancet, 116, 128, 130
Lecky, William, 62, 169; *The His-
  tory of European Morals*, 62

Lees, Edith, 53
Leigh, Mary, 198-199
lesbianism, 22, 51-53, 217
Leslie, Marion, 92
L'Esperance, Jean, 38, 39
Lewis, Jane, 49, 50, 58, 227
Liddington, Jill, 16
Lloyd, Mary, 82
Lloyd George, David, 174, 200, 202
London Medical Journal, 42
London National Society for Women's Suffrage, 186, 193
London *Times*, 28, 203
Lynn Linton, Eliza, 52, 103, 172, 176-179; *The Rebel of the Family*, 52
Lytton, Lady Constance, 147

McGregor, O. R., 6, 7, 62
McIlquham, Harriet, 14, 93
Madden, T. More, 108
Malthusian League, 21
Manchester Ladies' Literary Society, 186-187
Manchester Women's Suffrage Committee, 185, 186
marriage, 6, 22, 26, 27, 49, 50, 63, 79, 80-113, 141, 157; as a trade, 50, 86-87, 100; as prostitution, 70, 80, 87-88, 99-102; as slavery, 89, 92, 97; attacks on, 20, 81, 83-86, 88, 89, 99, 101, 103, 111; rape in, 92-94
Married Women's Property Acts, 18, 28, 50, 186, 194, 195, 207
Marsden, Dora, 217
Martindale, Louisa, 106, 134, 150-151; *Beneath the Surface*, 106
Martineau, Harriet, 185
masculinity, 67, 97, 99, 103, 111,

115, 164, 175, 212, 224. *See also* sexual ideology; sexuality, male
masturbation, 47, 62
Matrimonial Causes Act, of 1857, 29, 50; of 1923, 29, 221. *See also* divorce
Matthews, Vera Laughton, 170
Maudsley, Henry, 43-46, 136; *Sex in Mind and Education*, 136
Maxwell, Edith, 101-102
Meakin, Annette, 74, 97, 213
medical profession, 15, 16, 22, 32, 114-139, 157, 192; abuse by, 115, 116, 119-125, 127, 132; and suffrage, 133; women's admission to, 9, 14, 17, 19, 114-115, 122-123, 131, 158, 189, 195
Medico-Churigical and Obstetric Society, 42
Meikle, Wilma, 19, 21, 158, 159, 216
menstruation, 22, 110, 111, 135-137, 217
Mill, Harriet Taylor, 188-192; *The Enfranchisement of Women*, 188, 189
Mill, John Stuart, 55, 185, 187-189, 191, 192, 194, 195; *The Subjection of Women*, 188, 189
Millett, Kate, 188, 189, 227
Mitchell, David, 7, 174, 200; *Queen Christabel*, 174
Mitchell, Juliet, 228, 229; *Psychoanalysis and Feminism*, 229
Morgan-Brown, Laura, 157, 169
Morning Chronicle, 176
motherhood, 60, 62, 80, 91, 94, 98; compulsory, 91, 93-95, 98-99, 104-105
Mud March, 197
Murray, Eunice, 151

National Association for the Promotion of Social Science, 185, 186

National League for Opposing Woman Suffrage, 180

National Organization for Women, 227

National Society for Women's Suffrage, 192

National Union of Societies for Equal Citizenship (NUSEC), 221, 222, 225, 226

National Union of Women's Suffrage Societies (NUWSS), 9, 11, 18, 20, 21, 106, 141, 144, 170, 173, 197, 215, 220, 221

"new feminism," 225, 226

New Freewoman. See *Freewoman*

"new woman," 20, 51, 53, 82-83, 145

New York Medical Board, 75

Newnham College, 28, 195

Nichol, T. L., 105; *Human Physiology*, 105

Nightingale, Florence, 185

Norris, Jill, 16

North of England Council, 18

North of London Collegiate School for Ladies, 28

Norton, Caroline, 27

Obstetrical Society of London, 116-118, 128, 129

Ogston, Helen, 173

Oliver, Kathlyn, 94

O'Neill, William, 7, 69

Ortner, Sherry, 45, 48

ovariotomies, 47, 117. *See also* gynecological surgery; medical profession, abuse by

Pall Mall Gazette, 128, 142, 196

Pankhurst, Christabel, 5-7, 20, 21, 84, 106-111, 155, 156, 172-174, 197, 201-204, 207-208, 210-212, 216; "The Great Scourge," 5-7, 203, 211

Pankhurst, Emmeline, 21, 84, 156, 160, 174, 197, 200, 201

Pankhurst, Sylvia, 19, 20, 82, 148, 160, 174, 201, 216, 225

Parkes, Bessie Raynor, 182, 186

Parr, Olive, 178, 179

Patmore, Coventry, 33

Pearce, I. D., 98-99

Pearson, Karl, 146

Pechey, Edith, 126-127

Pethick Lawrence, Emmeline, 20, 149, 157, 200-202, 210, 212

Pethick Lawrence, Frederick, 20, 56-67

Petrie, Glen, 119

physicians, 15, 22, 37, 41-43, 46-47, 53, 58, 61, 114-139; and venereal disease, 64; female, 113, 115. *See also* medical profession

Piccadilly Flat case, 155, 156

Praeger, Arnold, 48

prostitution, 7, 14, 19, 22, 32, 60-79, 80, 81, 84, 86, 88, 99, 100, 113, 119, 141, 143, 157-160, 162, 196, 200, 201, 204, 208

psychoanalytic theory, 224, 225, 227-230

Queen v. Jackson, 28

Queen's College, 28

Rathbone, Eleanor, 225, 226

Re-Bartlett, Lucy, 175

Reform Act, of 1832, 26, 29; of

1867, 29, 148, 184, 188; of 1884, 29

Regina v. Clarence, 93

Representation of the People Bill, 221

Rosen, Andrew, 6, 7, 233-234n

Rossi, Alice, 188

Rover, Constance, 207

Rowbotham, Sheila, 216, 224

Royal Commission investigating the operation of the Contagious Diseases Acts, 68

Royal Commission on Divorce, 29, 50, 142

Royal Commission on Sanitary Law, 185

Royal Commission on Venereal Disease, 7, 107

Royden, A. Maude, 20, 21, 215, 217-219

Ruskin, John, 33

Russell, Lord John, 185

Sarah, Elizabeth, 208

Saturday Review, 90

Savill, Agnes, 130

Scharlieb, Mary, 102-103, 109; *What It Means to Marry*, 109

Schreiner, Olive, 11, 20, 67, 102, 145-147, 162-163, 168, 177, 206-207, 217, 218, 220; *The Story of an African Farm*, 20, 102; *Woman and Labour*, 146, 147, 162, 177, 207

Scotsman, 124

Scott, Ann, 146

Scott, Joan, 234n, 238n

separate sphere ideology, 5, 17, 30, 33-34, 57-60, 65, 66, 70, 76, 78, 85-86, 88, 89, 91-92, 94, 96, 99, 123, 130, 131, 141, 149, 157, 162, 163, 168, 175, 176, 178, 179, 183, 189-191, 193, 195, 200, 203-208, 219, 223-225; attack on, 22, 74, 85-86; private/domestic sphere, 16, 30, 34, 58, 65, 73, 79, 85-86, 91, 94-96; public/political sphere, 16, 30, 34, 58, 66, 79, 85-86, 91, 94-96; women's sphere, 31-32, 46, 77. *See also* sexual ideology, Victorian ideology

Sewall, Mrs. S. A., 239n

"Sex, the," 4, 13-59, 76, 114, 115, 134, 136, 146, 155, 162, 168, 189, 195, 196. *See also* sexual ideology

sex and politics, 3, 10, 14, 59, 84-85, 111, 209

Sex Disqualification Removal Act, 221

sex war, 5, 8, 23, 57, 103, 157-183, 200

sexual abuse, 7, 22, 32, 58, 68, 110, 111, 116, 121, 132, 143, 151, 152, 160, 162, 174, 196, 200, 227. *See also* medical profession, abuse by

sexual discourse, 15, 16, 20, 23-25, 38, 41, 85, 114

sexual identity, 7, 9, 15, 16, 58, 116, 134, 138, 218

sexual ideology, 14, 35-37, 40-41, 50, 53, 58, 60, 119, 121-122. *See also* separate sphere ideology, sexuality, Victorian ideology

sexual morality, 63, 136, 141, 149, 163, 205, 206

sexual politics, 188, 189, 192, 228

sexual relations, 11, 14, 103

sexuality, 10, 14-17, 19, 21, 32; female, 22, 37-39, 41-44, 48, 50-51, 60-63, 66, 73, 80, 84, 96, 98, 132, 134, 136-139, 145-148, 204, 212-215, 217, 224, 227; male, 22, 51, 60-66, 70, 71, 76, 79, 85, 86, 92, 96, 97, 103, 109, 111-112, 114, 119, 132, 134, 135, 143, 144, 147, 148, 151, 162, 164, 169, 170, 172, 173, 177, 179-182, 204, 212, 213, 224, 227

Shaftsbury, Lord, 185
Shanley, Mary Lyndon, 25
Shaw, George Bernard, 21, 165
Shaw, Hudson, 21
Shield, 68, 122
Shore, Arabella, 193, 194
Sims, J. Marion, 42; *Clinical Notes on Uterine Surgery*, 42
Sinclair, William, 108; *On Gonorrheal Infection in Women*, 108
Six Point Group, 226
Smedley, Constance, 151, 166
Smith, F. E., 54, 55
Smith, Louisa Garrett, 186
Smith, W. Tyler, 42
Smith-Rosenberg, Carroll, 39, 48-49
Snowdon, Ethel, 13, 64, 112, 129, 133, 169, 176, 210, 219
Social Evil with Suggestions for Its Suppression, The, 66
social purity movement, 18, 20, 63. *See also* Contagious Diseases Acts repeal campaign
Social Science Association. *See* National Association for the Promotion of Social Science
Somerville College, 176
Spencer, Herbert, 34, 35, 45, 49, 164

Stanford, Mrs. J., 34
Stead, W. T., 142, 196
Stone, Lawrence, 25
Storer, Horatio, 42; *The Obstetric Memoirs and Contributions of James Y. Simpson, M.D.*, 42
Strachey, Ray, 10, 14, 184, 194-195, 197, 198, 222, 223
Suffragette, 5, 202, 203
Swan, Annie, 164-165
Swanick, Helena, 3, 11, 20, 145, 173
Swiney, Frances, 11, 18, 69, 76, 97, 105, 110, 111, 143, 144, 150, 151, 156, 161-165, 169, 206

Tait, Lawson, 108
Taylor, Barbara, 67
Taylor, Gordon Rattray, 65
Taylor, Helen, 186, 192, 193
Taylor, Mary, 69
Thomas, T. Gaillard, 108
Thomson, J. Arthur. *See* Geddes, Patrick, and J. Arthur Thomson
Tilt, Edward J., 130; *Handbook on Uterine Therapeutics*, 130
Trumbach, Randolph, 25, 26, 29
Turner, Victor, 39

University of Edinburgh, 126
University of London, 28

venereal disease, 5-7, 22, 64, 84, 105-109, 119, 131, 133, 159, 160. *See also* Contagious Diseases Acts
Venturi, Emilie, 9
Vicinus, Martha, 145, 226
Victorian ideology, 34-35, 39, 50, 51, 60, 66, 80, 82-83, 89, 94, 102, 114, 157, 210, 213, 216, 217.

See also separate sphere ideology, sexual ideology
Vote, 152

Walkowitz, Judith, 7-9, 64-65, 67, 69, 76-77, 107, 119, 145, 243n, 243-244n
Ward, Lester, 161, 162
Ward, Mary (Mrs. Humphry), 176
Waring, Lily, 106, 133
Weeks, Jeffrey, 39, 44, 50, 216
Weininger, Otto, 24
Wells, H. G., 21, 54, 217
West, Rebecca, 171, 217
Westminster Review, 81, 101, 188
Westphal, Carl von, 53
white slavery, 142, 159, 196
"wild women," 52, 179
Wilkinson, J. J. Garth, 125
Wilson, Charlotte, 72
Wilson, Henry, 9, 72
Wolstenholme, Elizabeth. *See* Elizabeth Wolstenholme Elmy
Woman's Herald, 112, 151
women: as property, 26, 27, 29-31, 76, 88, 89, 92, 100, 150; as sexual objects, 7, 9, 69, 71, 150, 158; nature of, 31-32, 45-46
Women's Freedom League (WFL), 12, 140, 144, 151, 152, 160, 220
Women's National Anti-Suffrage League, 172, 180, 181
Women's Penny Paper, 92
Women's Social and Political Union (WSPU), 6, 12, 18, 20, 21, 56, 84, 149, 171, 197, 199, 201, 202, 217, 220
women's sphere. *See* separate sphere ideology, sexual ideology, Victorian ideology
women's suffrage campaign, 3, 4, 8, 9, 11, 13, 14, 16, 19, 22, 23, 29, 31, 55, 56, 59, 69, 81, 86, 89-91, 93, 96, 111, 114, 115, 133, 142, 144, 147, 156, 158-160, 164, 165, 169-175, 180, 184-219, 220, 222, 227, 230; militant, 8, 20, 56, 171-175, 181, 184, 196-203
Women's Suffrage Society, 188
Wright, Ada, 173
Wright, Sir Almroth, 203, 204; *The Unexpurgated Case against Woman Suffrage*, 203

Library of Congress Cataloging-in-Publication Data

Kent, Susan, 1952-
Sex and suffrage in Britain, 1860-1914.

Bibliography: p.
Includes index.
1. Women—Suffrage—Great Britain—History. 2. Women—Great Britain—
History. 3. Feminism—Great Britain—History. I. Title.
JN979.K43 1987   324.6′23′0941   86-25307
ISBN 0-691-05497-5 (alk. paper)